WARLORD SURVIVAL

WARLORD SURVIVAL

The Delusion of State Building in Afghanistan

ROMAIN MALEJACQ

CORNELL UNIVERSITY PRESS
ITHACA AND LONDON

First published 2019 by Cornell University Press

Printed in the United States of America

Library of Congress Cataloging-in-Publication Data

Names: Malejacq, Romain, 1983– author.
Title: Warlord survival : the delusion of state building in Afghanistan /
    Romain Malejacq.
Description: Ithaca [New York] : Cornell University Press, 2019. | Includes
    bibliographical references and index.
Identifiers: LCCN 2019012612 (print) | LCCN 2019014502 (ebook) |
    ISBN 9781501746437 (pdf) | ISBN 9781501746444 (epub/mobi) |
    ISBN 9781501746420 | ISBN 9781501746420 (cloth ; alk. paper)
Subjects: LCSH: Warlordism—Afghanistan—History. | Warlordism
    and international relations—Afghanistan. | Nation-building—
    Afghanistan. | Political culture—Afghanistan. | Afghanistan—Politics
    and government—1989–2001. | Afghanistan—Politics and
    government—2001–
Classification: LCC JQ1763.5.P65 (ebook) | LCC JQ1763.5.P65 M35 2019
    (print) | DDC 958.104/7—dc23
LC record available at https://lccn.loc.gov/2019012612

CONTENTS

ACKNOWLEDGMENTS

This book would not have seen the light of day without the support and generosity of more people than I can name. Above all, I owe a great deal to the many Afghans who made this work possible, each in their own way, from the passersby who gave me directions in the streets of Kabul, Herat, and Mazar-i Sharif to the friends who have shared their ideas and shaped mine year after year. Because my research deals with sensitive issues, I decided to maintain the anonymity of anyone who could be affected by being associated with me and my work in any way. I hope that they will forgive me for not giving them the credit they deserve. I am especially thankful to the interpreters, Dari teachers, and drivers I have worked with over the years, to those who gave me a roof and kept me safe, and to those who taught me how to navigate the culture and politics of their amazing country. I am eternally grateful to the people who shared their life stories with me. There would be no book without them.

I also extend my gratitude to all those who helped me during my fieldwork. In Kabul, the people of the Délégation Archéologique Française en

Afghanistan gave me a home away from home. I received warm welcomes at the Altai guesthouse and the French House in Kabul as well as the Acted guesthouse in Mazar-i Sharif. Special thanks go to the friends who let me use their apartment during my latest trip to Herat. I would not have been able to conduct my fieldwork without the support of a European Union Marie Curie fellowship and the generous funding of the French embassy in Afghanistan, the mairie de Paris, the Institut de Recherche Stratégique de l'École Militaire, and the American Institute for Afghanistan Studies. At Radboud University Nijmegen, the Institute for Management Research and the GLOCAL research group provided additional financial support.

This work would also not have been possible without the mentorship, friendship, and unwavering support of Bertrand Badie and William Reno. They have both inspired me and challenged me for over a decade now. It has been a privilege to work with and learn from them. A few other scholars deserve specific mention. None has broadened my intellectual horizons the way Georgi Derluguian has. His influence can certainly be felt throughout this book, and for this and more, I will always be deeply appreciative. At Northwestern University, Jon Caverley and Hendrik Spruyt also hold a special place. And so does Judith Wilks, my Farsi teacher. At Sciences Po, I am greatly indebted to Shahrbanou Tadjbakhsh, who first gave me the opportunity to conduct research in Afghanistan. My gratitude also goes to my fellow graduate students at Sciences Po and Northwestern University, as well as to Maud Biancardi, Danielle Leroux, and Courtney Syskowski, who kept me away from the administrative pitfalls of graduate training.

At Radboud University Nijmegen, the Centre for International Conflict Analysis & Management (CICAM) was the perfect place to finish the book. Not only was I very lucky to find an amazing group of scholars with whom to exchange ideas, but I could not have hoped for a more supportive environment and more encouraging colleagues. Willemijn Verkoren has been the best boss anyone could wish for. She gave me the time and freedom to work on the book, as well as the opportunity to develop my own course on Afghanistan. Maarten Cras is the heart and soul of our team. His unfaltering flexibility and kindness have been a constant delight to me and my family. At CICAM, I also commend the students of our Political and Geographical Conflict Resolution course, War and State Building in Afghanistan course, and Current Issues of War and Peace course for listening to and critiquing some of the ideas developed in *Warlord Survival*.

I cannot overstate the role of the many scholars who have listened to, discussed, or critiqued my work at conferences over the years. I am especially thankful to the ones who invited me to present the latest version of my book manuscript: Ursula Daxecker and Abbey Steele at the Amsterdam Conflict Club, Adrian Florea at the University of Glasgow, Annette Idler at the University of Oxford, and Corinna Jentzsch at Leiden University. I am also grateful to people at the Harriman Institute and the Saltzman Institute for War and Peace Studies at Columbia University for giving me a place to work from and present my ideas in New York City, and to Kimberly Marten in particular for giving great comments on some of the ideas that later made it into the book. I also would like to acknowledge *Security Studies*, *Small Wars & Insurgencies*, Stanford University Press, and *Political Violence at a Glance* for letting me use copyrighted material, as well as *Jane's Intelligence Review* and the Swedish Committee for Afghanistan for providing me with free copies of documents I needed to consult.

My gratitude likewise goes to the friends and colleagues who have critiqued and edited my work, recently and in the past: Dipali Mukhopadhyay and Christian Olsson have been great coauthors and fieldwork buddies; Ariel Ahram, Chris Day, Imke Harbers, Jana Krause, Sean Lee, Zach Mampilly, Ingrid Samset, Adam Sandor, Michael Semple, Lee Seymour, and Niels Terpstra gave me fantastic comments. Ben Goodwin and Joe Lukey's careful reading of the entire manuscript and clear-sighted perspectives greatly improved the book. Paul Staniland and Haley Swedlund gave me sound advice on the publication process.

I was fortunate to work with five outstanding research assistants: Daniel DeRock, Irem Dilbaz, John Jacobs, Max Mommers, and Ilse Renkens helped me tremendously. Daniel's editing and proofreading, in particular, made the book much stronger. My thanks go equally to Linda Haartsen, who showed extreme patience and designed outstanding maps. I am also enormously grateful to Roger Haydon, my editor, who provided sensible and thoughtful suggestions throughout, to the two anonymous reviewers, who gave me razor sharp comments, as well as to Karen Hwa, Ellen Murphy, Ange Romeo-Hall, Carmen Torrado Gonzalez, and the many others at Cornell University Press who have worked hard on turning the manuscript into a book. Special thanks go to Liz Schueler and Michelle Witkowski, at Westchester Publishing Services, for their meticulous editing, and to Judy Kip for indexing the book. Of course, I alone am responsible for any mistakes and for the views conveyed in this book.

Finally, I thank my family and friends. Many over the years have helped me cope with my vagabond life, sometimes offering a temporary roof, always blessing me with true friendship. Michael, in particular, has always been here for me. I also could not have made it without my parents and my brother, whose love and support have encouraged me throughout the years. And of course, I am forever grateful to my wife. I could not have completed this book without her love, extraordinary patience, and affection. Our son gave me a reason and the energy to push through. This book is for them.

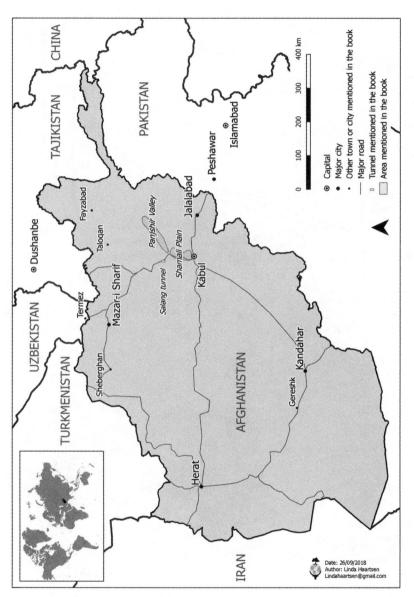

Areas of relevance mentioned in the book

Afghanistan provinces

Date: 26/09/2018
Author: Linda Haartsen
Lindahaartsen@gmail.com

Legend:
- Provincial capital
- Province in which fieldwork was conducted

Scale: 0 100 200 300 400 km

Countries labeled: UZBEKISTAN, TURKMENISTAN, TAJIKISTAN, CHINA, PAKISTAN, IRAN

Provinces labeled: BADAKHSHAN, TAKHAR, KUNDUZ, BAGHLAN, PANJSHIR, NURISTAN, KUNAR, KAPISA, LAGHMAN, NANGARHAR, KABUL, PARWAN, LOGAR, PAKTYA, KHOST, WARDAK, BAMYAN, SAMANGAN, BALKH, JOWZJAN, SAR-I PUL, FARYAB, BADGHIS, GHOR, DAYKUNDI, GHAZNI, PAKTIKA, ZABUL, URUZGAN, HERAT, FARAH, NIMROZ, HELMAND, KANDAHAR

Warlord Survival

INTRODUCTION

Why Warlord Survival?

On the night of February 2, 2008, Abdul Rashid Dostum, the Uzbek warlord of northern Afghanistan, was spotted on the roof of his Kabul mansion, armed and seemingly inebriated. One of the country's most feared and
powerful warlords, he faced a siege of his heavily guarded compound after
the police received word that his men had beaten and kidnapped Akbar Bai,
a former ally turned political rival. The standoff between his forces and the
police lasted all night, until, in the early morning of February 3, the police
withdrew. They had been ordered to do so by President Hamid Karzai, after
Turkey's minister of foreign affairs had threatened to remove all Turkish
forces from Afghanistan and end all aid projects in the country if Dostum
were arrested. President Karzai and the Turkish government struck a deal
that should have been the death knell for Dostum's political career. Per Turkey's request, Dostum was not brought to justice, but, to accommodate Karzai, he was to remain in exile in Ankara until further notice. Yet, only a few
months later, an unapologetic General Dostum was back in Afghanistan.
Karzai had allowed his return in exchange for his support in the 2009

presidential election, and against the urging of prominent members of the international community, who hoped to keep the warlord at bay. Dostum would not be sidelined so easily. In fact, he was here to stay.

Over the past four decades, General Dostum has lived through several transformations, but he has always played a major role in Afghan politics. In the 1980s, he exploited the communist regime's willingness to build pro-government militias to establish himself as the leader of an ethnicity-based armed group while increasing his own power within the Afghan Turkic community (which includes mainly ethnic Uzbeks and Turkmens).[1] As the regime grew weaker after the fall of the Soviet Union, he switched sides and allied with the rebels (the mujahideen) to take the Afghan capital in April 1992. He then created his own ministate in northern Afghanistan, which he had to abandon to the Taliban in 1998, spending the next three years in exile. Dostum returned to Afghanistan to join the resistance to the Taliban a few months before 9/11 and quickly remobilized his men. He then served the United States as a powerful ally on the ground, collaborating with US forces to turn his situation around financially and militarily. It was not long, however, before the US-backed administration tried to undermine his authority and Dostum lost his grip over northern Afghanistan. And yet, he has remained integral to Afghan politics, to such an extent that he was sworn in as first vice president of the Islamic Republic of Afghanistan in September 2014.

I first traveled to Afghanistan in 2007, less than six months before the roof incident. I wanted to study how men like General Dostum, who once controlled entire regions, exert authority in the midst of a state-building enterprise. I hoped to understand how these violent political entrepreneurs could survive for so long and be so remarkably savvy at adapting to changing environments. Peculiar incidents like Dostum raging on the roof of his mansion only piqued my curiosity further. How do warlords survive and even thrive in contexts that are explicitly set up to undermine them? How do they rise after each fall, despite the multiple shocks they experience and the deadly challenges they face? Many international actors involved in war-torn countries (for instance, foreign militaries and governments, aid agencies, and international organizations) would prefer that these violent political actors quietly disappear as central states assert their authority. Yet, in states such as Afghanistan, Iraq, and Somalia, warlords continue to shape the political landscape, exerting authority in parallel or in opposition to the state. They experience major shifts within their political environments, but many, such as the ones I follow in this book, reinvent themselves and continue to exert authority, from one regime to another.

This book is the result of a decade spent trying to solve this puzzle. I spent months in the field and conducted hundreds of interviews to understand the calculations warlords make to navigate changing political contexts and maintain their political authority. Here, I explain how they survive, during and after war. Warlords persist thanks to their ability to cross political orders and harness different sources of power, often in ways that escape state domination. Not only do they remain influential in the political system, but they also hold power that goes far beyond simple military might and endures long past the moment they have ceased to command a credible force. They adapt to new political regimes and offer "alternative forms of governance."[2] In other words, warlords maintain authority despite massive state-building efforts. *Warlord Survival* sheds light on why external interventions that aim at centralizing and monopolizing the exercise of authority, in places like Afghanistan, are more illusion than reality.

What Warlords Do

Most Afghan warlords do not appreciate being referred to as warlords. They even find the term offensive. In any case, they would certainly not call themselves that. The only exception may be General Dostum, who, in 2002, acknowledged that he had been a warlord, "when it was necessary to be a warlord," but only to stress that he now considered himself a "peacelord" instead.[3] In the Afghan context, the term has been employed by foreigners, in particular after 2001, to "vilify these figures as thugs who have long depended on intimidation and coercion to sustain their influence over civilians, their stake in illicit industries and their search for personal wealth."[4] The Persian word *jangsalar* (a literal translation of the English *war-lord*) is rarely used by Afghans—who typically opt for the more neutral *qumandan* (commandant)—but carries an even more pejorative undertone.[5] *Jangsalar* evokes the violent criminal behavior of what an Afghan scholar once described to me as "killers struggling for power."[6]

Warlords have been portrayed in less than flattering terms in other parts of the world too—for example, the "hyena[s] of the conflict zone" or "the virus[es] of the new strategic era."[7] To be sure, most warlords have been implicated in a range of human rights abuses. But seeing warlords merely as predators and spoilers misses the many roles that they play.[8] Men like Dostum are not simply the ugly symptoms of diseases that need to be diagnosed and treated. Some of them might support peace-building initiatives as long as they are compatible with preserving or extending their authority. This does not mean that one should expect warlords to comply with liberal and democratic norms of behavior and promote the construction of bureaucratic institutions once conflict ends. Warlords try to maximize their interests, but the way they do so depends on the context in which they operate at a given moment in time. In fact, their interests are constantly shifting.

In this book, I aim to adopt a definition of warlords that is detached from normativity and the "lasting influence of Orientalist thought" and focuses on what they do (their actual behavior) instead of what is assumed of them.[9] Warlords are astute political entrepreneurs with a proven ability to organize violence and control territory, who exert and transform authority across different spheres (ideological, economic, military, social, and political) and at different levels of political affairs (local, national, and international). As such, warlords remain, first and foremost, "autonomous and powerful *individuals*," not members of armed organizations bound by institutionalized forms of collective decision making (such as the Taliban or the so-called Islamic State), even though some of these organizations may have originally started as warlord enterprises.[10] I conceive of warlords as violent political entrepreneurs who control power resources (which I unpack in chapter 2) and develop complex survival strategies that extend beyond their territory, even as far as conducting effective interactions with international actors.[11] In Iraq, in the aftermath of the fall of Saddam Hussein's regime, the Shia cleric Muqtada al-Sadr harnessed Iranian support to create his own armed group, the Mahdi Army, and establish his own fiefdom.[12] And to survive the above-mentioned Akbar Bai incident, Dostum directly secured Turkey's protection.

In practice, warlords often play critical roles in people's access to political and economic opportunities and act as the principal suppliers of governance in their communities: in the 1990s, Mohammad Ismail Khan sustained administrative systems, schools, and hospitals in western Afghanistan; and at his peak, around the same period, even Charles Taylor, Africa's most notorious warlord, maintained state-like infrastructures and services (such as a currency, a banking system, and an international airfield) in "Taylorland," the part of Liberia under his control.[13] These men (they are almost always men) often act in self-interested ways, in particular since they operate in unstable environments that foster self-centered behaviors and short-term strategies. Their interests may at times lead them to protect specific communities—such as General Dostum's protection of the Uzbek population—and focus on building their personal authority. They often switch sides and hedge their bets, breaking agreements and seeking out new allies in the midst of conflict, thus adopting duplicitous behaviors in the eyes of the international community.[14] General Khalifa Haftar, the head of the Libyan National Army that took control over most of eastern Libya in 2014, for example, has been depicted as a man who "has fought with and against nearly every significant faction in the country's conflicts, leading to a reputation for unrivalled military experience and for a highly flexible sense of personal allegiance."[15]

In fact, warlords represent elements of continuity to their supporters in an otherwise fluid environment. Dostum may be portrayed by Western media as a compulsive side switcher prone to betrayal but, for many Uzbeks, he remains the only leader able to protect and provide. Rais Baghrani, a commander from Helmand Province, in southern Afghanistan, is another good example. Originally a member of the hardline faction of the People's Democratic Party of Afghanistan, he successively affiliated himself with a number of mujahideen groups during the Soviet-Afghan war, then with the Taliban, and eventually with the Karzai administration after 2001. "Each change in organisational 'membership,'" wrote former British Army officer Mike Martin, "was due to evolutions of his local political context, which he needed to either exploit or not be destroyed by."[16] In chapter 1, I unpack the relationships between warlords and states and show that men like Haftar, Dostum, and Rais Baghrani often operate in realms of authority that are beyond the grasp of the formal state to ensure their survival. Political orders change, regimes come and go, but many warlords remain.

Warlords undertake a *fonction totale*, exerting a monopoly over all sources of power on their territory simultaneously, in states that are "incapable of projecting power and asserting authority within their own borders, leaving their territories governmentally empty" (failed states) or at least in areas where state power is completely absent (areas of failed statehood).[17] Indeed, only the absence of state power in a given territory provides those who are "psychologically disposed to become self-interested specialists in violence" with the opportunity to exert and maximize their authority across all different realms (ideological, economic, military, social, and political) simultaneously.[18] It is in these environments, where the divides between the various realms of authority have withered and the state is unable to provide goods and services to its citizens, that warlords become fully operational, or active.

Where "a spectrum of conventional bureaucratic state capabilities [exist] alongside (generally very strong) informal political networks" (weak states and areas of weak statehood), warlords will be dormant, operating across only certain realms of authority.[19] "These guys are sleepers. . . . They change their colors," I was told about Somali warlords.[20] Warlords combine and convert different forms of power to acquire the resources they need to survive in a given environment (e.g., institutional positions or development aid), but they remain warlords—contrary to what the definitions that emphasize the "territorial nature of warlords" imply.[21] They reinvent themselves and exploit what most westerners perceive (and many locals experience) as social disorder to reconstitute their realm of reference and increase their chances of survival across different political orders.[22]

Warlord survival, in turn, is a warlord's ability to wield substantial political influence over time at the subnational, national, and international levels. It can be described as the resilience of power over time, the warlords' ability to affect political outcomes and maintain their autonomy to act in defiance of and in ways that are consequential to their central state, even after being subjected to exogenous shocks such as the post-2001 US-led intervention. Warlord survival is the ability to remain relevant in a new political environment or, in other words, to resist the central state's pressure for centralization and maintain influence in a given political system, during and after war. It is enduring warlord authority. This does not mean that warlords systematically maximize their authority. Few, if any, durably concentrate all sources of power, but many survive even when an alternative outcome should have plausibly occurred, such as military defeat or absorption into the state's institutions.

Warlord Authority

When asked whether warlords were powerful, most of the Afghans I spoke to over the years initially responded that they were not because, they explained, warlords no longer control the territories that they once claimed.

And indeed, for populations that have experienced civil war, power is often equated with control—that is, the ability to "establish exclusive rule on a territory."[23] It is an understanding of power that takes the state (centralized and monopolistic) as a point of reference and territory as the main object of contention. It rests on the idea that the state exerts (or should exert) uncontested domestic sovereignty—"the formal organization of political authority within the state and the ability of public authorities to exercise effective control within the borders of their own polity."[24] In this conception, the state is perceived as a "dominant, integrated, autonomous entity that controls, in a given territory, all rule making."[25] Even when it does not, this image of the state persists as a "symbolic reality" that exists "in people's heads."[26]

Yet, as conversations went on, the same interlocutors that claimed that warlords no longer held power usually expanded on their first answers by telling me that warlords in fact maintained influence—*nafuz* in the local vernacular. An acute observer of Afghan politics explains: "[*Nafuz*] can be acquired through tribal rank, charisma, command over resources and the possession of a body of followers or clients. It does not simply attach itself to an official rank, which only confers *salayat*, or authority and competence. In the Afghan context, official authority is ephemeral and often curtailed by the citizens' alienation and disengagement from government."[27] In other words, power, in Afghanistan and elsewhere, can be exercised in a different fashion. It need not be materialized through formal institutions or territorial control to be real, even though the warlords' bases of political support are concentrated in particular places. Influence (*nafuz*) is also a form of power. If we accept that power "is measured by the mastery that a leader exercises over others" and that influence is "*a relation among actors* in which an actor induces other actors to act in some way that they would not otherwise do," then influence can in fact be taken as "a measure of power."[28]

Authority can then be defined as "a mutual relationship between two actors in which the subordinate actor willingly *consents* to a command by the dominant actor."[29] Warlord authority, in turn, is based on what Whitney Azoy, a leading anthropologist of Afghanistan, describes as "the reciprocal process of reputation and followers," with reputation constituting "the ultimate source of political authority." This may seem overly simplistic, even naive. Yet, it explains why warlord authority is not solely a story of capacities and why materialistic explanations fail to make sense of the outcomes of the many wars and power struggles in Afghanistan. Azoy relates how he was at first disconcerted by the circular nature of this "politics by reputation":

> "Why," I would ask, "is that man so important?"
> "Because," the answer would come, "he has a name (*nam*)."
> "What good is a name?"
> "It gives a man supporters."
> "What good are supporters?"
> "They help a man succeed with his 'work.'"
> "What happens when his 'work' is successful?"
> "It gives a man a name."

During his research, Azoy kept looking for formal institutions and the clearly defined positions within them that westerners are so accustomed to using to explain the locus of political authority. I found myself in a very similar situation, trying to make sense of Afghan warlords. "My fieldwork search for neatly defined institutions of authority," Azoy confessed, "ultimately revealed no such thing." Such institutions, in fact, do not exist: "The Afghan form of authority resides neither in permanent corporations nor in formal statuses, but rather in individual men who relate to each other in transient patterns of cooperation and competition."[30]

This reality helps explain how warlords can rise up again after we think they are eliminated, or wield power even when they lack material resources such as territory, money, or weapons. While these material resources cannot be ignored altogether, they do not adequately encapsulate the complexity of warlord politics. Immaterial resources are also key to a warlord's authority. This explains why a man like Dostum, for example, invests in symbolic displays of power that will increase his local legitimacy, from the lion statues guarding his Kabul mansion to the dozens of self-promoting billboards in his hometown of Sheberghan. Ismail Khan, the warlord of western Afghanistan, even ordered the construction of a jihad museum, a tribute to and a reminder of his leadership and courage during the Soviet-Afghan war. Indeed, he once rebuked me for failing to mention *his* museum as my favorite monument in the city of Herat.

This form of authority and the type of behaviors it incentivizes are not restricted to Afghanistan. Similar interactions can be observed in places as varied as Yemen, Georgia, and the Democratic Republic of the Congo, where warlords systematically attempt to maximize their authority. The rationalist assumptions regarding warlords' strategies in fact suggest that this book's conclusions may be transferable beyond Afghanistan's idiosyncrasies. And this work aims at formulating general hypotheses beyond this specific case. The mechanisms I identify may be most illustrative of cases like Afghanistan, where foreign interveners try to build a capable central authority while depending on local actors to provide stability. Yet, this book provides a framework to explain variation in the political trajectories and survival strategies of warlords in general. Thus, it should still offer valuable insights into cases of state weakness in the absence of intrusive, ambitious, international intervention and contemporary state building, and could help academics and policymakers understand other parts of the world where political authority remains deeply fragmented.

Prevailing Approaches to Warlord Survival

Above I highlighted a common misunderstanding surrounding the way warlords exert authority. This misunderstanding has resulted in an inability to account for their survival in settings that are hostile to them or even designed explicitly to destroy them. Afghan warlords are often referred to as "paper tigers" in both academic and policy circles, remnants of the past who could and should have been crushed by the central government and its allies after 2001.[31] While the international community (and the United States in particular) played an undeniable role in empowering Afghan warlords in the early days of the post-9/11 intervention—for instance, providing Dostum and others with millions of dollars in cash—the "paper tiger" argument falls into a broader category of analyses that tend to focus on the demand for what warlords can provide: "the demand of the overburdened state for franchisees to which it can devolve responsibility for organized violence; the demand by local citizens for protection or public goods; the demand by external patrons for local clients who can provide stability and a modicum of security in a war-torn region."[32]

The demand is real and plays an important role in warlord survival. Yet, most scholars who agree with this characterization see warlords as malignant appendages to the state, feeding on foreign resources and colluding with state officials who benefit from either informal business partnerships (and clandestine commercial gains) or political alliances (and shared local power bases). Those who hold this view thus question the central government's and the international community's willingness to bolster state authority against them. Marten, for example, considers warlords as "parasitic creatures of the state" and wonders "what [it would] take to get rid of [them]."[33] Yet, she cannot account for the emergence and survival of warlords in the absence of a state or foreign patron to feed on.

This normative approach tends to ignore the warlords' ability to exploit sovereign states and adapt their strategies. It neglects both their exercise of agency and their variability of interests. Advocates of this line of argument assume that warlords are simple tools that states could easily get rid of if they were to summon the political will and focus of resources to do so. But warlord survival does not exclusively rest on the will of sovereign states. The United States, for instance, did not make Dostum a leader. Rather, the Uzbek warlord benefited from and could then use foreign support *because* he is a leader. As the American anthropologist Thomas Barfield once told me: "In egalitarian societies like Afghanistan, it is hard to become a leader. Once things are established, it is a default mechanism. Look at Dostum!"[34] And neither foreign actors nor state authorities can simply decide to banish him, because warlords are in fact integral to how states like Afghanistan exercise authority.

A recent wave of literature focuses on organizational features to explain variation in the fate of nonstate armed groups. Abdulkader Sinno, for example, contends that the success (and hence survival) of a nonstate armed organization in civil war rests on the distribution of power within the organization. His argument follows that the right organizational structure is one that is suitable to the specific circumstances an organization must deal with, in particular the availability of a territorial safe haven.[35] Even more recently, scholars such as Paul Staniland, Sarah Zukerman Daly, and Christopher Day have highlighted the role of the social networks that underpin armed organizations in order to account for their evolution, fortune, and misfortune.[36] Day, for instance, explains the fate of rebel organizations by the degree of embeddedness in state institutions, where "insiders" (former regime elites) are more likely to achieve military victory or reach a political settlement with incumbents than "outsiders" to the existing political system.[37]

Studies that emphasize the organizational features of armed groups are particularly helpful for understanding very specific outcomes, such as remobilization patterns or group fragmentation, typically within relatively stable structural arrangements.[38] However, they cannot account for individual life trajectories, especially when actors experience multiple reversals of fortune and fundamental changes in their sociopolitical environments, as has been the case in Afghanistan since 1978.[39] Taking individual warlords as the unit of analysis allows for more historical contingency, even if their behaviors are constrained by the larger political setting. A major innovation of this book is to investigate the sources of power of specific individuals who "live by the gun" across different political orders. Following Marielle Debos's example, I "attempt to think in terms of non-linear, interwoven processes that lie outside the framework of the transition between war and peace."[40]

The reason organizational approaches cannot fully explain warlord survival, I argue, is that they are less suitable to the study of fragmented, patronage-based societies, where personal relationships and patrimonial networks are often more important than institutional arrangements.[41] "In the absence of institutions which specify authority," writes Azoy, "this critical element is vested instead in individuals who cast themselves as leaders and bolster their claims by the acquisition of followers."[42] Warlords do not require formal or even visible political structures to maintain a local power base and followers to whom they remain relevant. In Herat, in 2011, I witnessed hundreds of men, young and old, gathered to support and listen to Ismail Khan. And, as of my last visit, in the summer of 2018, although he no longer assumed any formal position, he was still holding court and adjudicating disputes.

Organizational approaches cannot make sense, for instance, of why Mohammad Ashraf Ghani Ahmadzai (henceforth Ashraf Ghani), a former academic and World Bank technocrat, took General Dostum as one of his two running mates in the 2014 presidential election, paving the way for him to become first vice president of the Islamic Republic of Afghanistan. Dostum's selection was surprising as Ghani had recently coauthored a book on fixing failed states, in which he decried that "government failure to establish uniform and trusted practices across state territory allow[ed] large swathes of the country to fall into the hands of local militias and warlords."[43] The appointment was all the more unexpected given that, a decade earlier, during his tenure as minister of finance, Ghani had engaged in a struggle against the dominant Afghan warlords (including Dostum) to deprive them of custom revenues, increase state resources, and strengthen central institutions. In a letter to the *London Times* dated August 29, 2009, he had even criticized President Karzai for "welcom[ing] General Abdul Rashid Dostum, a known killer, back to Afghanistan to endorse his re-election bid." His later change of heart indicates that he adapted to the realities of Afghan politics. He certainly realized the need for political muscle and a larger electoral base, two things that General Dostum could provide.

In these circumstances, Dostum can hardly be described as powerless. In fact, Ghani's decision shows that he has some sort of power, a kind of power that is extremely valuable to a presidential candidate and indeed a president. Warlords are part of the political fabric. In Afghanistan, they have continued to exert power even after the externally led state-building project deprived them of their territorial control. It is thus misleading to assume that warlords can easily be disposed of or tamed by encouraging them to don a Western suit and tie and placing them in an office in a ministry. It is a misunderstanding that rests on a narrow definition of power and ignores the true nature of these men's authority. In this book, I build on the classic literature on (neo) patrimonialism and the most recent findings of civil war scholarship to shed light on the inner workings of the endogenous relationship between warlords and states.

The Mechanisms of Warlord Survival

My argument, which I develop further in chapter 2, is that warlord survival is a function of an individual's ability to make himself indispensable at different levels of politics (local, national, and international) and exploit the gaps and interactions between them. Turkish officials do not support Dostum because they like him. They in fact tried to empower alternative leaders after 2001 but none of them could command the same following or enjoy comparable support in the Afghan Turkic community. Turkish officials support Dostum because he has repeatedly demonstrated that he is the only person able to lead and keep this community together. In their eyes, he has become irreplaceable. Ashraf Ghani did not pick Dostum as his running mate out of political preference but because no one else can rally the Uzbek (and, to a lesser extent, the Turkmen) vote. Locally, people do not necessarily like the warlords they support either. Yet, they will vote for men they despise as long as they believe that these leaders can protect them and promote their interests, and "[remain] their best chance for patronage and access to what the government may have to offer in terms of jobs, services and some form of justice."[44]

As mentioned above, warlords survive because there is a need for people who can organize violence and provide trust, security, and employment along the way. In Afghanistan, the very skilled purposely create disorder, fear, and unpredictability to increase the requirement for those who can deliver political stability. In 2003, a US official explained: "At least some of these incidents (mortar attacks), especially those around Bagram [home of the largest US military base in Afghanistan], are crude attempts at extortion. . . . The extortion theory argues that the warlord is behind the rocket incidents, and that he thinks the rockets will scare the U.S. into paying him more to provide even more security."[45]

Such strategies can also be adopted to get rid of a rival, now deemed incapable of bringing stability. In 2004, in the southern province of Helmand, Mir Wali, one of the local warlords previously in charge of the highway police, attacked the checkpoints he used to control immediately after he was replaced by a private security contractor, meanwhile claiming that these attacks had been committed by the Taliban. In 2008, in the same province, local political brokers reportedly organized a fake Taliban attack to "create chaos and prove they were the only people who could lead the province."[46]

Warlords also eliminate or weaken cumbersome rivals who could compete for the same resources and use the same repertoires of action in the same "political marketplace."[47] As an observer of Afghan politics aptly put it: "They use whatever is at their disposal to marginalize and beat the rivals into submission until they are no longer considered a threat."[48] General Dostum used violence to defeat Akbar Bai; Sher Mohammad Akhunzada, a former mujahid and recently appointed governor of Helmand Province, manipulated US and British ignorance of the southern Afghan terrain to eradicate his rivals' poppy fields in the early days of the post 9/11 intervention.[49] In sum, the resilience of Afghan warlords is not simply a story of financial and military capacities but also a story of shrewd individuals who make themselves irreplaceable.

Warlords maintain their position through two mechanisms in particular: power conversion and power projection. Power conversion is the mechanism through which warlords transform, adjust, and bide their time. Warlords accumulate power resources, as well as convert preexisting ones, to adapt to changing political settings. They use these resources and convert them into something that suits their new environment (for instance, money and institutional positions). In other words, they cherry-pick the resources they need (and can acquire) to survive in a particular context. They take new social functions at the local, national, and international levels, even when they assume formal offices in the central state's apparent attempts to co-opt them. They find alternative social spaces to exert power, and hence survive shocks that are exogenous to their own ecosystem. In short, they survive as long as they "can manipulate changing circumstances to their own advantage."[50]

Power projection is the way warlords convince sovereign actors (both foreign states and their own) and local communities that they have authority. It is the mechanism through which they present themselves as legitimate political leaders—whose legitimacy rests mostly on their ability to organize violence and deliver services—and thereby perpetuate their power. Unlike Antonio Giustozzi, I do not consider that warlords necessarily have "little or no political legitimacy" (as opposed to military legitimacy).[51] On the contrary, I show in this book that political legitimacy, whether real or perceived, is actually key to a warlord's ability to sustain power. As a foreign analyst aptly notes, "Afghan politics is shaped by political posturing, inflated claims of strength and/or support, and unstable alliances."[52] Thus, warlord authority is real but at the same time fragile. This precarious equilibrium makes power projection a necessity. In fact, "the moment that others cease to believe in one's prestige or charisma, it quite literally vanishes into thin air."[53]

Why Warlord Survival Matters

Warlord survival explains why states like Afghanistan fail to conform to Weberian bureaucratic ideals of institutional and territorial control. It affects both state formation—a historical, largely unplanned, uncoordinated, and violent process—and state building, "a deliberate means to contain and direct power" to create an "overpowering organization" in society.[54] I adopt an International Relations perspective to show that warlords shape state formation in places of fragmented authority, where substate actors can both negotiate with the center as equals and conduct their own international relations in defiance of the center's interests, such as in Yemen, Sudan, Somalia, and a significant portion of sub-Saharan Africa. Understanding warlord survival is therefore crucial to comprehending how a number of states actually work. Most studies of state formation and state building focus primarily on the state, but in fact, "the study of government could be enhanced by the study of warlords."[55]

State-building advocates promote what is historically a very narrow conception of how dominant political authority ought to be organized. While the emergence of states is most closely associated with the historical rise of Western states (and the subordination of the feudal lords), the political survival of Afghan warlords shows that there are alternative paths to statehood.[56] Contemporary state formation is shaped by interactions among the state, the international community, and de facto power holders such as General Dostum. That warlords endure and thrive compels state builders, external and domestic, to engage in hybridization as they attempt to construct bureaucratic institutions. Dipali Mukhopadhyay, for example, shows how the hybrid form of governance developed by Afghan warlords turned governors has contributed to strengthening state institutions in the post-Taliban era.[57] In this book, I focus on warlords to shed light on a more realistic relationship between their authority and a state-building process that is usually expressed in terms of the triumph of the central state as the locus of political decisions.

Since 2001, international efforts to build the Afghan state have given domestic actors the opportunity to capture and "indigenize" the new institutions, a practice through which warlords and others secure and perpetuate their power.[58] The resilience of Afghan warlords shows that they participate in shaping what is actually a different order, where personalities matter more than bureaucratic institutions. This personality-based type of order may lack characteristics that most Western observers expect or desire, and hence may seem extremely fragile. Yet, "it appears as disorder only because most paradigms are based on a notion of a form of social, economic and, therefore, political development which reflects the experience of Western societies."[59] In fact, this type of order might be more durable and flexible in the broader context of instability and violence.

Nonstate power holders such as warlords are commonly treated as foes of state power, engaged in a zero-sum competition for the right to control and influence people. Yet, warlord survival demonstrates that substate actors remain relevant, even in an international system that clashes with their attempts to play a significant role alongside states. These nonstate armed actors are important in local, state, and international politics. They assert their power despite a state-building process that is (ideally at least) aimed at establishing a Weberian bureaucratic administration. In fact, the personal relationships and networks that underlie warlord authority are not necessarily inimical to the construction of at least the semblance of state authority. Warlords need not be corrosive challengers to the state.

Afghanistan is a rhizome state: "an infinitely variable multiplicity of networks whose underground branches join together the scattered points of society," with no clear divide between state and society, or between public and private spheres.[60] Warlords are integral not only to Afghan politics but to the formation of the Afghan state. Their struggle for influence transforms how sovereignty is exerted, in a way that is not consistent with the conventional idea of the state. External interveners should accept this reality and recognize that they can only influence this state formation process but not replace it. They should acknowledge that external state building that seeks to monopolize the means of violence and build centralized bureaucratic institutions is severely limited in places like Afghanistan, where warlords never truly engage in a virtuous process of integration.

The Method of Studying Warlords

This book is an empirical study of state building, state formation, and political order informed by over two hundred interviews with high-profile political actors conducted between 2007 and 2018, and many more informal conversations.[61] These actors include warlords and their entourages (advisers and family members), a former president, current (at the time of the interview) or former vice presidents, ministers, governors, intelligence officers, opposition leaders, former mujahideen, foreign diplomats, nongovernmental organization (NGO) workers, journalists, local researchers, and more. I spoke with some of these people multiple times over the years, but also used journalistic accounts and interviews with political opponents to get the most accurate account of events and ensure the quality of information. It was important, for my research agenda (and my credibility) to be perceived as independent, and hence not be part of a warlord's power conversion or power projection endeavors. In fact, higher-profile informants asked me for favors or used my interest in them to exhibit their personal connection with a foreign scholar on more than one occasion.[62]

I study warlord survival through an intensive comparative analysis of a few case studies within the larger case of Afghanistan, from the 1978 coup to 2014 (but provide additional information about events up to 2019 where relevant). Not only did 2014 mark the end of the Karzai era as well as the end of North Atlantic Treaty Organization (NATO) combat operations, but it was also a milestone for the warlords under study. Ismail Khan left the government in October 2013, on the eve of the presidential election; Moham-mad Qasim Fahim passed away the following March; and Dostum became first vice president of Afghanistan a few months later. This time frame al-lows me to trace the processes through which warlords evolved and trans-formed their power when subjected to exogenous shocks. I look at warlords' personal histories and political trajectories to analyze the specific mechanisms that affect their survival and identify the core components of their author-ity. By taking individual warlords as the unit of analysis, I hope to carve out space for their oft-ignored agency in the study of state formation and state building.

My method is to follow a limited number of warlords to reconstruct how they combine different sources of power to survive rapidly changing envi-ronments. This approach fundamentally differs from Jesse Driscoll's lottery model, which "treats all warlords as essentially interchangeable in [the con-solidation] process—subordinating the causal weight of social networks, war-lord ideology and charisma, and clandestine foreign interventions."[63] By tracing individual trajectories, I show that warlord survival is *not* a lottery, while underscoring these men's extraordinary longevity and variability of in-terests.

In-depth case studies of warlords from western, northern, and northeast-ern Afghanistan (Herat, Sheberghan, and Panjshir), where warlordism found fertile ground, allow me to identify variation in the way these men have com-bined and converted their respective sources of power. I uncover different paths of warlord survival by focusing on real, imperfect, yet successful, war-lords, combined with anecdotal evidence of failure. I use variation within each trajectory to uncover causal relationships and test my argument, look-ing at their ups and downs, at times offering glimpses of warlord demise, instead of merely focusing on survival and demise as dichotomous outcomes.[64] Examples from the "Pashtun belt" of southern and eastern Afghanistan serve to illustrate my argument across regions and show that the process of inter-est also takes place in less exemplary cases.[65]

Ismail Khan rose to prominence during the Soviet-Afghan war and became an active warlord in the years after the collapse of the communist regime. In chapter 3, I demonstrate that the self-proclaimed amir of western Afghanistan is a typical warlord: when the conditions do not allow him to concentrate all sources of power simultaneously, he uses his authority to mediate between different levels of politics and make himself indispensable. Dostum, a former pro-government militia leader, at one point ruled over most of northern Afghanistan. I show in chapter 4 that he never broke free from either his Uzbek identity or his role as an ethnic entrepreneur. This has in turn allowed him to successfully project authority both domestically and internationally, and eventually survive. Ahmad Shah Massoud and Fahim, his successor, are both atypical warlords and the focus of chapter 5. The former was a "mix" between a patrimonial leader and an ideological one, a "militant" whose objective was to capture the central state, a particularity that is reflected in the way he accumulated and converted his power.[66] Fahim is also atypical. While Ismail Khan, Dostum, and Massoud at times managed to accumulate all sources of power and exert a *fonction totale* in the territories they controlled, he rose to power only after Massoud's death and the beginning of the US-led intervention. His ensuing lack of legitimacy deeply affected the way he exerted and converted power, putting a greater emphasis on the accumulation of economic resources.

In the conclusion, I further articulate the core implication of this book: state building is impossible in fragmented societies without significant concessions to nonstate power holders. State building that is aimed at centralizing and monopolizing political authority is a delusion because warlords are in fact integral to the way states like Afghanistan actually work.

Chapter 1

Warlords, States, and Political Orders

In the summer of 2015, General Abdul Rashid Dostum, first vice president of the Islamic Republic of Afghanistan, traveled to his hometown of She-berghan, turned his own palace into a command center, and announced that he would now be personally in charge of coordinating all anti-Taliban war efforts in the northern provinces of Jowzjan, Faryab, and Sar-i Pul. "That the man a heartbeat away from the Afghan presidency was on the front lines," wrote Mujib Mashal in the *New York Times* on August 18 of that year, "caused consternation in Afghanistan's military and political establishments, and deep concern among Western diplomats"—especially as the military force that Dostum had rallied was mostly made up of men who paid personal allegiance to him rather than to the state.

Yet, for the international relations adviser to the first vice president, whom I interviewed a few months later, General Dostum did what was required of a great Afghan leader. "Our message," he told me, "is that the situation in Afghanistan cannot be compared to the one in any other country, in partic-ular Western countries." This is how he described the situation:

Here, if a leader doesn't take serious action, people get seriously disappointed. Many people think that their leaders don't understand them, have neglected them, live behind walls. . . . Dostum even brought his sons to the battlefield. He said: "I'm here with my two young sons. Your blood is as important as my sons's. I'm a general and you are here with me."

People needed to see management and leadership from the top, something that General Dostum delivered. . . . He is a real leader. People know that, when General Dostum is there, everything is fine. He is much more equipped. He is a general. He is an expert. He did what he should have done.[1]

What this episode suggests is that warlords are not mere challengers to the state. They represent alternative forms of authority that are well suited to certain circumstances (at times better suited than states) and will not disappear under the increasing pressure of state centralization. State formation should therefore not be conceived as the monopolization of authority by the state culminating with the destruction of other forms of governance (that is, the defeat of the warlords). It is not a zero-sum "quest for predominance" in which either the state or the warlords will prevail and rule single-handedly.[2]

In this chapter, I first unpack the complex relationships between warlords and states and explain that warlords operate in realms of authority that go beyond the grasp of the formal state to ensure their survival. I then build a typology of political orders in areas of weak and failed statehood to identify the different types of structural environments in which warlords exert their agency. This typology forms the basis with which I analyze warlord survival mechanisms in chapter 2.

Beyond the Weberian State

Warlords are important to study because of their complex relationships with their host state and their role in state formation. These relationships have always been a crucial aspect of studies on warlords and, to some extent, are what distinguish warlords from other substate actors. Since warlords surfaced as research subjects, special attention has been given to the necessary conditions for them to emerge, from the *tuchün* of Republican China (1916–28) to the *jangsalar* of 1990s Afghanistan.[3] Some view warlords as a cause of state failure and hence focus on the personalization of authority and local power dynamics; others consider warlords to be a consequence of state failure and thus believe that warlords "take advantage of the disintegration of central authority."[4] Whether one sees warlord politics as a cause or as a consequence of state failure, warlords remain defined in relation to the central state. Warlords matter because they shed light on state formation, or its frustration. In fact, "the concept of the warlord is inextricably linked to the Weberian concept of state."[5]

Warlords and States

Dominant normative and policy-oriented views incorporate the idea of a zero-sum game in which warlords are opposed to the sovereign state and in which the state must come up with ways to regulate its relations with these peripheral actors. I argue that warlords are in fact integral to the kind of state one finds in Afghanistan. They refuse to accept the existence of a hierarchically superior Weberian state (and cause the exercise of sovereignty to change), but they do not necessarily want to overthrow the state. They do not even always question the existence of the state in which they find themselves.[6] Afghan warlords, for instance, never really did. They did not try to break away from the state in the 1990s, when the state was at its weakest, nor did they after 2001. Warlords often try to wrap themselves in the state's symbolic mantle, even when their activities are actually undermining it. Their struggle instead aims at earning recognition and achieving a favorable balance of power.[7]

At times, warlords attempt to accumulate resources across all realms of authority (ideological, economic, military, social, and political) to undertake a *fonction totale* and replace the state.[8] They can do it locally, through the construction of their own protostates. Their capacity to establish exclusive rule on a territory and provide security on that territory makes them alternatives to centralized states. The Russian civil war of 1917–22 provides many examples: the anarchist revolutionary Nestor Makhno attempted to establish a stateless political order over parts of Ukraine, the Free Territory, that aimed to replace the central state and completely reorganize society along anarchist principles; in eastern Siberia, a military leader named Grigory Semyonov took advantage of the October Revolution to establish an oppressive rule over the Transbaikal region while resisting the new Bolshevik regime; and in southwestern Siberia, Aleksandr Kolchak, a commander in the Russian Navy, established an anti-Soviet government called the Provisional All-Russian Government.[9] Post-Arab Spring Libya is one of the most striking examples of recent times: "It is almost as if one part of Libya were controlled by White Russians—that's Haftar—and another part were controlled by Bolsheviks," said a US administration official.[10]

Warlords can also undertake a *fonction totale* nationally, appropriating the state's resources and negotiating with other warlords as primus inter pares. In fact, "most of them probably would not mind" conquering the state.[11] Charles Taylor, the former leader of the National Patriotic Front of Liberia, who later became president of Liberia (1997–2003), is probably the best-known example of a warlord turned head of state. State power provides warlords with significant sources of revenues and authority. International legal sovereignty (or external sovereignty), based on official diplomatic recognition, provides armed groups and their leaders with the ability to attract both material resources (such as arms and ammunition and financial aid) and symbolic ones (such as embassies or a seat at the UN General Assembly), which in turn increase their ability to maintain their domestic sovereignty (or empirical sovereignty).[12] Taylor's recognition of Taiwan, as head of state, in exchange for $200 million in foreign aid is a perfect example.[13] The same could be said of Ahmad Shah Massoud, whose control of the Afghan state apparatus in the 1990s was essential to his symbolic quest for legitimacy and international stature.[14]

At other times, warlords rule alongside the central state, constructing political authority on a different plane from the state. They exist on the same territory and may carve out spaces from that territory, but their realms of authority do not coincide entirely. Some warlords might engage with the state in many different ways, as shown in the Dostum example. In some cases, they collude with state officials to "flout and undermine state capacity and state institutions."[15] Marten, for example, highlights how the Russian state outsourced security in Chechnya to the warlord Ramzan Kadyrov: "Indeed Moscow gave away so much to Ramzan that Russian authorities may never be able to take back control of Chechnya without another bloody war, this time against Ramzan's forces and their patronage networks."[16] Yet, this is only one strategy among others. Warlords exploit elements of their host state and use state power as a political resource not only to maximize their interests (not always for personal, self-aggrandizing purposes) but also to provide "discriminatory access to desired goods" to their community through patronage relations.[17]

These patronage politics are not restricted to warlords. Jean-François Médard, for example, described very similar practices in Kenya (*le système Kenyatta*), Gabon (*le système Bongo*), and the French city of Bordeaux (*le système Chaban*).[18] Ernest Gellner in fact posited that "patronage is only avoidable when relations are anonymous and specific, in a mass society; and that in an inevitably more intimate elite, where relations cannot be anonymous nor criteria universalistic, patronage must be endemic."[19] For Afghan warlords, this means acting as the dominant political authority in areas that they control and exercising this authority in channels that may but do not necessarily contend with those of the state. These two types of authority can be exerted in parallel to each other; they can overlap; they can even exist in synergy.

Warlords may have an interest in the central state, participate in the way it is being shaped, and change the nature of the state itself. As Ariel Ahram and Charles King point out, "The warlord seeks a privileged place within the existing legal system—wedging himself into a legal order provided by a recognized state or crafting his own (often arbitrary) code of behavior."[20] While William Reno considers that warlords "rule through control of commerce rather than by mobilizing a bureaucracy," I argue that what he describes is not a defining feature of warlord politics but rather a particular survival strategy used in a specific environment.[21] In many respects, Afghan warlords are part of the post-2001 state apparatus. They are pivotal actors between the state bureaucracy and their local patronage networks. Understanding the formation of the Afghan state under US supervision therefore requires looking at the interactions among peripheral power holders, the central state, and the international community.[22]

State Formation and Multilayered Authority

The state-warlords relations I identify in this book should prompt scholars to question the nature of political authority in places where "central governments with very limited power rely on a diverse range of local authorities to execute core functions of government and 'mediate' relations between local communities and the state."[23] In these locations, political authority is multi-layered: warlords and other nonstate actors exist in parallel to the state, on the same territory, but not necessarily in opposition to it. In this sense, the state represents only one of the many sources of authority that coexist in a given territory, a source of authority that is not always distinct from the type of authority exercised by warlords. In Somalia, for example, warlords often use the state as a facade for their political activities. And, in Georgia and Tajikistan, the state has been compared to "a semipermeable membrane for violence entrepreneurs—'warlords'—who weigh their life opportunities as social bandits against their life opportunities as agents of an internationally recognized sovereign."[24] Afghanistan is a kind of "mini-empire" where the central state operates as a first among equals to negotiate diverse political agreements with nonstate actors.[25] These agreements hence defy the homogenization and codification of authority consistent with the territorial logic of states.[26]

One might in turn conceive of contemporary state building as a deliberate project of accelerating state formation—the state's "attempt to enhance the capacity to rule"—thus turning mini-empires into nation-states.[27] Karen Barkey describes this as the "Ottoman route to state centralization."[28] She writes: "Once the multifarious settlements between state and different communities diminish and stabilize, and standardized relations apply to all segments of imperial society, we are not talking about empire anymore, and have moved toward an alternative political formation, perhaps on the way to the nation-state."[29] This process has not taken place in Afghanistan and elsewhere, where the state should not be seen "as a thing, as a collection of institutions, but as a set of social processes and relations."[30] Granted, the distinction between the Weberian state and the state as a set of social processes and relations is not a dichotomous one. Yet, some states more than others (Afghanistan among them) remain characterized by intricate personal relationships and political networks. The political reality in which Afghan warlords operate, in fact, challenges the idea that the state's social contract is accepted by all as permanent and state power understood as the organizing principle of society. Warlord survival confirms that "the state will coexist—for the foreseeable future—with significant transnational and subnational actors: these are not anomalies, and they aren't going to go away."[31] Warlords are not throwbacks of an earlier era. They are contemporary phenomena.

The process of warlord survival also questions the universalism of the Western state formation. Indeed, the trajectories of Afghan warlords and of the states they are embedded in greatly differ from the path of Western modernization. It is misleading to assume that the only path to modernization is the one experienced by Western Europe, where the growth of state control overcame parallel sources of authority, or, in Edward Shils's words, that "the model of modernity is a picture of the West detached in some way from its geographical origins and locus."[32] Historians have shown that Western European states emerged because they were more efficient at war making than the medieval lords they were competing against: "A system developed which led to the state taking control of an increasingly regulated and integrated military machine and all its operations."[33] The end of feudalism (warlordism) and the transition toward capitalism was driven by the rise of the absolutist state, followed by the rise of a new class of merchants (the bourgeoisie) that emerged as the nobility's main adversary. In Afghanistan, the international community is strongly opposing the emergence of an absolutist state—although the British ambassador to Afghanistan once called for the installation of an "acceptable dictator" in the country—while slowing down the emergence of a new class of merchants due to the illicit character of the product they trade (drugs).[34] Warlords are both capitalists and notables, and can, through the transformation of their power sources, operate within all realms of authority (as detailed in chapter 2). They undertake a much more encompassing function than medieval lords ever did. Whereas European notables were unable to prevent the emergence of the bourgeoisie, warlords impede the arising of rivals by occupying the political space, and hence participate in shaping their state in ways that greatly diverge from the process of the state formation experienced in Western Europe.[35]

States and societies indeed are shaped by idiosyncratic histories, which result from the specificities of their own social fabrics and political environments (domestic, regional, and international).[36] In Afghanistan, both the British and the Soviets failed to centralize power, as did domestic leaders such as Abdur Rahman Khan (1880–1901), "who abolished the decentralized governmental system in which tribes and regions maintained a high degree of autonomy in exchange for submitting to the legal authority of the Kabul government."[37] Likewise, the states of Somalia, Myanmar, and Sierra Leone have their own trajectories and historicities.

Warlords as Actors in the International System

As providers of alternative forms of governance, warlords challenge the internal state hierarchy on which the Weberian state is based and hence the conventional notion of the state as the ultimate arbiter of a social contract. They participate in shaping the process of state formation and impact the interstate system, whether they enjoy official recognition or not.[38] Yet, few studies consider warlords as actors in the international system.[39] The scholars who do are often limited in the way they see international links, as they privilege clandestine networks and do not consider how warlords try to influence the interests of international actors through diplomacy.[40] Diplomacy is widely understood as "the strategic use of talk *by states*" and by states only, hence depriving nonstate armed actors of important sources of legitimization and (legal) revenues.[41]

"Today's successful warlords," writes Mark Duffield, "think globally but act locally."[42] They are indeed able to "act financially and politically in the international system without interference from the state in which [they are] based" while exerting authority at the local level.[43] This is not necessarily a process of destabilization, even when this independent action involves participation in activities that are illicit (from the point of view of prevailing international rules) and involve war economies. The warlords' faculty to reinvent themselves time and again in part rests on their ability to conduct their own foreign policy in ways that are otherwise reserved for sovereign states (through high-level diplomacy, for example), as well as on their ability to conduct relations with (and infiltrate) their own state. In sum, they conduct their own diplomacy while instrumentalizing and subordinating elements of the state. This is perfectly illustrated by how Dostum leveraged first his relationship with Turkey and second his ability to provide votes to survive the events following the alleged beating and kidnapping of Akbar Bai described in the introduction.

Not only do warlords adapt to the international environment to resist its homogenizing pressure, but elements of the international system also facilitate facade behaviors. The international environment decisively alters patronage politics.[44] External state builders often despise warlords, but they frequently rely on them as a stopgap as they attempt to build central authority. Paradoxically, their reliance on warlords empowers these peripheral actors against the center, thus subverting their aims. In 2002, Sher Mohammad Akhunzada, former mujahid turned provincial governor, leveraged his proximity to the United States (and American money) to solidify his position in the local political economy and then extract additional resources from development projects.[45] Governor Gul Agha Sherzai did the same in Kandahar, taking advantage of US largesse to cultivate and expand his patronage networks and further establish his authority, at the expense of state centralization. In the words of the former journalist Sarah Chayes, "The U.S. forces were helplessly wrapped inside the [Sherzais's] friendly bear hug," hence "not working *for* the central government, but *against* it."[46] In fact, warlords defy the international community even when they cooperate with it. This is not to say that international intervention is a necessary condition for warlords to survive, but it does affect their strategies. The international system sustains warlords.

Warlords in turn exert agency to adapt to changing international structures—for example, by turning newly created bureaucratic institutions into patronage networks. They also affect the structure in other ways. Their interests and strategies are incorporated into the choices of very powerful external actors—such as NATO officials—so that warlords, who are supposedly weak and subordinate, manipulate interactions with seemingly more powerful actors to support their own strategies.[47] They also take advantage of the heterogeneity and complexity of an international system in which many competing actors with a variety of foreign policy agendas coexist.[48] For example, in Herat, Ismail Khan was particularly successful at balancing between Iran, his western neighbor, and the United States while exploiting their rivalry to receive support from both and increase his local autonomy in the process. In Afghanistan more generally, even the different branches of the Bush administration could not agree on a single position to adopt vis-à-vis warlords: the Department of Defense was building up the warlords, providing them with ample amounts of cash in the context of the so-called global war on terrorism, while the Department of State was promoting state centralization under Karzai's authority. In the words of a former Western diplomat: "DC was on many pages at the same time."[49] The Department of Defense was waging war, the Department of State was building peace, and the warlords were reaping the benefits.

A Typology of Political Orders

Paul Staniland defines political order as "the structure and distribution of authority between armed organizations: who rules, where, and through what understandings" and develops a typology based on the distribution of territorial control and the level of cooperation between insurgents and states.[50] In this section, I build an alternative, descriptive typology of political orders in areas of weak and failed statehood, which I use to trace the trajectories of a specific category of actors (warlords) whose "goals of inclusion, patronage, and local autonomy . . . do not map onto conventional goals of insurgent groups."[51] However, this typology should apply to nonstate armed groups more broadly, which is why I include examples of nonstate armed groups that might not necessarily be considered as typical warlords (at least at this stage of their existence) or might not see themselves as such, especially when they are claiming statehood (such as in Somaliland, Iraqi Kurdistan, and the so-called Islamic State).

I argue that the nature of political authority can be mapped according to the relative internal and external power resources of the state and the nonstate armed actors (warlords as well as other individuals and organizations). These power resources are placed on a continuum (from low to high) and broadly defined as any means at the disposal of a political actor that, when activated, push back his constraints, open up his possibilities, increase his autonomy, and facilitate the development of his strategies.[52] These internal and external resources are not always substitutable for each other but have different values in different contexts. They include but are not limited to weapons, drugs, money, information, patronage networks, institutional positions, personal militias, and so on (for more on power resources, see chapter 2).

Although the state is represented as a single actor in the typology, it is not conceived of as a neutral and monolithic entity. State elites control their own resources and, as Hamid Karzai's attitude toward Dostum showed, have the ability to exert agency in the system, in particular in their attempt to manage peripheral warlords.[53] Weak states, however, lack the ability to extract sufficient resources through taxation. For the most part, their resources (in particular, financial and military) will therefore be a function of international

Table 1. A typology of political orders in areas of weak and failed statehood

		State resources	
		Low	High
	High	**Regional authority**	**Parallel authority**
Warlord		*(1990s northern Afghanistan)*	*(post-2001 Afghanistan)*
resources	Low	**Fragmented authority**	**Consolidating authority**
		(1990s southern Afghanistan)	*(projected Afghanistan)*

support.[54] A state that benefits from a massive influx of foreign aid can thus be understood as possessing high resources even though it lacks indigenous and sustainable forms of revenue generation. It should also be noted that state capacity is not directly a function of a state's amount of resources but reflects its actual ability to "control [its] territor[y] and deliver a high order of political goods to [its] citizens."[55] Indeed, state resources do not imply state capacity (although the reverse is usually true, as state capacity requires a large amount of resources).

Here I follow an explanatory typology methodology, which I use as a complement to deductive approaches to uncover causal relationships.[56] The different categories (outcomes) are derived inductively from observations from the theory-generating case, Afghanistan, which I analyze below. The multiple combinations of warlord and state resources are simplified in four such combinations that produce four ideal types: fragmented authority, regional authority, parallel authority, and consolidating authority, which can in some cases overlap or coexist in different parts of the same state. In other words, the different forms of political order are in no way mutually exclusive. These four outcomes are systematically defined and described below, together with the political logics at work.

Fragmented Authority

The fragmentation of political authority is the result of low warlord resources combined with low state resources (bottom left cell), a situation of state failure that comes directly out of the competing failed political projects of states and warlords. In a situation in which power resources are relatively evenly distributed—that is, when no warlord is more powerful than the others in relative terms—no single actor manages to impose his own rule over large swaths of territory. In the absence of a state that has the necessary resources to expand its territorial control beyond the capital city, political authority tends to splinter into kaleidoscopic forms of local control. Warlords resemble the roving bandits described by Mancur Olson. They do not have the capacity to defeat the others and accumulate power resources through "uncoordinated competitive theft."[57] They coexist in a form of stalemate, each of them in control of only a small area, and typically engage in "symmetric, non-conventional wars."[58] In the contemporary world scene, we would associate this with the situation that most of southern Somalia has experienced since the early 1990s.[59]

Fragmented authority can result from a sharp and sudden crisis in resources in a consolidating and hence vulnerable state (from bottom right to bottom left cell). State elites who are suddenly deprived of important state resources can no longer co-opt or control political and military rivals and the state eventually collapses, leading to the fragmentation of political authority. This outcome may also result from the fragmentation of regionalized warlord polities (from top left to bottom left cell)—for example, through a seeding process in which the strongest warlord coalition splits.[60] Generally speaking, a sharp decline in warlord resources evens the field for a multitude of contenders seeking new opportunities. This is typically the case when external powers attempt to weaken the most powerful warlords and in so doing upset the current political equilibrium, create a relative power vacuum, and thus facilitate the emergence of smaller warlords and other nonstate armed groups.

Regional Authority

Regional warlord polities, in which political authority is concentrated in the hands of a few warlords, result from the combination of high warlord resources and low state resources (top left cell). Warlords, in this configuration, "transform into state-makers *at the local level*," in the sense that they accumulate and concentrate capital and means of coercion.[61] They behave like states, act as the principal suppliers of governance, goods, and services to people in the areas they control, and eventually start building embryonic state infrastructures.[62] Warlords, in this context, are in many ways similar to Olson's stationary bandits, who, up to a certain point, have an incentive to purvey goods and services to the population under their control.[63] Given the structure of the contemporary international system, norms of sovereignty inhibit warlords from challenging existing borders and creating new states that would receive international recognition, a phenomenon illustrated by the cases of Somaliland and Puntland, Somalia.

Regional authority can result from a sharp decrease in state capacity where existing warlords have managed to keep most of their resources by resisting the state's effort to weaken their authority (from top right to top left cell). In this scenario, the decrease in state resources (usually the result of an exogenous shock) reempowers the warlords, who then retake control of their former polities. The expansion of Iraqi Kurdistan and the emergence of the so-called Islamic State on Iraqi territory following the complete withdrawal of US forces are prime examples. This outcome may also surface from the consolidation of fragmented authority through an influx of resources (from bottom left to top left cell). Warlords who are powerful in relative terms use their resources to progressively concentrate power in the territories under their control.[64] They co-opt or defeat relatively weaker warlords, expand their control beyond their power bases, and rule over entire swaths of territory. In some extreme cases, they eventually replace and become the state, either de jure (by seizing the capital city) or de facto (by expanding their territorial control to the entire country) and hence benefit from significant additional resources.[65]

Parallel Authority

The combination of high warlord resources and high state resources results in parallel authority (top right cell). The state tries to impose its rule on the whole territory—that is, to expand its empirical sovereignty—but its authority is constantly challenged and renegotiated by existing warlords who accumulate and convert resources to ensure their survival in a changing political environment. This outcome typically results from a sharp increase in the state's resources, owing to either a massive injection of foreign capital (for example, from an ambitious state-building project) or the extraction of newly discovered natural resources (from top left to top right). The warlords who previously controlled large swaths of territory become dormant and find other ways of exerting their authority. They reinvent themselves by shifting their sources of power. They play different roles in their new environments: they can be ethnic entrepreneurs, political leaders, businessmen, or even infiltrate the state apparatus (and become state elites), using one type of resource to accumulate another (see chapter 2). Others can remain (or become) insurgents and exert parallel forms of authority, as in contemporary Afghanistan, where the state coexists with both insurgents and dormant warlords. Acknowledging this peculiar situation, a Western diplomat interviewed in February 2014 mentioned the existence of "two shadow governors" in the northern province of Jowzjan: the Taliban governor (insurgent) and Dostum (dormant warlord).[66]

It is also theoretically possible to reach a situation of stalemated insurgency or open warfare between well-matched equals, such as a resource-rich warlord and a state that is strong enough to resist but too weak to defeat the insurgency. However, it is expected that these unstable equilibriums will only be temporary and will not crystallize into permanent forms of political order, given that conventional warfare (which we are most likely to see with equally powerful opponents) tends to result in shifts in the balance of power that push the situation back to parallel authority (through a relative increase in state resources) or regional authority (through a relative decrease in state resources). Parallel authority may also result from an influx of warlord resources in a consolidating state (from bottom right to top right cell). This tends to be the case in Afghanistan, as rising insecurity creates a situation of uncertainty in which both external forces and the population turn to the strongest power holders (warlords) to provide stability, further strengthening their power in the process.

Consolidating Authority

Consolidated state authority (or "consolidated statehood"), the sort of order that international intervention seeks to build, results from the combination of low warlord resources and high state resources (bottom right cell).[67] When the state controls a plethora of resources and the warlords do not, there should be no impediments to the process of state consolidation. The state should have no difficulty in asserting territorial rule and extending its reach and domestic sovereignty—that is, engaging in the process of state making and neutralizing warlords. This outcome should theoretically result from an increase in state resources providing the state with the capabilities to ultimately defeat or co-opt a myriad of weak warlords (from bottom left to bottom right cell). This, Driscoll convincingly argues, is what happened in Georgia and Tajikistan after the collapse of the Soviet Union, where "political order arose out of violent anarchy."[68] A decrease in warlord resources should lead to the same outcome (from top right to bottom right cell). Either scenario should theoretically foster state consolidation. Yet, the process described above does not take place in countries such as Afghanistan, where warlords show a high degree of resilience and transform the state's exercise of sovereignty to accommodate their interests.

While warlords might in some cases seem financially poor (relative to the state), they remain valuable to outsiders (and thus benefit from external support) and almost always maintain enough social and symbolic resources to bolster their local legitimacy and control. They have the capacity to shift their bases of power and switch to realms of authority that may be beyond the ostensible grasp of the formal state (e.g., commercial, spiritual, or customary). This in turn explains why state elites may oppose them while at the same time using them to gain access and control in these important realms of authority. Warlords reinvent themselves and in doing so prevent the consolidation of a Weberian bureaucracy.[69]

The four quadrants are descriptive ideal types (and not strategic choices, as in Driscoll's stag hunt, for example).[70] Since the two dimensions are nondichotomous, the empirical reality is much more nuanced and fluid. Nonstate armed actors constantly move around these horizontal and vertical axes. For that reason, the outcomes are always temporary; they are products of overall trajectories that can be explained in terms of the processes that I examine. Trajectories and processes matter, I argue, because in situations like Afghanistan, "the ruler [and the central state this ruler is supposed to represent are] only as strong as today's bargains with members of the political elite [such as Ismail Khan, Dostum, and Fahim], who retain a great deal of autonomy."[71]

Time and cases therefore provide variation. I study the political trajectories of four warlords and show how they move along the two axes. This examination of trajectories uncovers the processes that allow warlords to transform their power and survive, more than the causality (and outcomes) per se. Warlords are not clear cases of failure or success, but their chaotic trajectories and phoenix-like tendencies illustrate failure, or success, as shaped by the international environment of a particular time and their abilities to master these changes (or failure to do so). In other words, I look at survival, which I define as the process by which warlords manage to maintain authority.

Political Order in Afghanistan's Wars (1978–2014)

In this section, I consider the fit between the conceptual typology developed above and Afghanistan, the theory-generating case, which, given the country's geostrategic location (magnified by the so-called global war on terrorism) and the unprecedented state-building effort of the post-Taliban era, can be considered a paradigmatic case. The analytic narrative of the Afghanistan case fills the gap between macrolevel outcomes (the failure to consolidate) and microlevel explanations (warlords shifting resources). Careful process tracing shows how shifts in resources generate different political orders. It sheds light on warlord strategies and survival mechanisms, which in turn explain the absence of state consolidation.[72]

Throughout the 1980s (period 1), the Afghan political order evolved from a situation in which a weak, yet consolidating state (in the 1960s and 1970s) shifted toward one teetering on the brink of failure. This situation of parallel authority, characterized by the combination of a foreign invasion with a strengthening but fragmented insurgency, shows how rebels were able to play the international system to their advantage. The Soviet withdrawal crucially weakened the Afghan central state, which in 1992 gave way to a fragmentation of political order and the progressive regionalization of warlord polities (period 2). This development culminated in the Taliban controlling most of the territory and engaging in a process of state consolidation that was stopped only by the post-9/11 US-led intervention (period 3). In the absence of a central state, former warlords were able to swiftly retake the regional polities they controlled in the 1990s (period 4). Their relative weakening, combined with the massive injection of external resources and the emergence of the Taliban insurgency, led to a situation of parallel authority where the state coexisted with both dormant warlords and insurgents (period 5). This situation has started to change with the announcement of NATO troops' withdrawal: warlords have been preparing to transform once again and have been increasingly relying on military resources (period 6).

Period 1: Soviet-Afghan War (1978–1988)

In the summer of 1973, Mohammad Daoud Khan launched a bloodless coup against his cousin King Zahir Shah, marking the end of the Afghan monarchy. The coup, in conjunction with the rise of Islamist and communist radicalism, began a period of profound political instability in Afghanistan. In April 1978, the pro-Soviet People's Democratic Party of Afghanistan (PDPA), soon to be dominated by its more extreme Khalq branch, came to power in yet another coup (also known as the Saur Revolution) that caused uncoordinated uprisings across the country. This was followed by the invasion of Afghanistan by the Soviet Union in December 1979, an attempt to support and ultimately steer the new communist regime in favor of the more moderate Parcham branch of the PDPA. Pakistan reacted by officially recognizing and providing seven Sunni political parties with financial and military support for their jihad against the Soviet Union. These parties' nationalism, in line with Pakistani interests (and against the interests of the Afghan government), opposed the idea of Pashtunistan—that is, the proposal to unite Pashtun populations from both sides of the Pakistan-Afghanistan border, either to join the Afghan state or to form a newly independent entity.[73] This was also compatible with Pakistan's interest in establishing a friendly Islamic regime in Kabul to provide strategic depth and counterbalance India's military and demographic superiority. The strengthening of the insurgency, combined with the Soviet Union's effort to bolster the communist regime, fostered a situation of parallel authority.

While most mujahideen commanders and fighters were operating from Afghanistan, the leaders of the political parties were based in Peshawar, Pakistan, where they could gather support from the Inter-Services Intelligence, Pakistan's main intelligence agency, as well as from Saudi Arabia and the United States.[74] They would then redistribute the weapons and financial resources they received to their commanders based in different parts of Afghanistan. All the leaders and commanders who later participated in the warlord politics of the 1990s took part in the Soviet-Afghan war of the 1980s. Both Ismail Khan and Massoud belonged to one of the political parties waging the jihad, the Jamiat-i Islami (henceforth Jamiat), a political party inspired by the Egyptian Muslim Brotherhood that aimed at establishing a state founded on Sharia law. They both progressively established their grip over entire regions while increasing their autonomy vis-à-vis the party: Ismail Khan became known as the amir of western Afghanistan, Massoud as the lion of Panjshir.[75] Dostum, on the contrary, was a pro-government militia leader fighting the mujahideen. He also grew increasingly autonomous, to the point where, after the collapse of the Soviet Union had caused a sharp decline in state resources, he allied with Massoud against his former patron and turned into an orphan warlord, a "former regional [commander] of the central state army who faced with a political crisis at the centre opted to set up [his] own [fiefdom]" (see below).[76]

Period 2: Warlord Era (1988–1994)

On April 14, 1988, Pakistan, Afghanistan, the United States, and the Soviet Union signed the Geneva Accords, by which the latter agreed to remove all of its troops. The full withdrawal started on May 15, 1988, and was completed on February 15, 1989.[77] Contrary to expectations, the PDPA regime survived over three years after the departure of Soviet troops. After the collapse of the Soviet Union in December 1991, Moscow cut off supplies to Afghanistan's puppet government, and the United States stopped supporting its former clients. The PDPA regime could no longer survive in these conditions and eventually fell a few months later, in April 1992. Both warlord and state resources declined simultaneously, leading, in the following months and years, to a highly fragmented political order (what Barnett Rubin coined the "fragmentation of Afghanistan").[78]

The collapse of the government of Mohammad Najibullah effectively started when a group of non-Pashtun militia leaders and army generals from the North (including General Dostum) rebelled and, allied with a few mujahideen leaders, took control of Mazar-i Sharif, Afghanistan's second-largest city, in March 1992. A month later, the northern rebels concluded an agreement with Massoud, Abdul Ali Mazari (leader of the Hezb-i Wahdat, henceforth Wahdat), and other mujahideen commanders to form an alliance against Gulbuddin Hekmatyar's Hezb-i Islami (henceforth Hezb) and jointly enter Kabul. On April 24, the main party leaders, gathered in Peshawar, Pakistan, signed a power-sharing agreement (the Peshawar Accords) stipulating that Sibghatullah Mujadidi, leader of a party named Jebh-i Nejat-i Mili, would be president for the first two months, followed by Burhanuddin Rabbani, the leader of Jamiat, for four months, after which an interim government would be appointed for the next eighteen months, and then an election would be held. The following day, violent combat for the control of Kabul ensued between Massoud's and Dostum's forces (joined by some regime forces) on one side and Hekmatyar's forces (joined by other regime forces) on the other side. Massoud's and Dostum's forces eventually gained the upper hand and pushed Hekmatyar and his men out of the capital.

From that point on, Massoud, selected to become the next defense minister under the Peshawar Accords, and Rabbani, once he had taken over from Mujadidi on June 28, 1992, controlled the most important buildings in Kabul. They were accepted by the international community as the official government of Afghanistan, hence benefiting from all the symbolic resources that international diplomatic recognition can provide. However, Rabbani's government could not meet the demands of empirical statehood. Not only was the new government unable to control and exert effective power over the entire territory—after all, no Afghan ruler has ever met this standard—but it could not even control the whole capital city.

Kabul rapidly became the scene of intense combat and remained divided between different armed factions throughout the period. Gulbuddin Hekmatyar, new prime minister of the mujahideen government under the Peshawar Accords, in fact started to bomb the city with rockets as early as May 1992. In the beginning of 1994, he joined forces with Dostum's Junbesh-i Mili and Wahdat, which had become disillusioned with Massoud, through the creation of the Shura-i Hamahangi, an alliance aimed at defeating him. "Until he died," a former official in the mujahideen government told me, "Massoud refused to share the benefits with other parties. He did not accept Mohaqiq, Mazari or Hekmatyar."[79] Once considered heroes of the Cold War, the mujahideen started being depicted, both locally and internationally, as violent thugs and bandits, in line with an emerging literature on irrational and barbaric conflicts.[80]

Some commanders, like Massoud, captured what was left of the central state; others, including Dostum, formed alliances to defeat those in control and seize state institutions; and still others, like Ismail Khan, strictly focused on expanding their zones of influence. This situation led to a progressive concentration of power with the emergence of regional warlord polities, what I depicted above as regional authority.[81] Protostate makers (active warlords) started to rule autonomously over significant parts of the state's territory on which they had established political civilian structures, while developing their own foreign relations to acquire both symbolic and material resources. They all levied taxes and provided public services. They established access to capital (through international patronage networks) to wage war more effectively, defeat their rivals, and extend their territorial control, whether through grabbing the center and trying to expand (like Massoud), or by running and expanding their own fiefdom and creating a "state-within-a-state" (like Dostum and Ismail Khan).[82] In other regions, in particular in the south of Afghanistan, authority remained deeply fragmented. In Helmand, for instance, local commanders, who had started fighting among themselves only shortly after the beginning of the Soviet-Afghan war, kept doing so after the Soviet withdrawal, until the Taliban provided a new form of political order (regional authority) in the province.[83]

Period 3: Taliban Era (1994–2001)

The emergence of the Taliban in the South and their conquest of Afghanistan signaled the end of the warlord era. Contrary to a very common interpretation, the Taliban, an Islamic fundamentalist militant movement created in 1994, did not (solely) become popular as a reaction to warlordism. It was the absence of a strong warlord able to concentrate power around Kandahar that gave the Taliban the space they needed to rise as a response to the chronic insecurity that affected the region—as opposed to other warlord-controlled regions. It was the absence of a strong warlord, in conjunction with the existence of other nonstate armed actors (from petty criminals to small warlords), that gave space for a violent political entrepreneur with great knowledge of the local political dynamics (Mullah Omar and his Taliban movement) to emerge. Pakistan's logistical support and financial resources (in addition to drug money and road taxes) gave the Taliban the means they needed to defeat most of their domestic rivals (including Ismail Khan in 1995 and Dostum in 1997–98) and rapidly enlarge their zone of influence through fighting, co-optation, and bandwagoning.[84] The Taliban took control of most of Afghanistan between 1994 and 1998, further expanding their regional polity and showing early signs of state consolidation.[85]

The Taliban, however, never gained international recognition. Despite controlling most of the country (including Kabul since 1996), only Pakistan, Saudi Arabia, and the United Arab Emirates recognized the movement as the official government of Afghanistan. Rabbani's government remained the official representative of the Islamic State of Afghanistan throughout the war, even though it no longer controlled Kabul and had to move to the northeast of the country, still controlled by Massoud and his men, in 1996. From then onward, Tajikistan became of tremendous strategic value as a way to remain in contact with the outside. The government of Afghanistan was given access to Tajik airports as well as permission to enter Tajik territory without visas. Tajikistan also provided a safe haven and a transit route for Russian and Iranian supplies. Massoud simultaneously created the United Front—better known as the Northern Alliance—a disparate coalition of warlords and commanders who had fought each other throughout the 1990s (including Dostum and Ismail Khan).[86] This alliance successfully resisted the Taliban until the end of 2001, hence preventing the completion of the state consolidation process by the movement.[87]

Period 4: Interim and Transitional Governments (2001–2004)

The 9/11 attacks on New York and Washington, combined with the assassination of Massoud two days earlier, fundamentally changed the dynamics of the conflict once again. The US-led intervention and the adoption of the so-called Afghan model of warfare—"in which indigenous allies replace American conventional ground troops by exploiting US airpower and small numbers of American special operations forces"[88]—completely disrupted Afghanistan's political order, leading to the collapse of the central state and the regionalization of the former warlord polities. The Bush administration worked closely with the warlords who accepted cooperation with the United States, including Dostum, Ismail Khan, and Fahim (who had replaced Massoud as leader of the Northern Alliance after his death), using the Northern Alliance's fighters as proxies on the ground, working with the same individuals they previously depicted as thugs and greedy warlords. Teams of CIA operatives were sent to Afghanistan and embedded with warlords, creating lasting personal relationships with them and relying on them to control and secure the provinces.[89] Washington's focus on short-term stability and the so-called global war on terrorism encouraged these men to fill the security vacuum left by the defeat of the Taliban and take control of state institutions, hence converting their military power into institutionalized forms of political power that would be more sustainable in the new international environment (for more on power conversion, see chapter 2).[90] These individuals (or their representatives) were then invited to Bonn, Germany, in December 2001 to take part in a conference—from which the Taliban were excluded—organized by the UN to make decisions regarding the establishment of a provisional government. An emergency *loya jirga*—a national constitutional assembly—was convened the following June to ratify the decisions made in Germany and confer more legitimacy to the Bonn Agreement.[91]

The sudden infusion of resources that came with the US-led intervention and the creation of the International Security Assistance Force in December 2001, along with the collapse of state institutions, allowed former warlords to retake their regional polities, shifting the political order from a consolidating Taliban state to a state made of multiple regional polities de facto recognized by the center—what I depicted above as regional authority. According to a UN official, "Neither in the north, west or east, any appointment by Kabul authorities was considered binding, but always required the approval of the regional strongman." In his words, "To counter centrifugal tendencies, Karzai granted regional leaders the power to appoint civilian officials in their regions, reminiscent of the regionalism prevailing after 1992."[92] Karzai, selected as chairman of the Afghan Interim Authority during the Bonn conference and later confirmed as president of the Afghan Transitional Administration during the 2002 *loya jirga*, chose to acknowledge the warlords's authority rather than challenge them and risk losing to them in a showdown. "If the Americans had armed them," asked the warlords, "who was Karzai to tell them to disarm?"[93] The same kind of logic was followed by US policymakers. This warlord strategy required "living with ambiguity."[94] A US diplomat mentioned that, at times, "these militia, these power bases . . . [were] the only force against chaos and lawlessness."[95] In 2003, Colonel Roger King, spokesman for the US Army in Afghanistan, declared that protecting the population from warlords was not part of the

US mission and that nothing would be done to disarm them: "It's not our purpose. We're not here on a security or stability mission. . . . [Warlords] are part of the landscape . . . part of the situation."[96]

Period 5: The New Rules of the Game (2004–2009)

Things changed around 2004, as most in the Bush administration believed the war in Afghanistan was already won. Warlords were soon deemed incompatible with the state that the international community was trying to build. With the "stigmatization of the mujahideen by human rights and woman's [*sic*] rights organizations" under way, Western policymakers started to impose what former US ambassador to Afghanistan Zalmay Khalilzad called "new rules of the game" that emphasized channeling resources through the government in Kabul and bolstering state authority, while trying to co-opt the most dominant warlords.[97] These new rules also increased the state's resources while decreasing the warlords', not least, in the absence of a centralized taxation system, by centralizing custom revenues: "We are trying to get Ismail Khan, Dostum and the others to hand over the largest possible share of their revenues to the central government through negotiations," declared Karzai in an October 2002 interview.[98]

This state centralization process deprived the warlords of their territorial control and led to a situation of parallel authority, along with disarmament, demobilization, and reintegration processes, a broader security sector reform, and a general attempt at establishing practices of good governance according to Western standards (the rules of the game). Abandoned by the United States and international organizations to favor the construction of the central state over strictly military considerations, Afghan warlords had no alternative but to switch their bases of power, become more discreet, and rely on resources more adapted to the new environment—for example, distributing some of the land that their militias had grabbed to invest in real estate development, thus converting military power into economic power, a mechanism I explain further in the following chapter.[99] With the progressive monopolization of the legitimate use of force by the central government, jihadist credentials became "a liability."[100] Warlords had to develop more subtle strategies to remain indispensable in the eyes of the central state and the international community, and still appear as the only ones who mattered in their own fiefdoms. In this context of increasing pressure, Afghan warlords switched from being active, in control of large swaths of territory, to dormant, thus exerting their power in different ways. They might have been engaged in business, civil society, and other activities, but all of this contributed to their survival and consolidation of authority, with consequences for the international effort to foster the creation of a stronger state.

Period 6: NATO Withdrawal (2009–2014)

The situation started to change on the eve of the 2009 presidential election. The tensions between the Afghan president and the international community led the former, in need of local power holders able to deliver votes, to bring the main warlords back into the loop. In 2009, according to an Afghan political analyst, "Karzai understood that Afghanistan was conservative and traditional. . . . He called the important leaders [Dostum and Fahim], the political brokers," to win the presidential election.[101] These warlords in turn took advantage of the conflicting agendas of domestic and foreign actors to promote their interests. With the growing influence of the Taliban insurgency and the announced departure of US troops, political dynamics radically changed.

In those years, the growing ambiguity of the international community's intentions in Afghanistan created a high level of domestic uncertainty. As Jan Koehler perceptively points out: "The patron-client arrangement might also include *armed* support if all else goes wrong."[102] This environment led warlords to switch their power bases once again to increasingly invest in more military sources. Ismail Khan has been said to be bringing his most trustworthy lieutenants back from Kabul to Herat to fill strategic positions in the local security apparatus. "If the Taliban manage to make the government collapse," he told me, "then we will find weapons. . . . It's a fact and it's a truth."[103] We can mobilize "just like that," one of Massoud's former commanders asserted, snapping his fingers. "If you bring a big van," said another confidently, "I can fill it up. . . . If something happens in the afternoon, we find weapons in the evening."[104]

In the meantime, the US policy of arming and financing local militias to fight the Taliban has been going against the state-building project, and "it is highly unclear whether the state will later be able to revoke such partial

autonomy and reintegrate such organizations into official security structures."[105] The creation of pro-government militias as a response to the rising
Taliban insurgency actually "recycled some of the security actors' armed
interests away from the 'Taliban' and temporarily towards the 'government.'"[106] But the formation of pro-government militias is a strategy of tension that promotes fragmentation at the expense of state consolidation (and
at the expense of active warlords). It creates a situation similar to that of southern Afghanistan after the fall of the Najibullah regime in 1992, in which a
plethora of nonstate armed groups coexisted, which gave rise to the Taliban
and their conquest of most of Afghanistan. As Sinno aptly put it: "The currency to buy the short-term loyalty of Afghan local leaders, weapons and
money, has always been the means to strengthen their long-term independence, which goes a long way to explain the fragility of such arrangements."[107]

In this chapter, I mapped out a typology of political orders in areas of weak
and failed statehood that provides the basis for comparative analysis and is
able to explain variation in outcomes across shifting contexts. I showed that
Afghanistan is marked by cycles of authority in which warlord authority persists and overlaps with that of the state regardless of ambitious state-building
missions. This is not unique to Afghanistan. In most cases, external intervention fails to enhance state consolidation and instead empowers and creates ties with the very actors it aims to weaken, which in turn explains why
Afghanistan, South Sudan, Libya, and other states cannot be expected to fully
adopt Western-style institutions anytime soon, as a result of intervention or
otherwise. The collapse of the Iraqi army in the face of the advance of the
so-called Islamic State on Mosul in June 2014 tends to confirm that, consistent with my findings, outsiders can only temporarily bolster state institutions, which will then likely break down once foreign aid and resources dry
out. External state building is a conundrum: a collective action problem that
cannot be solved permanently.

In Afghanistan, warlords have started to remobilize and rearm their
followers, even though the US administration, in fear of a repeat of what
happened in Iraq with the collapse of the national army and the rise of the
so-called Islamic State, could end up maintaining troops in the near future,
despite frequent declarations to the contrary. If and when NATO eventually pulls out (especially in case of successful negotiations with the Taliban),
warlords will remain businessmen and political leaders connected to global

economic processes and networks but will shift to more military bases of power. Post-NATO Afghanistan is likely to resemble 1990s Afghanistan and feature a mix of fragmented and regional political orders. Should the central state be strong enough to resist both external and internal pressures and avoid implosion, it would then still be characterized by the existence of parallel authorities, with clear tendencies toward regionalization and fragmentation in the provinces.

In the following chapter, I explain how warlords navigate within the typology: I introduce the game of survival and further explain the power conversion and power projection mechanisms by which warlords ensure their survival. In short, I demonstrate the existence of a political logic according to which they shape-shift (agency) to adapt to changing political environments (structure).[108]

Chapter 2

The Game of Survival

On the last day of the 2011 winter, I was invited by Ismail Khan (and driven in his convoy) to attend a gathering of former mujahideen held in celebration of the Herat uprising of 1979, in which he, among others, played a prominent role. Here are a few excerpts of the speech he gave that day:

> My dear courageous brothers, proud mujahideen . . . you were the people who defeated the Soviets many times. . . . Looking at each of your faces reminds me of different events. . . . God allowed us to stay alive to pass on what we, the mujahideen, did during the jihad, to the new generation. . . . Let's tell them the history of the mujahideen to keep the memory of the mujahideen alive in the hearts and minds of the new generation.

> In the past, we were united because we only believed in jihad and God. Now we are divided. . . . Have you forgotten we were not afraid of tanks? . . . Why are we scared of ourselves today? Why should a person who fought tanks be afraid now? What happened to us? . . . Don't you remember when our

families could go outside at night? That's because we were united. . . . Let's unite. . . . We've had enough with the disagreements.

The Taliban think that they can take control of our region when the international community leaves. It's a dream. We won't let them. . . . The government should use individuals who have influence over others and who can mobilize them to fight against the enemy. The government should use those leaders who have influence and know this region.[1]

This speech tells us three things about the mechanics of warlord survival. The first extract illustrates that Ismail Khan builds on his glorious past to legitimize his authority; it shows how he uses his jihadist credentials (and military legitimacy) as a source of power. The second indicates the need for unity and, implicitly, leadership in Afghanistan's current context of instability and uncertainty. The last one expresses why he, Ismail Khan, is the right person to provide this leadership: he fought on behalf of the people before and will be ready to do it again when the time comes. The message is clear: in the current security environment, he is indispensable.

In this chapter, I demonstrate that men like Ismail Khan are skilled political entrepreneurs who best exploit the means at their disposal to make themselves indispensable well beyond the battlefield. Warlord survival is a game in which political entrepreneurs express their power through a variety of resources, which they convert and project to maximize their chances of winning. In the following pages, I first show that warlords are political entrepreneurs who mobilize their different sources of power through the corresponding power resources. I then develop the survival mechanisms, power conversion and power projection, to explain how warlords survive across the different types of political orders identified in the previous chapter. Finally, I illustrate how warlords have typically converted and projected power since 2001 to exert their authority as armed notables. In other words, I show how warlords win the game of survival.

Warlords as Political Entrepreneurs

Of Greed and Self-Interest

As political entrepreneurs, warlords possess different sources of power that they express and mobilize through a variety of power resources (which I unpack below). They accumulate what they need to build up their own power bases and carry out their designs. It is therefore misleading to assume that a warlord's actions are necessarily (and solely) motivated by greed and self-interest.[2] Warlords are political entrepreneurs, not in the sense that they run the day-to-day business of their polities, but because they accumulate and invest in resources that can be useful to them in the future.[3] As such, the fact that warlords constantly seek out additional revenues is not surprising. In many cases, the warlords' drive for profit is a function of their need to reward followers and maintain forces (their political communities).[4]

Warlords develop diverse political strategies to, at a minimum, survive and, at a maximum, undertake a *fonction totale*. As such, they accumulate and invest in resources that in many cases extend beyond those of the state. In fact, it is rational for the political actors trying to maximize their chances of winning the game of survival to accumulate and mobilize power resources to adapt to the changes taking place in their environment. In the words of the American journalist Bob Woodward: "The warlords flourished in a culture of survival—meaning they would do anything necessary."[5] The warlords' need to accumulate resources had already been stressed by experts of Republican China: "It was soon apparent to the commanders that not only were they, through the control of their armies, in a position to achieve political and economic power, but indeed it was absolutely essential that they maintain their power if they were to continue to be active in political life. Thus, whatever may have been the long-range objectives of the particular military commanders, they soon all found themselves prisoners of the need to maintain and expand their personal power. This need was the basic driving force behind the distinctive politics of warlordism."[6]

I show below that warlords accumulate different sources of power (ideological, economic, military, social, and political) that they must then express, mobilize, and operationalize through the corresponding power resources.

Sources of Power

When asked about Ismail Khan's current power, a Herat resident said to me: "Ismail Khan doesn't have power. He only has skills."[7] The skills that this man referred to are what Pierre Bourdieu called a serious understanding of the game. A former rugby player, Bourdieu suggested that social life was a high-stake game, with players, rules, and a field structured by the unequal distribution of capital (the sources of power). Since "the social world is accumulated history," it is the accumulation of these sources of power that makes "the games of society . . . something other than simple games of chance."[8] Politics is in fact "a competitive game" that skilled individuals like Ismail Khan, who have developed an intuitive understanding of their society, have the best chance of winning.[9] Over time, players accumulate different sources of power and convert them into "the type of power effective in the field in question."[10] Building on work by Michael Mann and Timothy Earle, I distinguish five largely fungible, nonexclusive, and mutually reinforcing sources of power: ideological power, military power, economic power, political power, and social power.[11]

"Ideological power," as Mann defines it, "derives from the human need to find ultimate meaning in life, to share norms and values, and to participate in aesthetic and ritual practices."[12] Warlords and other nonstate armed actors invest in it as a way to cultivate their legitimacy through the use of symbolic processes. The Liberation Tigers of Tamil Eelam, for example, developed an ethnonationalist agenda that materialized through a new national flag, a new national anthem, and a number of other new symbols, such as a national bird and a national flower, all for the sake of legitimizing their rule over the Tamil population of Sri Lanka.[13] Military power comes from the control of armed men. It is the backbone of warlord authority. Economic power, "immediately and directly convertible into money," is "at the root of all the other types of capital."[14] Social power, which I broadly conceive of as similar to Bourdieu's definition of social capital, "consists of resources based on connections and group membership."[15] In other words, an actor's social power depends on who they know, how well they know them, and how much they can benefit from them. In a patronage-based society like Afghanistan, social power is essential.[16] Finally, political power is defined as "centralized, institutionalized, territorial regulation," that is, the power that comes from controlling the state.[17]

Power Resources

Power resources are the medium through which political entrepreneurs express the five sources of power identified above. In other words, power resources are the concrete elements that political actors use to exert their power in the different realms. As defined in chapter 1, these power resources are any means at the disposal of a political actor that, when activated, push back his constraints, open up his possibilities, increase his autonomy, and facilitate the development of his strategies. In sum, power resources are "means by which one person can influence the behavior of other persons."[18] They take the same forms as the sources of power (ideological, economic, military, social, and political) and include all the tangibles that political entrepreneurs can tap into to reward, punish, or induce others.[19] In fact, "it is through the shrewd investment of these resources that [patrons] may build and maintain their personal clientele."[20] It is therefore through the mobilization of these specific and concrete power resources, enhanced when a warlord is able to apply them across domestic and international environments, that political entrepreneurs can operationalize their sources of power.

Ideological resources are less fluid than other types but allow access to other resources, both domestically and internationally. In Afghanistan, Islam probably remains the most common ideological repertoire in the pursuit of local legitimacy, while jihadism, communism, and ethnocentrism (to name but a few) have been widely used by nonstate armed actors for the benefit of complex extraversion strategies.[21] Economic resources include (but are not limited to) business contracts and networks (both domestic and international), employment opportunities, and, of course, money. For example, a former US ambassador in Afghanistan interviewed in 2011 believed that Ismail Khan still "control[led] all the jobs in Herat."[22] If this was most certainly an overstatement, Ismail Khan's ability to influence employment opportunities remains real and gives him leverage over his clients. Military resources consist of any resources that are derived from the ability to mobilize armed men (e.g., militias and private military contractors), a defining feature of warlord authority. Social resources include the reputation of one's name and family status, international patronage (and hence international protection), "positions in the prewar political networks," and any information collected through such networks (and the development of an intuitive understanding of society).[23] Finally, political resources consist of all the resources that come from holding an official position in the state apparatus—for example, the right to make laws, access to the center of power (the presidency) and the international community, and political appointments.

Survival Mechanisms

In the introduction, I identified two mechanisms that warlords use to maximize their interest and ensure their survival: power conversion and power projection. These two mechanisms, sometimes hard to distinguish in practice, are intimately related to who the warlords are and what they do to survive.

Power Conversion

Warlords convert their existing sources of power into ones that are compatible (and less costly) in a new political setting.[24] They must accumulate, diversify, and combine the corresponding resources to maximize their chances of survival. They select the ones that they deem necessary (or that they can secure) to survive in a particular environment, given that they already have resources they can use to acquire the new ones. Driscoll aptly describes how, for the warlords of post-Soviet Georgia and Tajikistan, the "challenge was to convert their ability to organize armed social capital into wealth, power, and possibly even job security and respect over the long term."[25]

After the collapse of the Taliban regime and the imminent establishment of a new political order, Afghan warlords did not have much time left to rely on their military power (because of both state centralization and popular pressure).[26] They would soon have to become dormant and therefore had to use their armed forces while they still could to strategically acquire resources more adapted to their new environment—namely, money and political appointments (e.g., governor, vice president, or police chief)—and survive this abrupt transition. Ismail Khan, for example, used his armed followers to impose his favored candidates during the *loya jirga* elections of 2002.[27] Despite initial reluctance, most warlords eventually came to the conclusion that "avoiding direct confrontation [with the United States was] even worth giving up a portion of their arsenals, particularly when future income would easily allow them to purchase better weapons."[28] Those who did not (and failed to adapt to the new environment) progressively faded away—in particular, those who underwent disarmament, demobilization, and reintegration processes and were removed from their original fiefdoms. An acute observer of northern Afghanistan, for example, notes that Mir Alam, once the strongest commander in Kunduz Province, "did not manage to successfully transform his military power and legitimacy into the less-violent form that was required in the Karzai era."[29]

Numerous warlords specialized in violent entrepreneurship, what Vadim Volkov defines as "the way in which groups and organizations that specialize in the use of force make money."[30] The economic liberalization (and security vacuum) that followed the beginning of the US-led intervention created opportunities for extortion—"activities aimed at appropriating someone's property or property rights under threat of violence or damage to that subject's property or under threat of dissemination of harmful or derogatory information."[31] Some Afghan warlords used their military power (armed forces) to grab valuable land in urban and peri-urban areas and their social capital (government connections) to legalize their ownership of said land (private extortion).[32] Others (including Fahim) took advantage of controlling the state institutions to not only seize land but also officially reallocate it as a form of patronage politics (institutional extortion).

The skills warlords and their men had acquired during the previous two decades have been used to provide protection. Like "vigilantes, former soldiers, private guards, bandits, and prison inmates," former mujahideen indeed "nurture the skills a person needs to become a 'protector.'"[33] Their leaders have therefore used them to become involved in what Diego Gambetta calls "the business of private protection" (essentially racketeering), using violence to provide (coerced and illegal) protection.[34] Warlords also took advantage of this *"ready supply of people willing and able to carry out violent and protective duties"* (combined with the absence of a credible central authority capable of providing trust and security) to enter the private military sector, with the creation of numerous private military and security companies in the first years of the intervention.[35]

Since 2001, Afghan warlords have frequently used the political power they have acquired through institutional positions to secure business deals, not only in the private military sector but in all kinds of other trades as well. Fahim, for instance, used his position as vice president (2002–4) to obtain a number of lucrative reconstruction contracts in the early days of the intervention. Governor Gul Agha Sherzai is another great example: not only did he take advantage of his position as an official representative of the Afghan government to collect foreign aid, but, according to Chayes, he spent it all on consolidating his own power base in and around Kandahar.[36] The same applies to parliamentarians: "Many of those elected to the 249-seat parliament," writes Sinno, "are local leaders with unchecked influence in their home regions; they perceive official positions as yet another dimension of their relation of clientage with the state and international donors."[37] The American anthropologist Noah Coburn explains: "Even simply having close connections with men such as [commanders turned members of parliament Anwar Khan and Haji Almas] facilitated a wide array of opportunities for local residents, whether it was finding employment or using their connections in the government to secure a contract. As the intervention wore on, Anwar Khan and Haji Almas became known for having connections to a variety of resources as well as still possessing reputations as mujahideen fighters, and it became increasingly difficult to do business in the area without working with them."[38]

Such practices allow warlords to accumulate economic capital that they can in turn dispense throughout their patronage networks, as warlords operate as job providers vis-à-vis their followers, or as a source of favors, to reward their political clients and create obligations. Jennifer Brick Murtazashvili, in her book on informal governance, notes that more than half of the people she interviewed in one district of Kabul Province claimed that they, or their relatives, worked as "bodyguards" for the warlord Abdul Rasul Sayyaf. "From observations," she writes, "it did not seem as if being a bodyguard for Sayyaf involved much work, but instead was a source of income for the family in exchange for loyalty."[39] Giustozzi mentions how businessmen who started as smugglers in the 1980s and 1990s "mostly retain a strong connection with the warlords and the factions and they rely especially on the control exercised by many warlords over the local authorities as a way to get favours and privileges."[40]

In addition, the wisest warlords invested in social and ideological power, two types of power that do not necessarily need to be used to be effective. This lowers the "costs of power," because, as Walter Korpi points out, "prudent managers of power resources have strong incentives to avoid the exercise of power."[41] A former Herat resident, for example, told me that warlords are now "opinion leaders and community leaders, and that's what gives them legitimacy."[42] For example, when Hazara villagers were killed over grazing rights by Kuchi nomads in the central highlands of Afghanistan in the summer of 2008, the Hazara warlord Mohammad Mohaqiq took the initiative, went on a hunger strike, and demanded action from the government, hence acting as a community leader.[43] Over the years, warlords have become well-placed individuals entangled in their communities: former mujahideen, co-opted by elders, have infiltrated local councils (*shuras*) and now fully belong to the local social fabric.[44]

Alternatively, when the state gets weaker and the future becomes uncertain, warlords tend to favor military power, which they can in turn use to establish control over territory and acquire other sources of power. In the previous chapter, I explained how Dostum took advantage of the uncertain security situation to reaffirm his military authority in three northern provinces in the summer of 2015. In Kunduz, Mir Alam instrumentalized the reemergence of the Taliban to reaffirm his position as a military leader locally, which in turn made him, for a time, the recipient of important means of patronage from both the central state and the international community.[45]

It is important to recognize that the different sources of power are only partially fungible. They remain fungible only for as long as their overall distribution remains relatively balanced. In other words, acquiring too much of one, economic power in particular, can be damaging to the accumulation of others. Coburn explains how it worked in the market town of Istalif: "Economic capital helped build social capital, but wealth was still a dangerous thing. . . . If a leader acquired significant capital without redistributing a great deal of it, his followers accused him of greed and he lost social capital, no longer able to claim that he was *primus inter pares*."[46] This claim of being first among equals does not apply with the same immediacy to warlords, who, as noted earlier, are less beholden to community expectations than local leaders due to their larger power bases. However, failing to redistribute the wealth will still damage their reputation in the long term. I show in chapter 5 how this was the case for Fahim.

Ultimately, the process of power conversion allows warlords to exercise authority in different realms at the same time as they take on multiple roles in various power-related fields (straddling).[47] For example, the same individual can be both a businessman and a public official, or use his religious credentials to further his legitimacy in other domains. Feng Yü-hsiang, the "Christian General" of Republican China used religion "as a tool for the achievement of great things."[48] And, in the Caucasus, Yuri Shanibov "change[d] his name to the more native form, Musa Shanib, and donned the traditional tall sheepskin hat (*papaha*) of a Circassian prince" to legitimize his authority.[49] In Afghanistan, warlords have adopted different faces (such as mujahid, notable, or minister) simultaneously to reach specific audiences and take advantage of international actors looking for pure ideal types—a Pashtun elder in traditional outfits, a fierce warlord in military fatigues, or a westernized bureaucrat wearing a suit, for example—but who lack the necessary skills, expertise, and flexibility to comprehend the local environment.[50]

Power Projection

Warlords transform their power to continue projecting authority and ensure their survival. They develop strategies to remain indispensable in the eyes of those who need what they can provide (e.g., protection, trust, security, votes, or information), sometimes in ways that are at odds with their actual capacities. To be sure, material conditions matter to a warlord's authority. But warlord authority is in part a social construct that does not necessarily reflect these material conditions. Warlords also need to acquire (and maintain) what Bourdieu called symbolic power, "a power which exists because the person who submits to it believes that it exists."[51] In other words, symbolic forms of power, such as prestige and charisma, reside primarily in the perceptions of other people.

As Max Weber explained, "Men do not obey [the charismatic leader] by virtue of tradition or statute, but because they believe in him."[52] Charisma is "the absolutely personal devotion and personal confidence in revelation, heroism, or other qualities of individual leadership."[53] James Scott also emphasizes the relational and constructed nature of charisma: "Although we often speak as if an individual had charisma the way she might have a house," he wrote, "what we mean is that others respond to her with an awe and enthusiasm that suggest charisma."[54] This stands out clearly in the account I gave of my first meeting with Ismail Khan in 2011: "Ismail Khan is the most impressive individual I have ever seen. . . . There is something very distinctive about Ismail Khan. He has a very unique way of looking into someone's eyes. His tiny half-closed eyes seem to see right through your soul: threatening black eyes that exude intelligence and power."[55]

Since all forms of symbolic power depend on recognition from others, they are, by their very nature, vulnerable to disenchantment. This is precisely why warlords constantly resort to symbolic displays of power. Prestige and charisma, on which warlords rest much of their authority, require regular public performance to be accepted as legitimate. In Bourdieu's words, "No domination can maintain itself without making itself recognized by making the arbitrary that is at its basis be misrecognized."[56] As Scott puts it: "Prestige can be thought of as the public face of domination."[57]

To increase their prestige, warlords typically try to portray themselves as the strongest actors on the local scene. This in turn gives them the means to acquire additional resources and thus become stronger. "The belief that a person will be successful (or a failure) is self-fulfilling," says Barfield. "The belief that you have power is very important. That is why you can lose power so quickly and why Afghan politics is so unpredictable."[58] In Afghanistan, reputation is indeed "a man's greatest weapon and greatest vulnerability."[59] Reputation is not only about patronage (expected norms of reciprocity and remuneration); it is also about appearing as the strongest actor on the scene to the international community, central elites, and the local population. Warlords exude power. They remain powerful only as long as all the actors who are part of the environment *believe* that they are.[60] As Thomas Hobbes aptly put it, "Reputation of power is power."[61]

This aspect of power is reflected, for example, in seemingly odd patterns of fighting. It helps make sense of why "sometimes the fighting of Afghans resembles a kind of stylized theater."[62] This behavior has been well described by the renowned Afghanistan expert Olivier Roy: "Patterns of fighting are closely linked to the social structures behind the power of an individual warlord. This explains why territorial control is not ensured through conquest involving pitched battles, but mostly through negotiations and targeted assassinations. Sudden changes of fortune are very common. The battle is won or lost, not on the day but on the day before: if one side feels that the situation is not in its favour because local commanders have changed their allegiance, it will suddenly withdraw."[63]

This constructed dimension of power illuminates similarly puzzling political events and outcomes in the post-2001 environment. For example, it explains how, in 2005, the Taliban took control of the village of Baram Chah, in Helmand Province, without a fight. Instead, they turned Baluch militiamen against their former ally, the provincial governor Sher Mohammad Akhunzada.[64] It also accounts for the sidelining of Ismail Khan in 2004, when the amir of western Afghanistan, supposedly the strongest actor in his region, was defeated by smaller commanders, had to request Kabul's help, and then was forced to leave his fiefdom and accept a position in the capital (a clear example of co-optation) after US planes flew over his compound in a demonstration of force and resolve.[65] The strength of men like Ismail Khan rests on an unstable equilibrium: their power depends above all on the allegiance of their commanders. *"Avoiding any public display of insubordination"* is therefore critical to a warlord's ability to control his troops.[66] Indeed, "open insubordination represents a dramatic contradiction of the smooth surface of euphemized power."[67] This is also why rumors are so important (in particular the ones regarding a leader's death, or sickness, which automatically weaken him in the eyes of his constituency).

Warlords thrive when the state no longer holds a monopoly on legitimate violence and is not able to provide crucial services, when "its reputation as a defender of its population" has been damaged.[68] Their survival in fact lies on the shared assumption—itself based on past experience—that they will be able to provide the security that the state is no longer able to supply. In some cases, the warlords' mere existence is enough to appear as a symbol of protection (a lesser evil sometimes) against others or against the state, in particular for marginalized, persecuted, peripheral communities. As Karl Deutsch pointed out: "Prestige is then to power as credit is to cash."[69] The reputation of power becomes a factor of power that prevents the power holder from actually exerting it, in a self-enforcing manner.

Most actors, and foreigners in particular, are in fact incapable of assessing a warlord's authority. Warlord survival in turn rests on a warlord's ability to exploit this opaqueness and project an image of strength. The fact that most actors involved in the Afghan conflict disagree on the actual sources of warlord authority shows that the warlords' material bases of power are indeed hard to assess. A warlord's power cannot be numerically quantified. While money, weapons, and armed followers all constitute resources that warlords can mobilize to wield authority, warlord survival cannot be reduced to a story of capacity. Power cannot simply be defined as control over material resources. A warlord's authority rests essentially on his reputation, and his reputation is characterized by a certain inertia. Indeed, as Abner Cohen once noted, "Subjects do not start their lives every morning examining the dispositions of power in their society." And, to paraphrase his analysis of regime survival, a warlord's ability to maintain his authority depends, to a large extent, on representing himself as "a 'natural' part of the universe."[70]

The difficulty in assessing a warlord's sources of power in turn pushes sovereign actors to deal with them in a conservative manner, as they fear the consequences for confronting them may include political instability and calls for deeper military and financial commitment. Coburn similarly notes that unpredictability can, in some cases, "*decrease* violence, because it creates a situation in which the consequences of violence are potentially so serious and destabilizing that even enemies agree to work to contain conflict."[71] I show in chapter 4 how Dostum organizes uprisings to destabilize governors he disapproves of in his fiefdom, and in chapter 5 how Fahim made himself indispensable after 9/11, threatening President Karzai to "divide Afghanistan and split."[72] In fact, "privileges are given in exchange for political support, in particular to those who can threaten the status quo."[73] Driscoll notes how, "in the 1990s, Georgian and Tajik warlords realized they had the ability to replace presidents, trigger investor pullouts, and drag their countries into anarchy . . . [and they] had only to make these threats credible to be bought off—not to actually make good on them."[74]

Those who portray themselves as potential rivals to the regime (e.g., by running for office in presidential elections) often do so in "the hope that they will be considered threatening enough to be courted and co-opted."[75] Dostum's candidacy in the 2004 presidential election is a good example of such practices. Afghan warlords have therefore developed strategies aimed at convincing first the international community, and then domestic actors, that they remain the most powerful actors on the local scene. It is also why, for example, General Dostum was involved in what seemed like a trivial dispute with his main rival in the North, the warlord turned governor Ata Mohammad Noor, after the latter had allegedly ordered the removal of Dostum's photograph from two large billboards in the center of Mazar-i Sharif.[76]

It has been argued that reputation is "the key currency in central Asian politics, especially the reputation for controlling events."[77] It is also true elsewhere. Image is key to warlords who need to develop strategies to convince all actors that they have and should have the "right and responsibility to lead," regardless of their actual capacities.[78] Scott captures this dimension of the exercise of power very eloquently: "There is a certain amount of bluff and pretense in almost any display of power. The successful communication of power and authority is freighted with consequences inasmuch as it contributes to something like a self-fulfilling prophecy. If subordinates believe their superior to be powerful, the impression will help him impose himself and, in turn, contribute to his actual power. Ceremonies dramatizing the majesty of power are integral to the accumulation of power. Appearances do matter."[79] This explains why, as Marten put it, "warlords may sometimes be more pretense than peril."[80] Power is not exclusively a question of force and manipulation but a question of persuasion and propaganda.

Warlords as Armed Notables

In the following chapters, I show how a warlord's trajectory depends not only on the environment in which he operates but also on his initial endowment in capital (his sources of power) and on the choices he makes given the options available in each specific environment (his strategies). In other words, I identify sources of agency within the context of a particular structure and shed light on the specific trajectories of the warlords under study. Here, however, I focus on the commonalities: I explain how the successive environments in which Afghan warlords have had to convert, project, and exert power since 1978 have led them all to eventually transform into armed notables.

In the absence of a state able to provide extensive services to the population, Afghan warlords have typically made use of specific contextual resources (an easily accessible supply of armed men) to acquire new social functions in response to a very specific security context (a high demand for trust and protection), aggravated by a deep crisis of leadership. More specifically, since the beginning of the Afghan wars, and even more so since 2001, warlords have frequently converted their power to take over functions that were previously performed by traditional leaders. Roy describes how warlords have started to take the place and fulfill the functions of traditional khans during the Soviet-Afghan war: "The changes in social status caused by the war do not imply the abandonment of the traditional conception of the exercise of authority: the newly promoted people adopt the way of life and behavior of the ancient notables (significantly the title of khan is attached to the name of commanders, which were in the past students with no prestige but who are today at the head of large fronts: Basir Khan, Ismail Khan, Bashir Khan). The sociological origin of the chief has changed from the past but not the behavior of the one who is now perceived as the new khan."[81] The fact that some warlords affix the title to their name is significant. As Frederick Barth notes, "The title khan, even apart from its formal courtesy use, does not denote incumbency of any formal office. . . . The title merely implies a claim to authority over others."[82]

A traditional khan may be described as follows: "A local notable who exercises an influence related to his status as a landowner or as a tribal leader. He maintains a clientele whose size is measured by those who are obliged to him, from among the relationships in which he is dominant. He feeds others and obtains services for them: he cannot operate without an open table, gifts to the local *mullah* and so on."[83] Based on this definition, Afghan warlords can indeed be considered as a new form of khans.[84] They share a number of characteristics with the old ones: they have a network of relationships (social power), they acquire prestige rather than material benefits in the first instance, and their power consists primarily in their capacity to influence. They behave in similar ways: they hold court, address grievances, and adjudicate disputes.[85] Although the scale of their power differs, parallels between traditional khans and warlords also appear in their relations to the center, as seen in this mid-nineteenth-century account of the traveler and writer Joseph Pierre Ferrier: "[The khans] recognize the suzerainty of the princes . . . only because they have not sufficient power to throw it off, or, that occasionally it happens to be in their interest to acknowledge it."[86]

Warlords also differ from the traditional khans in a number of ways. When they are at their peak (as active warlords), they have much more autonomy than the old khans ever had. The latter, while "typically operat[ing] at a level above the village, imposing order over wide swaths of territory," still had a smaller power base, limited to a rural economy within a well-defined geographical area and tribal structure.[87] As a result, the old khans were more tightly bound to the obligations to their communities that came with their power. These communities had expectations about how they would behave, particularly in their roles as protectors and patrons, which left them with much less leeway and fewer opportunities to extract resources and prestige from external actors.

Most importantly, the traditional khans typically had no networks within state institutions and therefore no way to influence them. In Afghanistan, the role of "bridge between the people and the government" has traditionally been assigned to the *maliks* (or *arbabs*), individuals who "[represent] community interests to the outside world and [since 2001] the international donor community."[88] Warlords also perform this function. In fact, they do so at a higher level than the *maliks* do. They can connect their communities to the central power because they benefit from unprecedented access to state political elites and have the ability to influence institutions, which they gained by converting their pre-2001 sources of power. They serve as mediators between their communities (or their followers) and the outside world.

Afghan warlords at least want to give the impression that they do mediate, which explains why foreign visitors are given such a high status—through the seat they are being assigned to, for example—and why warlords (and other local political actors) often brag over the visits of foreign delegations, journalists, and scholars. In her study of warlords turned governors, Mukhopadhyay notes how Sherzai, as governor of Nangarhar, made use of US presidential candidate Barack Obama's visit to draw attention to his own role in the stabilization of the province.[89] This also happens with much less significant international actors. For instance, my 2011 visit with Ismail Khan was mentioned during one of the speeches given during a gathering of former mujahideen he had invited me to attend. A handshake I shared with a provincial governor I had barely met was even broadcast on Afghan television. Warlords need to show their followers that they have access to external networks and resources. Local legitimacy is in fact strengthened by international connections and reputation.[90] The reverse is also true: warlords need to demonstrate their local clout. In the fall of 2008, Ata, the "warlord-governor" of Balkh Province (and rival of General Dostum) had me sit through hours of him adjudicating disputes and listening to people's grievances before our formal interview could commence.[91]

In Afghanistan, the warlords' ability to mediate between different levels of politics is key to their authority (and to their ability to appear as indispensable) in the post-2001 era. Warlords, in post-Taliban Afghanistan, operate in ways reminiscent of the notables described by scholars of patrimonial and neopatrimonial politics, local leaders who can mediate between the different levels of politics and derive much of their power from this ability.[92] "The idea of mediation," wrote Jean-François Médard, "is at the heart of the concept of the notable; there is no notable without mediation. But not all mediators are notables. There is, in addition, another element, which involves reputation, prestige, or some kind of locally rooted legitimacy."[93] In short, the warlord is both *malik* and khan.

Warlords are more than this. They are armed notables. They have access to means of coercion (and hence the ability to provide security) that were never available to traditional *maliks* and khans. The idea of Afghan warlords being armed notables is well conveyed by the American social scientist Michael Bhatia:

> In many ways, the strongman seeks to reference symbolically (but in fact far transcends) the role of the traditional tribal *khan* as an arbiter of local disputes and distributor of resources. The traditional tribal *khan* seeks to acquire authority through the distribution of resources, the maintenance of a sizeable retinue of loyalists and the ability to arbitrate disputes (Anderson, 1983). For Ismail Khan, Dostum and Sayyaf, these traditional roles are further supplemented by their role in securing their communities (while persecuting others) and securing the interests of their ethnic minorities from competing regional groups or in the national government. . . . In reality, while he may position himself as a contemporary manifestation of the traditional *khan*, the contemporary strongman (or warlord) holds far greater power and has been able to restrict or reduce the traditional checks on his power.[94]

As Ahmad Shah Massoud once put it, "[The commanders] have taken the place of the old *khans*, but they are more powerful!"[95]

Afghan warlords are believed to have lost their legitimacy after 2001 because they were no longer viewed as providing protection against a bigger threat (such as the Soviets, other ethnic groups, or the Taliban) and were now merely seen as predators.[96] Although this interpretation is partially true, it overly simplifies the relationship between warlords and their environment and reifies the threat. The situation is more fluid. The importance of warlords in the political landscape varies across time and space. It is a function of an international environment that is much more heterogeneous and dynamic than this explanation leads us to believe. This argument also omits other bases for authority. Warlords who hold religious authority positions, develop nationalist agendas, or occupy prime locations in commercial networks have other ways of conferring benefits on supporters than strict protection.

In his seminal study of Chinese warlords, Lucian Pye argued that warlords play a "dual role," being both military and political leaders.[97] In this book, I show that warlord authority is not strictly military and political but also economic, social, and ideological. Warlords are sometimes even more, up to, ideally, undertaking a *fonction totale*, in which they exert a monopoly over all the sources of power in their territory. In Ahram and King's words, warlords are "uniquely gifted boundary-crossers, conducting both violent and non-violent transactions across political, economic, and cultural dividing lines."[98] They operate in environments in which ideological, economic, military, social, and political affairs are intricately enmeshed, and have a strong interest in keeping it that way.[99] Confronted with a changing environment after 2001, Afghan warlords were no longer able to combine all sources of power simultaneously to remain active warlords. They had to shape-shift and become dormant.

In the following chapters, I show that different warlords operate along different modalities, depending on their own social background, social capital, and personal trajectories. All these elements in turn determine their respective survival strategies and political positionings. To put it differently, a warlord's background helps explain the way he combines and uses his different faces. Warlord survival is a story of shrewd individuals who develop creative political strategies to survive in a hostile environment, in which international and state actors are attempting to centralize and normalize the exercise of power. They adapt to the domestic and international environments and transform their power accordingly. In sum, warlord survival "is a game of favours, obligations and portrayal of threat, in which mutual loyalty is consolidated through the regular confirmation of the ability to deliver (protection, hospitality, favours, services)."[100] Here, I demonstrate that, contrary to common expectations, the warlords' solid understanding of the Afghan political game has allowed them to successfully invest in the right power resources in order to convert their pre-2001 sources of power and survive in a totally different international environment.

Chapter 3

Ismail Khan, the Armed Notable of Western Afghanistan

As of 2019, Mohammad Ismail Khan is one of the most feared and powerful warlords of Afghanistan, the self-proclaimed amir of western Afghanistan. Both times we met, in 2011 and 2018, he was sporting an immaculate white traditional outfit, a pair of comfortable black loafers, and a long snow-white beard, all of which contrasts with the military fatigues and the pitch-black beard of his jihad days. He lives in the center of Herat, surrounded by deer, ostriches, and peacocks. Yet, Ismail Khan remains a force to be reckoned with. His piercing black eyes exude intelligence and fierceness. In fact, many still fear him and are reluctant to talk about him. A man I once interviewed, scared of being overheard, asked me to speak softly and not mention Ismail Khan by name. "Walls have mice and mice have ears," he said.[1] Ismail Khan holds court in the same luxurious four-story white marble palace he had built after 2001, addressing demands and grievances, always attended by a substantial entourage. A few times a year, for big celebrations, he adorns the city with huge posters of himself and his late son. He regularly rallies hundreds, if not thousands, of supporters. They come to hear

The author interviewing Ismail Khan in his palace, Herat (photograph by friend of the author).

him speak, take pictures of him with their cell phones, and kiss his hand to pay their respects. He feeds them with lavish meals of rice, mutton, spinach, and bread. They listen to him; he listens to them. He offers leadership.

Ismail Khan rose to prominence with the Herat rebellion of March 1979 and the Soviet occupation of the 1980s. He went on to establish his own emirate, independent of the central state, during the Afghan civil war. After he lost his domain to the Taliban, he entered the resistance and eventually ruled over a large part of western Afghanistan once again in the early days of the US-led intervention. Ismail Khan soon faced strong international and domestic pressure to fit into the confines of a more conventional state, but his ability to act in the international system allowed him to resist for almost three years. He ultimately had to change course, leave his governorship, and move to Kabul as minister of energy and water in the new Karzai cabinet in December 2004. He held this position for almost ten years before resigning in October 2013 to enter the presidential campaign as the running mate of another mujahideen leader, Abdul Rasul Sayyaf. Ismail Khan can no longer be considered an active warlord in the current international environment and has held no official position in Herat for over a decade. Yet, he still holds significant political authority in the region, as he successfully reinvented himself to become the epitome of the armed notable, a powerful individual who mediates between the local level and the outside world, provides security and opportunities to his followers, but is also able to coerce opponents and recalcitrant populations.

Rise and Fall of the First Emirate (1979–2001)

The Mujahideen Leader

Ismail Khan was born around 1950, into a modest Tajik family from the Shindand District, in the western province of Herat.[2] After attending primary school in his village, he enrolled in a military high school in Kabul and then entered the military academy. In his early twenties, freshly graduated, he was stationed in Herat for the best part of a decade, before taking an active role in the Herat rebellion of 1979. On March 15 of that year, almost a year after the coup that brought the pro-Soviet People's Democratic Party of Afghanistan to power, residents of Herat's rural districts, encouraged and coordinated by local mullahs, massacred civil servants before converging on the city. There, they attacked symbols of the central state and killed communist officers and Soviet advisers in protest against the new agrarian reform and the persecution of religious and traditional elites by the new regime. Officers of Herat's Seventeenth Division—including the one known at the time as Turan Ismail (Captain Ismail), then still sporting a mustache—soon joined the rebels and seized all governmental buildings.[3] Less than a week later, government forces regained control of the city, forcing the mutineers to seek refuge in the abutting mountains west of the city, before crossing the border into Iran.

Ismail Khan, more than anyone else, was able to capitalize on his participation in the Herat rebellion. With the support of Iran's Revolutionary Guard, he established his operational base in Sharshari, on the Afghan side of the border, while keeping his logistics in Taybad, on the Iranian side, where he opened an office to recruit and mobilize militants.[4] After meeting with the leadership of the Jamiat-i Islami (henceforth Jamiat) in Peshawar, he was eventually selected to be the party's leader (amir) for western Afghanistan.

This position gave him a monopoly over the party's regional supplies and turned him into the region's most powerful military patron.[5] Now at the top of Jamiat's regional chain of command, Ismail Khan grew stronger, progressively concentrating power among the mujahideen of western Afghanistan. Turan Ismail had become Amir Ismail Khan.

Ismail Khan supported and equipped some groups, excluded and disarmed others, and eventually managed to concentrate power in most of the region (although the city was still under the control of government forces) while setting up for a new political order (from fragmented authority to regional authority) that would only truly materialize after the fall of the regime. He reestablished a functioning parallel administration with services (e.g., hospitals, schools, and courts) and created committees responsible for various areas of governance, such as culture, justice, health, and education. He showed how the right individual could convert his existing social capital (as a homegrown army captain) and careful cultivation of networks into command over armed soldiers to become the dominant political force of an entire region, long before the fall of the communist regime.

Ismail Khan spent the 1980s battling the Soviets and their local allies while building a parallel administration in western Afghanistan. His strategy was based on mobilizing resources through networks of associates and subordinates in the political, commercial, military, and religious domains. This strategy created an authority that was driven by the principles of patrimonial rule—Ismail Khan's control over the distribution of resources in exchange for loyalty. Though bureaucratic institutions may have superior means at their command to mobilize resources, particularly for warfare, Ismail Khan showed that a rebel force based on patron-client ties could assert authority and undermine its enemies.[6]

Warlord Governance

Although he established a parallel administration while the communists were still in power, Ismail Khan fully consolidated his warlord polity only after the fall of the regime, which marked the complete realization of the new political order (from fragmented to regional authority) and the coming of age of active warlords exerting power across all the different realms of authority simultaneously (hence undertaking a *fonction totale*). On April 18, 1992, a week before the fall of Kabul, Ismail Khan's forces entered Herat with ease, quickly defeated weaker rival groups, and, a Herat resident remembers, "took control of everything."[7] Ismail Khan and his associates seized a large reserve of arms and ammunition left behind by the communist government and captured the revenue-generating border posts with Iran and, later, with Turkmenistan. These border posts provided Ismail Khan with enough revenues to establish his own, nearly autonomous, emirate in Herat and the neighboring provinces of Farah, Badghis, Ghor, and Nimroz, where he held most if not all executive powers. "All positions were in his hands," said a religious leader from Herat.[8] As one of my respondents put it: he had built his own "mini-kingdom."[9]

Like most mujahideen leaders, Ismail Khan recruited mainly from his existing networks, which quickly created tensions among the ruling coalition. For the son of a poor Tajik family from Shindand (south of Herat) who received his education at the Kabul military academy and later joined Jamiat, social capital meant rural Tajiks, army soldiers, and Jamiati partisans. This in turn led traditional and urban elites to question his legitimacy, in particular in the ethnically diverse city of Herat. Ismail Khan, now nicknamed the lion of Herat, chose to concentrate authority by disarming those he could not (or did not want to) co-opt while integrating the others into the political and military structure he had created. This strategy turned other commanders into subordinates and may have alienated a section of the military class, but it also proved to all that he could provide security. In fact, it gave him "a degree of popularity with the population at large, because it implied a higher degree of discipline and better behaviour on the part of the militiamen."[10] Ismail Khan's rule was autocratic and repressive but nonetheless represented the establishment of a new political order.

The amir of western Afghanistan maintained the existing official administrative system, hence grafting his regional authority onto the defunct Afghan state. "We just changed the members," he told me.[11] Schools were reopened along with the university, which hosted 450 students and 30 professors. Ahmed Rashid, an influential journalist personally acquainted with Ismail Khan, claims that, under Ismail Khan's rule, 45,000 children (half of them girls) were going to school in the city of Herat alone.[12] The amir of western Afghanistan also distributed social benefits, improved the infrastructure, and supported local businesses. Under his patronage, shops that had been destroyed or damaged during the Soviet-Afghan war were repaired, rebuilt, and improved to restore the merchants' confidence and boost the local economy.

Ismail Khan was also careful to project authority and improve his reputation through symbolic displays of power. He took care of important celebrations, paid daily visits to the different administrative services under his jurisdiction, and made sure that his activities were reported by the local television channel. This carefully crafted projection of power is well described by Giustozzi: "His cult of personality was propagated by provincial media, such as state radio and TV and newspaper. . . . He paid much attention to the choreography of power and his circle arranged large demonstrations of support on many occasions, as well as for large crowds to be shepherded to greet him or support his claims. His militias would force shopkeepers and shop-owners to shut down business and attend the gatherings."[13] On top of this, Ismail Khan had his men write slogans celebrating the jihad and the mujahideen on the walls of public buildings. "That was a way of legitimizing himself," said a former Herat resident, because "[jihad is] how he got his power."[14]

The amir of western Afghanistan never participated in the struggle for central power, at least not militarily. "It was useless," he told me.[15] Whether this was because of insufficient capabilities or because he never had any intention to do so remains unclear, but most observers agree that Ismail Khan was only interested in establishing his authority in the West. His autonomy often put him at odds with fellow Jamiatis in Kabul. His unwillingness to share revenues, follow directives—such as Massoud's injunction not to fight Dostum—or consult with the center before appointing provincial governors (even though, officially, he himself was only a provincial governor) created tension. In the summer of 1994, Ismail Khan further antagonized Kabul by organizing a large political gathering, to which he invited most Afghan leaders in and out of Afghanistan, in what appeared to be a concerted attempt to boost his own credibility and portray himself as an alternative to President Burhanuddin Rabbani. Yet, the amir of western Afghanistan did not try to break away from the state and acquire official international recognition either—probably in part because he knew he would never succeed—and instead developed a certain degree of legalism and nationalism, even keeping a picture of President Rabbani in his office. It appears that he always wanted to work "under the flag of Afghanistan."[16]

Warlord Diplomacy

Working under the flag of Afghanistan did not prevent Ismail Khan from asserting his own diplomacy. During the jihad, he had built relationships with foreign journalists (inviting some to Herat) and NGO workers and sent his own representatives to Pakistan or the US Congress to lobby on his behalf—obtaining Stinger missiles in the process. He had learned early on that he could use his personal networks (as in Iran) and exploit geostrategic interests (as in his relations with US officials) to conduct his own brand of international relations (outside Jamiat), bend domestic and international realms of authority, and ultimately consolidate his position. In the 1990s, he asserted his diplomacy further. Not only did the amir of western Afghanistan receive numerous foreign delegations (including from Saudi Arabia and European countries), but he also developed routines of diplomatic ties and connections with neighboring states and close relationships with NGOs and international organizations, which, in dealing directly with him, became complicit in bolstering his authority.

Due to their geographic, historical, and cultural ties with Iran, Heratis have always had close relationships with their neighbors to the west. Iran, for its part, has long considered Afghanistan as belonging to its natural sphere of influence. Most goods sold on the Herati bazaars in the 1990s in fact came from Iran, with only a few items, such as cars and tires, imported from elsewhere. Ismail Khan is no exception and has maintained friendly relationships with the Islamic Republic of Iran for decades, especially since its Revolutionary Guard protected him and built him up during the Soviet-Afghan war. Yet, once in control of the western region, he was willing to diversify his international connections and commercial ties to limit and counterbalance Iran's influence and support—for example, by developing close relationships with Turkmenistan and Pakistan. The government of Turkmenistan provided oil and fuel to the emirate in exchange for access to the road leading to Pakistan (via Herat), and, in November 1993, Ismail Khan signed a business cooperation agreement with the president of Turkmenistan in Ashgabat—hence proving that he could be a patron of business as well as a significant international player. In a bid for penetrating Central Asian markets and increasing Pakistan's influence in the region, the Pakistani minister of interior and the Pakistani ambassador to Afghanistan inaugurated a new consulate in Herat in September 1994.

Ismail Khan's last significant foreign relations accomplishment was to harness NGOs and international organizations operating in his fiefdom. Médecins du Monde, in cooperation with the Danish Afghanistan Committee, rehabilitated and ran Herat's hospital; the Danish Committee for Aid to Afghan Refugees worked on roads, schools, and water and sanitation projects, with funds from both the Danish government and the European Economic Community; the International Afghan Mission ran the ophthalmologic hospital; and Shelter Now ran a UN program. International organizations, such as the UN High Commissioner for Refugees, the UN Children's Fund, and the International Committee of the Red Cross, were also active in Herat.

Ismail Khan reaped the benefits of this international presence. He proved that he could recruit foreigners to provide the expertise and the services that he lacked and needed. This political strategy exploited the advantages of foreigners' relatively efficient and technocratic organizations and tapped new conduits for resources to bolster his personal authority. Hence the importance, for Ismail Khan and other warlords in similar positions, of claiming a monopoly over international relations within their fiefdom. Ismail Khan even used NGOs to promote his own rule. In 1993, for example, he invited Bernard Dupaigne, representing a French NGO called Afrane (Amitié franco-afghane), to visit him in Herat. The visit culminated in Afrane launching programs in the province and Dupaigne describing Herat as "a model and a chance for Afghanistan."[17]

The Resistance Leader

In the beginning of 1995, Ismail Khan was engaged on two military fronts: against Dostum, in the northeast part of the emirate (against Massoud's will); and against the Taliban, in the southeast. In March of that year, his troops took Gereshk, a city in Helmand Province on the way to Kandahar, the Taliban's stronghold. They were defeated on August 28 and returned to Herat, which was captured by the Taliban a week later, forcing Ismail Khan to flee. It is difficult to single out one explanation for how and why the once overly powerful amir of western Afghanistan could be defeated so quickly. Ismail Khan's fall was most likely due to a combination of factors: political maneuvering in Kabul to replace him with his deputy, Alauddin Khan (who also served as chief of Herat's military corps), military fatigue and low morale (which Ismail Khan exacerbated by overextending himself in fighting both Dostum and the Taliban simultaneously), deficient military tactics, a relative lack of resources (compared with the resource-rich and Pakistan-supported Taliban), and corruption within the ranks.

Ismail Khan's position was safe as long as he dominated the region's political and military landscapes. The amount of resources at his disposal to reward, punish, and induce others sharply decreased as a result of waging war on two different fronts. As Ismail Khan progressively lost his ability to win battles and project authority, it gave his rivals a window of opportunity. Being challenged by both the central government and his own deputy further damaged his reputation and helped undermine his waning authority, in particular among his military commanders. As soon as Ismail Khan started showing weakness, the many commanders that he had co-opted defected to the Taliban, which took advantage of the situation and captured Herat almost without a fight (on similar patterns of fighting, see chapter 2).

Accompanied by a few hundred men, Ismail Khan first fled to Mashhad, Iran, where he stayed while planning his political comeback. In 1996, he joined Massoud in Kabul before going to the northwestern provinces of Faryab and Badghis to fight the Taliban on their way to Mazar-i Sharif. Ismail Khan, rearmed and reequipped by Iran, had become a resistance leader. The following year, he was captured by the Taliban and sent to a prison in Kandahar, from which he escaped in March 2000—a move that contributed to building his reputation, as I explain later. He then went back to Mashhad, where the Revolutionary Guard helped him establish his military base and organize the fight against the Taliban inside Afghanistan, hence playing a pivotal role in restoring his military power. Less than two years later, a new exogenous shock would change his life by allowing him to shape-shift and become an active warlord once again.[18]

The Second Emirate (2001–2004)

US Intervention and Warlord Strategy

Upon his return, many westerners considered Ismail Khan as the epitome of a "'vanished golden age' in Afghanistan," a reputation he had gained by providing goods, services, and security to the population of Herat in the 1990s.[19] A few days after the terrorist attacks on New York and Washington, Rashid asserted that he was "the most credible anti-Taliban commander" following the death of Ahmad Shah Massoud.[20] "If [Ismail] Khan does return to his role as amir of Western Afghanistan, Herat will no doubt settle back happily into its tradition as a place of enlightenment and sophistication in the Islamic world," claimed Hamish McDonald in the *Sydney Morning Herald* on October 20, 2001. A month later, UN envoy to Afghanistan Sotiris Mousouris further praised Ismail Khan in a CNN interview: "I think that Ismail Khan has proven, when he was governor of Herat, that he's a patriot, a decent man, and a very competent administrator. . . . He's a man of clear vision and decency, and his ambitions are not overwhelming. I think he can be a source of future leadership for Afghanistan. . . . Ismail Khan is a person which I think we *should* rely upon."[21]

Ismail Khan used such international praise to portray himself as the ultimate bulwark against al-Qaeda and the Taliban. Projecting this image, in turn, allowed him to benefit from US support to retake control of his fiefdom. Yet, his position vis-à-vis the United States has been ambiguous and ambivalent from the very beginning of the US-led intervention. On the one hand, he has repeatedly expressed his willingness to cooperate with whoever could advance his interests. On the other hand, he has always publicly opposed the presence of foreign troops who would limit his ability to rule his fiefdom as he pleased. "To win, we need more money, men and weapons. We're willing to accept help from whoever has our best interest in mind," he said, as quoted by AFP on October 4, 2001. Interviewed via satellite phone a few days later, he declared: "We have no desire to see any foreign troops on our soil. The coalition's mission is to provide assistance for the liberation of Afghanistan from terrorist occupation by the Pakistanis and Arabs. The mission is not to impose a new type of foreign rule."[22] In other words, the US-led intervention should not aim at building a conventional state based on

Western models. "The solution for Afghanistan," Ismail Khan told reporters, "is for [the Americans] to militarily aid the Northern Alliance and not to send in soldiers."[23]

After he had regained control of Herat, Ismail Khan became more confrontational with the United States, calling the deployment of US and British soldiers "a mistake."[24] He dismissed the need for "the American experts" and reminded anyone who would listen that they had "gained enough experience from 23 years of war."[25] After the signing of the Bonn Agreement of December 2001 (see chapter 1), Ismail Khan stated that no international troops would be allowed to stay in *his* territory, making clear not only that he would not cooperate with the Bush administration but also that he considered western Afghanistan his personal fiefdom. He then reiterated his opposition to the presence of foreign troops in a January 2002 meeting with Francesc Vendrell, head of the UN Special Mission to Afghanistan, and then again to the commander of the International Security Assistance Force, British general John McColl. Of course, this public stance was compatible with accepting considerable financial resources and behind-the-scenes support from foreign forces. Ismail Khan in fact developed a close relationship with a team of US forces whom he hosted in "a brightly lit palace on a hilltop that the American troops have nicknamed Disneyland" and that locals call the "house of jihad."[26]

Ismail Khan simultaneously received strong support from Iran, especially in the early days of the intervention. Although he never officially admitted receiving weapons and ammunition from Iran, he did not conceal his good relationship with his neighbor to the west. "There are many reasons why we should have good relations with Iran. . . . Iran supported the Northern Alliance throughout our struggle. . . . We share a 600-mile-long border with them and they have welcomed more than 2 million Afghan refugees [as well as] many of our most famous mujahideen," he declared when asked about this relationship.[27] Iran in turn had an interest in using Ismail Khan as a proxy to extend its influence in an unstable region. In early 2002, observers reported that Ismail Khan's soldiers were trained by Iranian advisers, wore Iranian fatigues, and carried Iranian-made rifles. Iran even allegedly sent Ismail Khan Afghan currency for him to pay his soldiers and provided him with refurbished tanks captured from the Taliban.[28]

As the strongest armed actor in western Afghanistan, Ismail Khan found himself at the center of a power struggle between Iran and the United States.

This struggle reached its climax after President Bush labeled Iran a member of the "axis of evil" in the State of the Union address of January 29, 2002. "We do see things that clearly demonstrate Iran's interest in—at a minimum—the western portion of that country," declared US defense secretary Donald Rumsfeld two days later.[29] US Special Forces and Bush administration officials—including Rumsfeld and Secretary of State Colin Powell—then accused Ismail Khan of letting members of Iran's Revolutionary Guard into the country. Rumsfeld decided to pay him a visit, for he feared seeing Ismail Khan, whom he described as a "very interesting, deep man," courted by Iranian hardliners.[30] According to Robert Finn, then US ambassador to Afghanistan, visiting Ismail Khan in his own fiefdom was a mistake of high symbolic significance. It undermined Karzai's power and showed that the United States really treated the ruler of Herat as a head of state. It was like "making a statement," he said. In return, Ismail Khan welcomed Rumsfeld with all the ceremonial pomp attached to a diplomatic visit, in a clear display of symbolic power. "There were 40 people waiting at the airport, a band playing music, [and] people lined up in the streets," remembered Robert Finn.[31]

Playing both sides against the middle allowed Ismail Khan to regain his local autonomy, as both the United States and Iran were desperately in need of a strong ally in the border region while being in relatively weak bargaining positions. Rashid explains how Ismail Khan turned this power struggle to his advantage: "[Ismail Khan] is a master at this game. He's been playing it for the last 10, 15 years. And he frankly has been taking advantage of the Americans and the Iranians. He's getting them both to start reconstruction in the region he controls, building roads and other things. As far as he's concerned, and as far as the local Herati people are concerned, he's, you know, been playing a very wise game, which has been helping him and helping the territory under his control."[32] In this peculiar situation, both countries provided Ismail Khan with the economic and military support he needed to strengthen his power. "The wily Ismael Khan," the journalist notes, "made sure that the Iranians and the Americans spent most of the time watching each other rather than him, as he fed them tidbits of misinformation and gossip that kept their daggers drawn."[33] In sum, he benefited from Iranian and US largesse, as he played one actor against another, depending on the circumstances—so much so that his men wore American gear while carrying Iranian-made weaponry.

Ismail Khan also affirmed his international status through conducting high-level diplomacy of a sort commonly reserved for formally recognized sovereign states. For example, he met with aid agencies in Herat to demand they invest in welfare in his territory. "He basically presented us with a shopping list," recalled a UN official.[34] Ismail Khan also held private meetings with a number of foreign officials, including the Iranian president, Mohammad Khatami; the UN special representative for Afghanistan, Lakhdar Brahimi; President Bush's special envoy in Afghanistan, Zalmay Khalilzad; the US secretary of the treasury, John Taylor; and the commander of US military forces in Afghanistan, Lieutenant General Dan McNeill, who referred to him as "the Great Khan."[35] These meetings demonstrated to observers that he should be regarded as the one in charge of western Afghanistan. Through the conduct of a high-level diplomacy independent from the one promoted by the central government, Ismail Khan managed to portray himself as a leader able to deal on an equal footing with powerful heads of state and diplomats. Foreigners and the government in the capital were forced to negotiate with him as an autonomous political force whose interests had to be considered in any wider political arrangement. Ismail Khan was taking advantage of the international situation without paying the price—in this case, formal allegiance to the state.[36]

Warlord Governance

In this new international environment, and with the collapse of the Taliban regime (and a consequential decrease in state resources), Ismail Khan was likely to tip the balance of power in his favor. The financial, political, and military support he received from both the Iranians and the Americans provided him with enough resources to impose a new political order and reinstate his regional authority. Ismail Khan once again established himself as the amir of western Afghanistan: an active warlord dominating and controlling most sources of power in his fiefdom or, as Rashid put it, "a genuine warlord . . . both ruthless and popular, a provider of essential services to the people and a perpetrator of terror."[37]

Ismail Khan took control of Herat on November 12, 2001, captured the local state institutions, and immediately filled most of the government positions with his own people (as the Panjshiris were doing at the central level), ensuring his total control over all sources of power in the region. He then gathered thousands of supporters at the main mosque and pronounced himself governor of Herat—a self-appointment that was never contested by the central government and was even officially confirmed in February 2002. Ismail Khan also quickly asserted his military autonomy, in fact controlling what was believed to be the largest private army in Afghanistan at the time. In an interview with AFP in February 2002, he boasted: "Before the central government establishes a national army, we have already created one here in Herat. . . . All the mujahedin of Herat are members of divisions, they wear uniforms and live as an army."[38]

Ismail Khan's military might allowed him to secure control of the border posts (and custom revenues) in the same way it had after the fall of the communist regime in 1992.[39] Controlling the border posts provided Ismail Khan with the financial resources he needed to pay the salaries of his mujahideen, finance a gubernatorial bureaucracy, and invest in reconstruction projects. He used some of these revenues to provide goods and services to the inhabitants of Herat, which in turn increased his legitimacy. It also made him very popular among the business community, as Ismail Khan started to be perceived as a patron of business again. Years later, when asked about Ismail Khan in the early days of the US-led intervention, the governor of Herat at the time told me: "The perception is that Ismail Khan did some great things, unlike other warlords who enriched themselves: road construction, etc. but he did it with custom revenues. Now, as a governor, I understand: either you don't do anything, or you do like Ismail Khan. Either you play by the rules, or you become a beloved governor."[40]

Ismail Khan used this economic success to legitimize his very repressive and authoritative rule and, according to one of his local rivals, "remain known as the champion of Herat and the West."[41] According to an Afghan NGO worker I interviewed in Herat, he in fact came back with "a new face" in 2001 and built himself "a new image nationwide" by spending money on reconstruction.[42] "Yesterday, we had the jihad of the gun. Today, we are leading the jihad of reconstruction," Ismail Khan declared in August 2002, somehow acknowledging the necessity to convert his sources of power to shape-shift and survive in the new international environment.[43] By accumulating economic resources, he was not being greedy but rather "preparing for a future in which his sources of revenue might dry up, either because of the seizure of the custom posts or because of a change of trade patterns."[44]

Part of this investment (and power conversion) consisted of boosting his local legitimacy and ideological power by turning to a much harsher version of Islam. Observers indeed noted a net radicalization of Ismail Khan's religious discourse after 2001, a change most noticeable in his attitude and policies toward women. Some believe that he turned "from a religious conservative into a fanatic"; others argue that "Ismail Khan was never an Islamist in any real sense" and "became more of a traditionalist conservative Muslim than anything resembling a revolutionary Islamist."[45] Ismail Khan's use of religion as a tool to legitimize his authority is best understood in the context of his local rivalry with Mawlawi Khodadad. This influential Pashtun cleric uses his religious credentials to belittle Ismail Khan, who in turn reacts by further emphasizing his own religiosity—a reminder that Islam remains "the strongest unifying force in Afghan society," especially in an ethnically diverse city like Herat.[46] Before the Soviet-Afghan war, Ismail Khan was not known for being particularly religious. "He adjusted himself and created a religious character for himself," remembers one of his local opponents. "He made himself famous, the amir."[47]

In parallel, Ismail Khan invested in the projection and symbolic display of power, a process that was well described by Borzou Daragahi in the *Washington Times* on April 13, 2002: "Ismail Khan is everywhere in this city. His picture adorns the walls of government offices. It is on the desk of the manager of Afghan television and radio. Here's Mr. Khan visiting a girls' school. There he is giving a speech to teachers." His early promise to provide the equivalent of $25,000 to rebuild and refurbish a girls' school clearly illustrates Ismail Khan's need to appear as a liberal in the eyes of the international community, at least in the early stages of the US-led intervention.

In that period, it became clear just how adept Ismail Khan was at adjusting to various settings, calling on diverse social and material resources, and exhibiting different faces to different audiences: the "liberal warlord" visiting girls' schools to the international community; the religious conservative to his local constituency. In the absence of pressure from international forces to subordinate himself to the central government, he ruled as an alternative to the state—an active warlord. When pressure to conform grew, he drew on the resources at hand, such as his reputation as a defender of liberal values (in the eyes of outsiders) and as a provider of protection and services to local communities. And, when further pressure rendered these strategies unviable, Ismail Khan reemerged as a defender of faith. Yet, in spite of all these efforts, Ismail Khan partially failed to maintain his local legitimacy and reinitiate his emirate.[48]

Autonomy and Co-optation Attempts

During this period, Ismail Khan consistently remained the independent-minded warlord he had been in the 1990s. He soon started to criticize the Bonn Agreement of December 2001, which aimed to establish the new rules of the game, even though his son Mirwais had been appointed minister of labor and social affairs in the new transitional government. He accused his Panjshiri allies (who were overly represented in Bonn) of following their own agenda and keeping the most important positions for themselves. "Ismail Khan is in control of five provinces in Western Afghanistan and where is he in the government? He is not," complained his spokesman—hence supporting the views that former mujahideen leaders had a legitimate claim to rule post-Taliban Afghanistan.[49] Ismail Khan attended Karzai's inauguration as chairman of the Afghan Interim Authority only after both Iranian and US officials insisted he do so. He arrived an hour late, as a sign of defiance to the new Panjshiri-dominated political order. "I didn't even want to go," he told me.[50] In February 2002, he eventually pledged support for the new Afghan flag and for the *loya jirga*. In return, he was confirmed as governor of Herat and continued to run his fiefdom independently.

Ismail Khan's military capacity in fact allowed him to defy Kabul's directives and maintain his emirate's autonomy. Considering the challenge that Ismail Khan's authority represented to state centralization, it should come as no surprise that President Karzai made Herat his first domestic destination outside Kabul after taking office. He flew there in February 2002, accompanied by three ministers, to meet with his "good friend" Ismail Khan, "a brave man . . . whom [he trusted] not to make problems and work for the good of the country."[51] That Ismail Khan was calling himself amir was upsetting Karzai but, as a former mujahid pertinently pointed out, he had "too much power . . . too much money . . . too many soldiers" to need the president.[52] "On paper anyway," said an NPR reporter on November 6, 2002, "[Ismail] Khan is loyal to the fledgling US-backed central government of President Hamid Karzai, and is a friend of the [United States's] ongoing military campaign. But in reality, critics say, Ismail Khan answers only to Ismail Khan."[53]

Ismail Khan's relationship with the central government was marked by multiple attempts to co-opt him and bring him to Kabul to move him away from his power base—a strategy reminiscent of the one used by medieval European kings to tame unruly vassals. Ismail Khan resisted for as long as he could. He declared multiple times that he was not interested in a position in the central government: "To be a national man among the people of Afghanistan is far more worthy than holding an official post. . . . I do not hanker any post in Kabul," he declared after the formation of the interim cabinet.[54] A few months later, Ismail Khan turned down President Karzai's offer to appoint him minister of interior in the transitional government— an offer that was confirmed to me by Karzai himself.[55] In doing so, he reasserted his willingness to remain in Herat and mediate between his community and the central state: "I thought it would be better if I stayed here and brought the province closer to Kabul," he declared.[56] In a clear attempt to strengthen his local legitimacy, Ismail Khan repeated his love for Herat and "his people" ad nauseam: "I was offered a vice president position or one of the ministries, but I did not accept. . . . I preferred to be beside you, with the disabled and the mujahideen, than to accept a position there," he reaffirmed in August 2002.[57]

The amount of custom revenues the ruler of Herat was able to reap in part explains the government's attempts to rein in his power. His control of the border posts gave him tremendous economic power and vastly undermined central authority. As a Western diplomat told me years later: "The borders are where the money came from. Ismail Khan built schools with custom revenues but it should have been built by Kabul."[58] In May 2002, a seemingly worried customs department director general declared: "A lot of goods are coming from Iran and a lot are transiting through Iran from Dubai. . . . Ismail Khan is keeping all the money for himself. I sent him a letter telling him 'please send the physical money to Kabul'—I never got any answer. . . . The provinces help themselves and Kabul looks on."[59] In an apparent bid to resist centralizing pressures without antagonizing the government and its allies to a point where they would have to act on it, Ismail Khan declared in July 2002: "We will send them money in the future if they need it. . . . We have sent money in the past. And also during the near future, we plan to send some more money to the central government."[60] Ismail Khan's words sounded more like those of an equal partner than those of a subordinate but, a month later, he began paying custom duties to the central state. His ability to provide goods and services then progressively declined as the state affirmed its power and the amir gradually lost control over the border posts. This development ultimately required that he adapt, transform, and shift his bases of power to face Kabul's centralizing pressure—embodied by the minister of finance and future president of Afghanistan, Ashraf Ghani— and weather this challenge.[61]

State Centralization

The pressure on Ismail Khan intensified after the publication of a Human Rights Watch (HRW) report in November 2002 denouncing practices such as arbitrary arrests, intimidation, and torture, and the resulting "climate of fear" that existed in Herat under his rule.[62] A month later, a new HRW report criticized the United States' warlord strategy (see chapter 1).[63] Confronted with growing international pressure from human rights activists, the foreign forces that were comfortable with warlords playing a substantial political role in post-Taliban Afghanistan—namely, the US Department of Defense and the CIA—started to lose influence. The Bush administration reduced its support to Ismail Khan after US officials accused him of collaborating with Iran. US forces also refrained from getting involved in his armed confrontations with rival commanders. "Since 2004, the [United States] irrationally hates [Ismail Khan]," a UN official told me years later.[64] Iran, which needed Ismail Khan to counterbalance US influence at its border, in turn lost interest in using him as a proxy and readily dropped its support.[65]

Ismail Khan had long benefited from and taken advantage of his geopolitical position. Yet, he had little room to maneuver and shop for alternative international patrons. Therefore, losing support and protection from both Iran and the United States substantially weakened him to the extent that skirmishes with opposing commanders eventually led to the loss of his emirate. Once his international support had vanished, Ismail Khan could no longer resist state centralization. As Rashid explained to me, "He wasn't going to be anybody's stooge. . . . He was kind of resisting, trying to play this middle of the road thing," but eventually he had to give up and transform into something else once confronted with a new international environment.[66] His military power was no longer adequate to maintain his control over western Afghanistan. His economic power was almost entirely dependent on his ability to resist the central state's attempts to regain control over the border posts (and hence on his faltering military power). He had always faced tensions with other commanders and never consolidated his political control over all the factions in the area (especially the Pashtun ones). His strict Islamic policies, while increasing his local legitimacy among some, had also antagonized a number of actors in the liberal city of Herat.

Until then, the balance of power between Karzai and Ismail Khan had been largely in the warlord's favor. The central government had not been able to rein in his power and had instead preferred to act as a broker in the conflicts that opposed him to other commanders. Things changed in August 2004, when Ismail Khan had to request help from the central government against Amanullah Khan, one of his former allies. Officially, both the Karzai government and the United States backed Ismail Khan, who represented the government in the province and thus benefited from state legitimacy in his fight against other commanders. But in reality, Rashid told me, "there was no doubt that the government and the Americans were backing Amanullah Khan."[67] He had better connections in Kabul and "played his cards better."[68] By maintaining links with Iran and clashing with US troops on the ground, Ismail Khan had eventually managed to antagonize the United States. His call for help showed that the governor of Herat was no longer Karzai's equal. He had finally become a subordinate to the central state, prompting the creation of a new political order (from regional authority to parallel authority).

In an environment that puts a premium on perceptions and reputation, the whole event "both revealed and increased Ismail Khan's vulnerability."[69] No longer able to project authority, the strong and ferocious warlord of western Afghanistan appeared in everyone's eyes to be a giant with feet of clay. After the conflict with Amanullah Khan and the loss of international protection, Ismail Khan no longer had the capacity to resist Kabul's co-optation attempts and had to leave office in September 2004. Ismail Khan did not facilitate a peaceful transition in Herat, allegedly encouraging violent demonstrations by angry mobs who burned the compounds of several international organizations and NGOs—hence demonstrating his ability to disrupt political order.

However, at this stage, he no longer benefited from either US or Iranian protection and eventually had to accept his nomination as minister of energy and water in the new Karzai cabinet in December 2004. Sinno aptly points out that "political appointments under the leadership of a weak regime with an uncertain future are a poor substitute for governing autonomous fiefdoms," and warlords "would only accept such a deal on the verge of defeat, as Ismail Khan's experience has shown."[70] Or, in Karzai's words: "He was happier in Herat but, when I discussed with him, he accepted."[71]

Ismail Khan's skillful diplomacy, combined with his economic and military superiority (strengthened by Iranian and US support), had allowed him to remain an active warlord until 2004. Yet, his inability to maintain a *fonction totale* (that is, concentrate all sources of power simultaneously) in a changing international environment led to his partial downfall. Mukhopadhyay's argument, that Ismail Khan was too strong of a warlord to be kept in power in the midst of the state-building project, further emphasizes the importance of the shift.[72] In a process of state consolidation, Kabul (and the international community) could no longer afford to tolerate active warlords.[73]

The Armed Notable (2004–2014)

The growing centralizing power of the state (and its increased resources) and shifts in foreign interests and perceptions about Ismail Khan (and his decreased resources) resulted in a new political order of parallel authority. It forced Ismail Khan to find a new position in the social environment and finally transform his power from warlord-governor to armed notable, a leader who mediates between his community of followers and the outside (both the state and foreign actors) but also has the ability to coerce and provide security. Deprived of most of the authority he had acquired as a service provider on the basis of his military and economic dominance, Ismail Khan relied on what had always constituted the backbone of his power: his proven ability to organize violence. Unlike khans, whose power to operate as mediators came from tradition and land ownership, Ismail Khan and other warlords have relied on their military resources and personal charisma, itself based on the quasi-mythical characterization of their military careers and bravery in combat.

The Security Provider

Ismail Khan's inability to exert power the way he used to made finding new sources of legitimacy (or strengthening existing ones) a bigger concern after 2004. In a place where "followers seek leaders who offer them the greatest advantages and the most security," Ismail Khan logically built on his jihadist credentials.[74] His individual prestige still very much relies on his role as a military patron, the result of both military power and social capital. In the words of a human rights activist I interviewed in Herat: "[After years of] leading commanders, distributing weapons and resources, he is [powerful]. I don't know if he still has money and weapons, but the commanders still need him" (if only to benefit from the resources that his cabinet position was giving him access to, up to October 2013).[75]

The gathering of former mujahideen that Ismail Khan invited me to attend in 2011 perfectly illustrates that military legitimacy and the provision of security are at the core of Ismail Khan's authority. Not only did he make constant references to the jihad while praising his "courageous brothers," "the proud mujahideen," but he also pointed out the need to "tell [their children] the history of the mujahideen to keep their memory alive in the hearts and minds of the new generation."[76] In doing so, Ismail Khan plays into what Bhatia described as a "competition for legitimacy over the 'right to rule' and the 'right to conduct violence.'"[77] In other words, he projects authority to bolster his reputation.

Above all else, this military legitimacy, which Ismail Khan expresses through his jihadist credentials, is here to convince his followers of his pivotal role in establishing security, reminding his audience (at all levels of political affairs) that he already proved himself in the past and thus has the ability to provide security in the future. This way, the amir of western Afghanistan continues to appear as a leader with the ability to wage war in the eyes of the central state and the international community, even though he has held formal office in an apparent attempt by the state to co-opt him.[78] Ismail Khan emphasized this point at the gathering evoked above: "[The international community] may leave and that's our responsibility to defend Afghanistan. . . . We want the government to let experienced mujahideen take part in the Afghan National Army and the Afghan National Police to defeat the Taliban. Until then, Afghanistan won't be safe and secure."[79]

These gatherings—collectively referred to as Ismail Khan's *shura* or *shura-i jihadi*—are headed, funded, and run by Ismail Khan and serve to make sure that no one forgets about his military role. The same is true of the posters of him standing with Ahmad Shah Massoud, playing into "the image and iconography" of the late Panjshiri.[80] The gatherings take place in Herat's surroundings on a regular basis—about once or twice a month according to someone in Ismail Khan's entourage—and function as a platform to discuss social, political, and security issues among former mujahideen. As I witnessed myself in the summer of 2018, smaller and shorter gatherings (for commanders only) are organized in the confines of Ismail Khan's palace every week. This *shura* ("my *shura*," said Ismail Khan) serves as a permanent body for him to maintain his patronage networks among commanders—many of whom he has appointed to administrative positions or have been integrated into the local administration since—and show them that he defends their interests.[81] Ismail Khan also maintains individual contact with a number of his former commanders, who visit him regularly to, in the words of one of them, "pay their respects."[82]

Another useful way for Ismail Khan to project authority is the Jihad Museum he had built to assert his military legitimacy and remind all parties of his jihadist credentials. "He wants to keep his name," a Herati human rights activist told me. "When we talk about jihad in Herat, we talk about Ismail Khan."[83] Outside the museum, one sees some of the matériel and weapons that Afghan fighters used against the Soviets: helicopters and ground-to-air missiles among others. But the real treasure is inside. After some time strolling among the pictures of mujahideen leaders, one reaches the main room, covered by a circular fresco representing different events of the Soviet-Afghan war. Of particular importance is the Herat rebellion of March 1979, the single most celebrated event in the museum, in which Ismail Khan gives himself a prominent role. This rebellion, which played a major part in the early escalation of the war, is also celebrated every year in Herat and its surroundings. This is of course critical to the construction and reinforcement of Ismail Khan's legend, for the Herat rebellion is what really launched his political and military career. In the museum, one can only admire the shrewd display of symbolic power when the life-size statues of fighters respectfully listening to their leader catch the eye.

Ismail Khan never misses an opportunity to mention the museum. He did so during our first interview, as I narrated on my personal blog

Ismail Khan addressing his men, Jihad Museum, Herat (photograph by the author).

Herat rebellion (1979), Jihad Museum, Herat (photograph by the author).

(*Afghanopoly*), on July 20, 2011: "Ismail Khan is a very witty individual who likes asking questions (although I was the one looking for answers). He for example asked what my favorite place in Herat was. Caught by surprise, and knowing how serious Ismail Khan is about religion, I thought that talking about Herat's magnificent mosque was a smart move. Wrong again! That answer did not please him at all. Purposely ignoring me, Ismail Khan started to talk to my interpreter alone and asked him if I knew about the Jihad museum that he had built (as a tribute to his own courage and splendor). Unfortunately I did know about the museum. My interpreter and I actually went there a week earlier, during my last trip to Herat. But it totally slipped my mind." Ismail Khan also mentioned the museum at the gathering of former mujahideen I attended that year. He asked former mujahideen to donate any items, registers, and pictures dating back to the jihad to the museum and promised them to hire historians to write their stories—that is, his version of their stories—in yet another attempt to increase his own ideological capital.[84] When he was still governor of Herat, the city was festooned with posters of mujahideen martyrs (especially along the highways) and the walls covered with jihadist slogans. They were removed by his successor, as a way of showing that bureaucratic legitimacy had to replace military legitimacy. Ismail Khan also frequently portrays his son Mirwais as a martyr, even though he did not die during the jihad, and adorns Herat's main intersections with posters of him every year for the anniversary of his death.[85]

The Notable

Asked about Ismail Khan's authority since 2004 and the loss of his fiefdom, a Herat resident told me the following story:

> A special man was a close adviser to the king. He behaved so badly that the king decided to fire him. Understanding that he would eventually have to accept the king's decision, the special man asked one last favor. "Invite me to your next meeting" he told the king. "Curse in my ear and tell me to go away." Perplexed, the king accepted. When came the next meeting, the king stayed true to his promise: he summoned the former adviser; he cursed in his ear; and he ordered him to go away. While he was doing so, the special man looked intensely at the ministers and then left. After the meeting, he himself sum-

moned the ministers and told them that the king had ordered him to punish them. Scared, they begged the former adviser to do something to appease the king's wrath. "Don't worry," he told the ministers. "I will make sure that everything is OK. But in exchange, you will need to do something for me."

According to the Herat resident, the story of the special man encapsulates the way Ismail Khan wields authority in western Afghanistan, mediating to exert power. "Ismail Khan does not have power. . . . He has skills," he told me with a sarcastic grin.[86] The skills that my interviewee identified allow Ismail Khan to maximize his odds of survival. This fable does not illustrate the absence of power, but the ability of political actors to make themselves indispensable.

Ismail Khan's story is not one of capacity but a Bourdieusian tale of a shrewd individual who has the skills to shape-shift when the environment changes. While the new international environment did not allow him to wield uncontested authority over *his* territory after 2004, it has not prevented him from exerting power in a different form. Ismail Khan remains "the epitome of the warlord who learns the art of survival by being extremely flexible."[87] This ability ultimately rests on his past reputation and influence in a variety of networks. When some networks become less significant, such as when shared interests between Ismail Khan and foreign military waned, influence in commerce, for instance, becomes more significant. This change also shifts Ismail Khan's resource base. When custom revenue falls out of his control, subtle capacities to act as an intermediary and facilitator in business, for example, may replace these lost resources.

Being governor of Herat surely allowed Ismail Khan to accumulate and concentrate sources of power and re-exert a *fonction totale* for a short while. Yet, the fact that in 2019 he still remains the main political broker in the region years after he was sent to Kabul proves that his formal position did not constitute the core of his authority. It is his successful power conversion that has given him ways to hold new social functions at the local level to support his legitimacy. Ismail Khan survives because he manages to maintain his legitimacy as a leader (his reputation and his name). Hence why Ismail Khan prefers to be referred to by the honorary title of amir of western Afghanistan.

Ismail Khan is an Afghan notable, a khan, a title that has even become part of his name since the beginning of the jihad. This explains otherwise apparently irrational behaviors. Considering that, in Afghanistan, "[the horse] has kept its status value," it makes sense of Ismail Khan's earlier habit of riding his white horse through the city of Herat, "re-creating a legendary patrol by a long-ago emir."[88] It also helps one understand why Ismail Khan owns a private zoo. "In a landscape of political impressions, the compound of a powerful khan dominates all other works of man," writes Azoy.[89] Most importantly, "authority [in Afghanistan is] dependent on reputation and reputation on exploit."[90] Among other things, this illuminates why Ismail Khan's followers keep mentioning that their leader escaped from a Taliban jail, even though the escape may in fact have been negotiated (through bribes)—which would point to different sources of power altogether. In the words of one of his followers: "Ismail Khan is a great military intellect. He was wounded three or four times severely, but still escaped many times just by the skin of his teeth."[91]

Ismail Khan also exerts his social function by holding court, listening to his "subjects" complain, and trying to respond to their needs. "I solve the problems of the people," he told me in 2018.[92] His *shura*, for example, provides financial support to the families of martyrs, thanks to his personal "generosity" or through contributions from businessmen.[93] As of 2019, Ismail Khan receives elders late at night, is always surrounded by an extensive entourage, and, as a UN official put it, maintains a "backward middle-aged autocratic vision."[94] This type of politics is well described by Giustozzi: "Presenting himself as a nineteenth-century Afghan ruler suited Ismail Khan's political views to perfection, while at the same time also working as a form of customary legitimisation. He clearly enjoyed holding court at the governor's palace and receiving all sorts of supplicants, from people asking for his intervention in judicial affairs or in a family dispute, to others just begging for some practical or financial help."[95]

Ismail Khan can arbitrage: he takes "advantage of a price differential for political, economic, and cultural goods across terrains."[96] He occupies a mediating position that is legitimized by his ability to provide for his followers. Although he no longer has the capacity to provide services for the entire population, he still holds considerable sway in Herat. As a human rights activist I talked to in 2018 put it: "He solves problems for people, he calls the government."[97] In other words, he mediates. In that regard, it is interesting to note that, at the gathering of mujahideen I attended in 2011, alongside posters that showed Ismail Khan with Massoud were also posters of him with

President Karzai, potentially bolstering his legitimacy through his relationship to the state. Like traditional khans, Ismail Khan also "feeds others," both literally, by inviting large crowds to share a meal with him—in the context of his *shura*, for example—and metaphorically, by providing his men with jobs and other economic opportunities.[98]

Ismail Khan continues to act as a power broker over political nominations, at both the local and central levels. As a former governor who oversaw all post-2001 political nominations in the province, he still has leverage over local state institutions, in which his followers occupy prominent positions. Even after he was sacked from his governor position, Ismail Khan kept enough leverage to preclude the disarmament of his men and affect the Afghan National Security Forces recruitment process.[99] Ismail Khan also has influence over political elites in Kabul. After 2009, he was able to maintain his grip on his cabinet position, in spite of disapproval from parliament and US pressure to have him removed.[100] As of 2019, many still consider him as the main power holder in western Afghanistan and feared his potential for disruption—which he already proved when he lost his position as governor in 2004. President Karzai was known to consult him before making important political appointments in the province, even after he was dismissed from his gubernatorial position. In the words of a fellow Jamiati interviewed in 2018, "No one has replaced him, people who are appointed in Herat need to get Ismail Khan's support."[101]

In some circumstances, Ismail Khan uses an anti-US and anti-West rhetoric to strengthen his legitimacy. "It's disgusting to see that we are not able to ensure our own security," he told his followers in a speech he gave in 2011. "Why do we need people from foreign countries (the United States, France, and other European countries)? Why don't we say that we want the international community to leave? Aren't you ashamed to see a Canadian lady here as a military to ensure our security?"[102] Using the United States and others as scapegoats is a way for Ismail Khan to promote unity among the mujahideen of western Afghanistan (under his leadership). In the fragmented Herati context, it remains vital, for him, to appear as the only legitimate leader in the region. "There's been one person under one leadership over these past 23 years [in Herat] and there is no problem," he bragged back in 2002.[103]

According to the Afghanistan scholar Gilles Dorronsoro, Ismail Khan, in his search for unity, even managed for some time to allow doubts to persist as to which ethnic group he belongs to.[104] Unlike Dostum, for example,

Ismail Khan never portrayed himself as an ethnic leader (although he has had trouble being accepted by fellow Pashtun commanders in the region). Unity was a strong theme in the speech Ismail Khan gave at the gathering of mujahideen I attended in March 2011: "During the jihad, there were four or five mujahideen committees here, served by Shias, Tajiks, and Sunnis. We didn't talk about ethnicity back then. Why are we divided today? In the past, we were united because we only believed in jihad and God. Now we are divided because we are interested in material things such as money. That's how they are dividing us. . . . We have formed different *shuras* for ourselves now, criticizing each other. . . . We are having different *shuras* now, for Sunnis, for Shias, etc."[105] In other words, the people of Herat are unsafe because they are divided, and they should therefore unite again, preferably under Ismail Khan's leadership. Overall, Ismail Khan's ability to mediate, combined with the ability to deliver security and opportunities at the local level, allows him to remain relevant to actors willing to delegate responsibilities, as he continues to have relations with foreigners and the central government.

Ismail Khan's political career took off with the Herat rebellion of March 1979. The future amir of western Afghanistan accumulated power during the Soviet-Afghan war and reached his apogee in the 1990s, when he exerted a *fonction totale* over Herat and the surrounding provinces. After losing his fiefdom to the Taliban in 1995, he entered a life of exile and resistance that came to an end with the US-led intervention. From 2001 to 2004, Ismail Khan was once again able to rule as the amir of western Afghanistan. He was able to resist the state's centralizing pressure for a while, owing to his ability to act in the international system. He played Iran and the United States off one another to benefit from their international protection, and he increased his local legitimacy by conducting his own warlord diplomacy. His balancing act was tied to this effectiveness, and as he progressively lost this ability, he had to accommodate to the Weberian hierarchy of the state. Once the idea that he could no longer provide security started to take shape, it became self-fulfilling, and Ismail Khan eventually had to give up his fiefdom. As Barth put it, "A position of authority can be maintained only through a constant struggle for the control of the sources of authority."[106] By removing Ismail Khan from his gubernatorial position, the central state cut off most of his sources of revenue, thus diminishing his ability to remunerate his followers, and hence people's material reason for supporting him. Deprived of the legitimacy he had acquired as a service provider, Ismail Khan had to transform his power, reinvent himself, and find a new social space to exert his authority (power conversion).

As of 2019, Ismail Khan's authority rests on his ability to operate as an armed notable who mediates between the local level and the outside world (for example, by portraying himself as the preferred interlocutor to negotiate with the Taliban directly or by participating in the negotiations between the Taliban and representatives of the Afghan opposition in Moscow) and has the ability to coerce and provide security.[107] This ability in turn rests on his military legitimacy and the followers that come with it. Ismail Khan still has authority over his former commanders who hold sway in their local communities. He still maintains his military *shura*, as I personally witnessed during my latest visit. His survival is therefore a combination of many factors. He survives because he manages to maintain his legitimacy as a leader able to protect and provide: he is "indirectly in power, fixing and granting."[108] He has the ability to appear as the main locus of authority in western Afghanistan and thus benefit from all sorts of protection, thanks to the social capital he has acquired throughout the various Afghan conflicts. In the words of a Herat bureaucrat: "He has been in and out of Afghanistan [since 1979], he obviously has supporters in and out of Afghanistan."[109] In sum, Ismail Khan's survival is not only a story of military strength but also one of a shrewd individual who uses multiple repertoires to navigate in the complex post-2001 environment.

Authority of this kind is deeply rooted in the social fabric of western Afghanistan and is much broader than the authority that comes from holding state office. This authority blurs the boundaries between state and society that are the foundation of conventional notions of state building. It shows how truly different—and, to the extent that it is connected to the particular cultural milieu of western Afghanistan, truly heterogeneous—the authority and polity in which Ismail Khan holds sway are. Nevertheless, these differences do not prevent foreigners, even those who insist that they are promoting state building in Afghanistan, from dealing with Ismail Khan on his own terms and in his own political terrain.

In 2011, when asked if he would fight again should the Taliban return to power, Ismail Khan had told me: "As a matter of fact, it is an obligation for us to defend Afghanistan. . . . We are responsible and obligated to defend the country, as we have done in the past."[110] With the growing influence of the

Taliban insurgency and the end of NATO combat operations, political dynamics have drastically changed since then. The uncertainty surrounding the international community's intentions in Afghanistan has made warlords indispensable, which has in turn emboldened Ismail Khan to constantly criticize the Ghani government for sidelining the former mujahideen.[111] There is absolutely no reason to believe that Ismail Khan will stop playing a prominent role should the United States successfully negotiate a peace agreement with the Taliban and follow through with the complete withdrawal of its troops. In fact, given his ability to shape-shift and convert power, Ismail Khan will most likely maintain authority and play an active role in Afghan politics for the rest of his life.

Chapter 4

Dostum, the Ethnic Entrepreneur

In April 2016, US officials denied Afghan warlord turned vice president Abdul Rashid Dostum a visa to the United States. In doing so, they did not simply refuse entry to the second-ranking official of a regime the United States helped put in place. They also turned down a man who was instrumental in recapturing the northern city of Mazar-i Sharif from the Taliban in 2001, a man who had worked hand in glove with US Special Forces as part of the so-called global war on terrorism. Fifteen years later, the same man was barred from entering the United States. The decision to reject Dostum's visa application was indicative of the US government's double standards and lack of coherence when it comes to dealing with the violent political actors that it previously empowered. Western policymakers value indigenous allies; yet they are often at a loss about what to do with them once the conflict ends. Most importantly, maybe, for the purpose of this book, this anecdote is an example of the changing circumstances to which warlords must adapt. Dostum greatly benefited from the US-led intervention in

Afghanistan, but he has found other ways to survive when US support later turned into open hostility.[1]

Dostum has in fact been shape-shifting for the best part of the past four decades: from pro-government militia leader, to active warlord, to resistant, to US ally, to political pariah, and finally to first vice president of the Islamic Republic of Afghanistan. As a result, he has often been criticized for his lack of political loyalty. Since the beginning of the Soviet-Afghan war, he has indeed acquired a reputation as a side-switching, self-interested political butterfly, floating and flitting from patron to patron, from Russia and Uzbekistan (and before, the Soviet Union) to Iran, Pakistan, and Turkey. But his fickleness is actually a skill, one that has allowed him to survive through the various events that have shaken Afghanistan throughout his lifetime, and in which he has taken an active role. Dostum's trajectory, in and out of power, indeed demonstrates his ability to straddle different realms of authority.

However, Dostum has remained consistent in his lifelong attempt to be accepted by the political elites in the capital while maximizing his local autonomy. He has never betrayed his core clientele, and many ethnic Uzbeks continue to see him as the pasha, a fatherly figure who "has money and weapons [and] can defend them."[2] In Azoy's words, Dostum is "an ethnically loyal opportunist," and that is why he maintains "the loyalty—or at least the tolerance—of some very urbane fellow Uzbeks."[3] Dostum is in fact a typical ethnic entrepreneur: "[a political entrepreneur] within an ethnic group who seek[s] to enhance [his] power or influence through the political and/or military mobilization of [his] ethnic group."[4] He owes his survival, above all else, to his ability to maintain himself as the leader of the Afghan Turkic community—made mostly of ethnic Uzbeks and Turkmens—that is, his ability to portray himself as the one and only leader able to represent and protect a group whose members often see themselves as belonging to an oppressed minority.

Genesis of an Uzbek Warlord (1978–2001)

The Militia Leader

Abdul Rashid, who would earn the nickname "Dostum" ("my friend" in Persian) years later for his habit of calling everyone by that term, was born in the mid-1950s in Khuaja Dukuh, a village near Sheberghan, the capital of the northern province of Jowzjan.[5] Raised in a poor farmer's family, he had to drop out of school to work when he was a teenager, something he has been mocked and criticized for throughout his political career. In the mid-1970s, he completed his military service, during which he was assigned to train with an elite commando unit in the eastern city of Jalalabad—owing to "his physique and reputation as a leader" (if the origin story provided on his official Facebook page is to be believed). Back in Jowzjan a couple of years later, he was soon hired at Sheberghan's state-run oil and gas company, where he became increasingly involved with Parcham, the more moderate faction of the People's Democratic Party of Afghanistan (PDPA)—as opposed to the more extreme and more pro-Pashtun Khalq faction. There, he also acquired a reputation as a strong *kurash* wrestler and *buzkashi* rider, two traditional folk games that favor physical strength and aggression. I expand later on the role *buzkashi* has played in Dostum's political career.

Unlike the other warlords covered in this book, Dostum did not spend the following decade waging war against the pro-Soviet government. On the contrary, he fought on behalf of this government—which many Uzbeks saw as sympathetic to its oppressed minorities—against the mujahideen. Dostum enrolled in the armed forces after the PDPA coup of 1978 and was eventually given command of an all-Uzbek militia of several hundred men (soon nicknamed the Jowzjani militia) in charge of securing gas fields around Sheberghan, hence exploiting the government's willingness to recruit militias to build his own ethnic-based armed group. After a short hiatus following the purge of the Parcham faction from government, Dostum rejoined the army after the Soviets invaded Afghanistan and killed Hafizullah Amin, the Khalqi leader, to replace him with a Parchami, Babrak Karmal, in December 1979. He was soon given command of the 734th People's Self-Defense Regiment of Afghanistan's security and intelligence agency (KhAD). As part of KhAD, he then received KGB training in the Soviet Union, where he developed contacts that later proved instrumental to maintaining his power.

Nurtured by the Parchami regime throughout the 1980s, Dostum was made general and eventually "reached the pinnacle of his power within [the Najibullah] government [September 1987–April 1992]" with the formation of a mobile reserve unit, the Fifty-Third Infantry Division.[6] Yet, he complained about being marginalized and despised by the regular army because of his ethnic background and lack of formal education. After the full Soviet withdrawal, he began to oppose the regime as a reaction to Najibullah's attempt to "pashtunise" the military.[7] Now in possession of his own armed ethnic constituency, he formed an alliance with former pro-government commanders, army generals, and mujahideen leaders, with whom he took over Mazar-i Sharif in March 1992. Those new allies also gave him unprecedented access to ample economic and military resources—weaponry, vehicles (such as aircraft and tanks), and equipment that previously belonged to the army.[8] From then onward, Dostum ruled his fiefdom autonomously (while also being engaged in the fighting taking place in Kabul, as explained in chapter 1).[9]

Warlord Governance

Dostum's accumulation of power, combined with the collapse of the central state, led to the emergence of a new political order in the North (regional authority). Dostum became an active warlord. From the fall of the Najibullah government in 1992 to the capture of Mazar-i Sharif by the Taliban in 1997–98, Dostum ruled most of northern Afghanistan, controlled five to seven provinces (depending on the time period), and commanded tens of thousands of armed men. In fact, he was well on his way to building his own protostate. In 1992, out of the alliance formed to capture Mazar-i Sharif and the relationships that he had built before and during the Soviet-Afghan war, Dostum established Junbesh-i Mili (henceforth Junbesh), a political platform that regrouped people from all existing political parties in the North. Junbesh was initially created to promote unity among all these political forces and compel central elites to recognize the northerners as a force to be reckoned with. It eventually became the protogovernment structure that ruled northern Afghanistan.[10] Through the creation of Junbesh, Dostum tried to convert a primarily military power into a more overtly political one. As a scholar from Mazar-i Sharif put it, "He was only a military commander and wanted to become a political character."[11] In fact, Dostum attempted to "store" his power in institutional positions to lower the costs of exercising it militarily.[12]

Taking over the collapsed state's institutions and the former regime's personnel, Junbesh worked like an embryonic government. It had specialized committees providing different services (e.g., justice, economy, interior, foreign affairs, and intelligence) and its own version of the Afghan currency (the

Afghani), printed in Uzbekistan. The Junbesh Afghanis, soon nicknamed *junbeshis*, could be distinguished from the ones the government had printed in Russia by their serial numbers and were exchanged at a lower rate.[13] Yet, Dostum himself claimed (years later) that he "did not form a government of [his] own at the time, but had good contacts with the leadership of President [Burhanuddin] Rabbani in Kabul" (even though he fought against that government after the creation of the Shura-i Hamahangi in January 1994, as explained in chapter 1).[14] He was willing to acknowledge the central government's authority, provided that he could remain his own master and rule his fiefdom accordingly, in part because, as Giustozzi points out, "the chances of warlords receiving formal international recognition in the age of the 'international community' are virtually nil and Dostum was well aware of that."[15]

Mazar-i Sharif, under Dostum's rule, has been portrayed, retrospectively, as "a jewel in Afghanistan's battered crown," a place that "enjoyed peace, prosperity and hedonistic excess."[16] Rashid describes the city at that time as a major trading center in which the bazaars, supplied with smuggled goods by Dostum's own airline, were "stocked with high Russian vodka and French perfumes," girls "dressed in skirts and high heels" went to the university, and the administration ran efficient health and education services.[17] This picture is likely exaggerated. Yet, Dostum did manage to successfully establish a new and stable political order and remains popular today for the stability that he brought to his region, as well as for the services that he provided in the 1990s. In a very conservative society like Afghanistan, Dostum is remembered for his liberal and secular rule, compared with warlords with a mujahideen background such as Ahmad Shah Massoud and Ismail Khan. Yet, during that period, he also acquired the reputation of being ruthless, violent, and authoritarian. This reputation, due in part to the reproduction of stereotypes of Uzbeks as fierce and cruel fighters and in part to his own actions, later undermined his ability to shape-shift and hindered his position in post-2001 Afghanistan.

Warlord Diplomacy

Dostum was able, as head of his own protostate, to develop and expand his international networks. Junbesh had offices in Iran, Pakistan, Turkey, Uzbekistan, and the United States. Its foreign affairs representative, General

Abdul Malik Pahlawan (henceforth Malik) regularly visited foreign coun-tries to meet with ministers and heads of state. Consulates were opened in Mazar-i Sharif. Dostum himself received foreign diplomats and occasionally traveled, for example, to Saudi Arabia, Pakistan, Turkey, and the United States. Most importantly, he was able to convince foreign governments that he could serve their interests, developing particularly close relationships with Uzbekistan and Turkey, based on ethnic affiliations. Dostum in fact devel-oped a distinctive form of warlord diplomacy that exploited personal net-works as much as it did formal ties and was conducted to enhance his per-sonal authority. These relations later proved instrumental to his survival, as they allowed him to benefit from international protection when his physical survival was endangered.[18]

In the 1980s, during his days as a pro-government militia leader, he de-veloped networks abroad through regular contact with Soviet generals and KGB advisers pushing for a bigger role for Dostum ahead of Najibullah's fall. After the collapse of the Soviet Union, some of these individuals inte-grated Uzbekistan's newly formed intelligence agency, the National Security Service, also in charge of foreign policy toward Afghanistan. In the 1990s, thanks to these preexisting networks, Dostum was provided with war matériel (weapons, aircraft, fuel, and cash), while Junbesh forces were given access to the Termez airbase (directly across the Afghanistan-Uzbekistan border), and Junbesh members were allowed to freely enter Uzbekistan with-out visas. This "privileged status" was conducive to the development of what Giustozzi describes as a "mafia system": "Individuals in Junbesh (smugglers, traders) had connections with Central Asian bureaucracies and could then smuggle goods into Afghanistan. The government of Uzbekistan may well have known what was going on, but they also had interest in the system. Drug trafficking may well have started at that moment. It was easy for Junbesh to cross borders without checks."[19] In the end, Dostum was able to build ties and pursue foreign relations with actors who operated in parallel to the for-mal diplomatic channels of Uzbekistan and regarded him as an extension of their own domestic system.

Turkey has also offered great support to Dostum from the early 1990s on-ward. His relations with that country were conducted along more formal channels, though, in this case, personal networks also played a critical role. Dostum managed to develop contacts with Turkey through Azad Beg, a Turkic nationalist often considered as the father of Pan-Turkism in Afghanistan—"Turkic" referring to the ethno-linguistic group comprising not only Turkish people but also, among others, Uzbeks, Kazakhs, Turkmens, Kyrgyzs, and Azerbaidjanis. In the early 1980s, Beg created a Turkic nationalist group that was mobilizing ethnic Uzbeks and Turkmens from northern Afghanistan in the fight against the Soviet Union. Through his personal connections, Beg became the main line of contact between Dostum and Pakistani intelligence. Beg then developed ties with Turkey, which started to fund Junbesh financially and, from there on, helped Dostum with military and governance-related issues (e.g., culture and education).[20] Yet, Azad Beg's ambitions and international connections posed a challenge to the Uzbek leader. Unfortunately for Beg, in 1990s Afghanistan, military might was the most important source of power. And, "in terms of military strength Azad Beg was no match for Dostum."[21] Unlike Dostum, Beg was unable to combine the diverse sources of power necessary to secure his political and physical survival. He died in an airplane crash in 1997, under suspicious circumstances.[22]

The Resistance Leader

Things changed with the rise of the Taliban. Unlike Massoud and Ismail Khan, Dostum had managed, with Azad Beg's help, to develop good relations with Pakistan, the Taliban's main patron. For example, he met with Prime Minister Benazir Bhutto in October 1994. Pakistan tried very early on to forge an alliance between Dostum and the Taliban against commanders of Jamiat-i Islami. For Dostum, cooperating with the Taliban against their common enemies (Massoud and Ismail Khan in particular) was only logical (especially as he was involved in fights against them in Kabul and in the northwest, respectively). In 1995, the Junbesh air force helped the Taliban attack Herat by carrying out raids against Ismail Khan's forces. And, on another occasion, Junbesh mechanics were sent to Kandahar to repair Taliban aircraft. Dostum switched sides to join Massoud's Northern Alliance after the fall of Herat, when the Taliban made clear they would not grant him autonomy in the North.

The Taliban took Kabul in 1996. High-ranking officials from the Pakistani government then visited Dostum in Mazar-i Sharif to persuade him to switch alliances again. Faced with Dostum's refusal, Pakistan turned toward

General Malik, Junbesh's foreign affairs representative. Malik had held a personal grudge against Dostum (but remained officially part of Junbesh) since Dostum had allegedly ordered the assassination of his brother a year earlier.[23] On May 19, 1997, the Pakistani Inter-Services Intelligence (ISI), Malik, and the Taliban brokered a deal that, in hindsight, looked like a covert and concerted effort to dismantle Dostum's military organization and shatter the defense of northern Afghanistan. Dostum, who depended on some of the local commanders affiliated with Malik to secure Mazar-i Sharif, fled to Turkey (via Uzbekistan) with a handful of his men as the Taliban entered the city. Within days, Mazar-i Sharif residents mounted armed resistance. Malik eventually rejoined the Northern Alliance (in return for which he received the position of foreign affairs minister in the mujahideen government), and the Taliban were forced out of the city. However, Malik never fully established his leadership over the northern military commanders, who ended up supporting Dostum's comeback in September 1997. From then on, "Rabbani was the president," said the then governor of the northern province of Faryab, "but it [was] Dostum who made the decisions [in the North]."[24]

The Taliban recaptured Mazar-i Sharif in August 1998. Dostum fled Afghanistan again, leaving almost all his assets behind. He spent the next three years in exile in Ankara with his family, with the support of the Turkish government. Frustrated by Jamiat's lack of progress in the fight against the Taliban, Iran's Revolutionary Guard, which had provided Dostum with weapons before his exile, eventually helped Junbesh open several military fronts. Iran, along with Russia and Turkey (which also worried about the Taliban's growing power), also pushed the Northern Alliance to facilitate Dostum's return.

In the spring of 2001, a Northern Alliance helicopter fetched Dostum and thirty of his men at the border between Iran and Afghanistan. Dostum flew first to Fayzabad, in the northeastern province of Badakhshan, to meet with Rabbani and other leaders, and then to Panjshir, where, as an official member of the military of the Islamic Republic of Afghanistan, he swore allegiance to Ahmad Shah Massoud, the defense minister. In April, he was inserted by helicopter into Sar-i Pul Province, with a little more than a dozen men. A former European diplomat recalls: "There was a lot of excitement. . . . People were walking from far to meet with the Pasha. People were really excited. . . . Dostum had residual influence even in Balkh and [Mazar-i Sharif], even when they were under Taliban control, as he was organizing the resistance from abroad."[25]

Dostum's dazzling comeback illustrates that warlord survival is not a function of military and economic assets alone. On the contrary, his diplomatic skills, charisma, and ideological power (vis-à-vis the Turkic community) played the primary role. Dostum returned and remobilized his men and followers despite the loss of his military might. In the words of the French researcher Vincent Fourniau, he had "less legitimacy than any other party in the Northern Alliance . . . because he was not in Afghanistan (fighting) over the last years," but he had the "charisma to recapture his military strength."[26] For Giustozzi, in fact, "the most interesting feature of the reformation of warlord polities in Afghanistan from 2001 is the speed with which it took place."[27] In the period that followed, Dostum became an active warlord once again (although never as powerful as he once was), weathering very hostile international and local environments to emerge as soon as the conditions permitted.[28]

Back to Warlordism (2001–2004)

US Intervention and Warlord Strategy

The beginning of the US-led intervention made a remarkable difference in Dostum's life and political career. He provided the United States with a powerful ally on the ground to fight the Taliban. Incidentally, US support gave him the opportunity to rearm, remobilize, and reaffirm his authority in the North. In fact, he later confessed that he had been "saved" by the Americans.[29] US Special Forces worked closely with his men, creating what has been described as a "familial bond."[30] Together, and with the help of other Northern Alliance commanders, they recaptured Mazar-i Sharif in November 2001. Dostum later organized a farewell ceremony in honor of the US troops who had fought on his side, presenting them with numerous gifts such as Uzbek robes and carpets and horse blankets. He even erected a memorial to honor Mike Spann, a CIA paramilitary officer who had died in a Taliban prisoners uprising. Dostum's political rivals eventually started criticizing him for being an American stooge: "Dostum is like clay, [the Americans] can shape him however they wish," said a Northern Alliance source.[31]

But as subsequent events showed, the Americans also were clay in Dostum's hands. The Uzbek leader used his charisma and warrior ethos—which resonated particularly well with US Special Forces—to develop his networks within the US military. He told foreign forces what they wanted to hear to benefit from this new relationship and maintain his international connections.

Dostum also used his collaboration with the United States to legitimize and increase his local authority. Stanton, for example, recalls that when Dostum arrived in Mazar-i Sharif, he "wanted to be seen riding alongside the Americans as they entered the city. . . . He suggested that they hoist an American flag on a pole attached to the buggy."[32] An elite unit of US Special Forces continued advising Dostum long after the fall of Mazar-i Sharif and the signing of the Bonn Agreement, traveling in his car and standing by his side during meetings. One would imagine that the US exercise of power would occur along more formal bureaucratic lines and would be applied in support of a state-building project. Instead, Dostum's close personal ties, right down to individual soldiers accompanying him, showed how he could manipulate this set of foreign relations to bolster his authority.[33]

However, compared with Massoud and his successors, Dostum crucially suffered from an image deficit that, in the new international environment, could hinder his political career. Already, in the beginning of 2001, he had asked a European diplomat to help him design a website to improve his image. But Massoud had "quashed the idea of [Junbesh] having its independent media outlet," hence maintaining a quasi monopoly over the Northern Alliance's outgoing communication.[34] It should therefore come as no surprise that Dostum hired a Washington-based lobbyist immediately after he heard about the attacks on the World Trade Center. The lobbyist reportedly met with several congressmen and their staffers to plead Dostum's cause, in exchange for a percentage of any aid he managed to secure.[35]

In the immediate aftermath of 9/11, Dostum also launched a diplomatic campaign by talking to foreign journalists through his satellite phone. To the West, he was spreading the idea that he was no longer the man he used to be and was willing to play by the new rules of the game: democracy and the so-called global war on terrorism. In October 2001, in one of many such examples, one of Dostum's senior aides told the press that his leader dreamed "about peace and democracy" and was "ready to fight against terrorists."[36] After he and his rivals had retaken the North from the Taliban, he started to invite journalists to Sheberghan. Dostum presented a new face to the international community. He had his speeches translated into English and distributed to foreign journalists by an English-speaking adviser in charge of media relations. And the perception did in fact change, at least in some circles. On Christmas Eve 2001, a CNN journalist expressed: "There is a spirit of hope and progress under Dostum, a man who is moving from war maker to peace maker. From warlord to political leader, from alignment once with the enemies of America to its close ally." A news report indicates that Dostum even sent New Year's greeting cards to NGOs based in Mazar-i Sharif that year.[37]

Prior to that, Dostum had also used Karzai's inauguration ceremony of December 2001 to meet with Lakhdar Brahimi, the special representative of the UN secretary-general, the Uzbek minister of foreign affairs, the Pakistani minister of foreign affairs, the British chargé d'affaires, and a number of other high-ranking foreign guests. "Presiding over international relations," wrote Edward Cody in the *Washington Post* on January 16, 2002, "is all in a day's work for Dostum." There are multiple other examples of Dostum conducting his own diplomacy in the early post-Taliban period: he attended the reopening of the Uzbek consulate; he met with the Pakistani ambassador, the Indian consul, the US chargé d'affaires, the US assistant secretary of state for Southeast Asia, and many other foreign dignitaries; and he even received a delegation from the European Parliament in his Mazar-i Sharif residence in 2003. Dostum also talked to numerous foreign military officials, Western journalists, Afghan leaders, and government officials, always receiving them as if he were a head of state.

Most importantly, Dostum built on his relationship with Turkey, which, as he once put it, "always supported [him and his people] during the worst times."[38] Turkey has indeed always been crucial to his survival, as a safe haven when his life was in physical danger. Dostum took his first trip abroad after 9/11, in January 2002, to Ankara, where he visited his family and met with Turkish officials to discuss Turkey's offer to provide training to the Afghan military and to help build a new national army. The Turkish prime minister praised Dostum for saving the Afghan people from the Taliban regime as well as for his constructive role in post-2001 Afghanistan. Acting as a patron of business, Dostum also pointed out during that visit that Turkish companies should be involved in the reconstruction of northern Afghan cities, while helping them make deals with Afghan importers. More generally, there are indications that Turkey later financed the creation of Ayna TV and kept making monthly payments to Dostum for years.[39]

While it is common for leaders of a part of a country to conduct their own relations with officials in other countries, Dostum's actions were calculated to highlight to observers (both home and abroad) the extent to which he, rather than the government in Kabul, was the central authority responsible for northern Afghanistan's international affairs. This role, which was constantly underscored on Ayna TV, enhanced his image as a patron and as the apex of power in his region. To foreigners, these meetings may have appeared as pragmatic and routine measures; to Dostum, they were critical to his attempt to gain recognition in the center, maximize his local autonomy, and assert his power against the state-building enterprise.[40]

Warlord Governance

Overall, Dostum's diplomatic skills, combined with his relationship with US Special Forces, allowed him to regroup, develop international connections, and gain military strength, through which he now had leverage over the central government. By the end of 2001, his de facto authority in northern Afghanistan had been acknowledged by Karzai's interim government and the US administration ("I took note of Dostum's dominance in the North," wrote Khalilzad in his memoirs), and he had been appointed deputy defense minister.[41] Furthermore, a Pashtun from the Hezb-i Islami, but with a history of collaborating with Junbesh, Juma Khan Hamdard, had been granted control of the Eighth Army Corps to be deployed though the provinces of Balkh, Jowzjan, Faryab, and Sar-i Pul, which allowed Dostum to get his own commanders paid directly by the international community. His forces had risen from 1,200 men in November 2001 to around 20,000 men equipped with dozens of tanks in January 2002. He even claimed that he could mobilize as many as 40,000 troops—a likely inflated figure that demonstrates both his ambition and need for political posturing. Despite his initial military weakness, Dostum had successfully used his charisma (and US largesse) to run his old fiefdom as an active warlord once again.[42]

This time, however, Dostum faced unprecedented competition from rival warlords (the Tajik, Ata Mohammad Noor, and the Hazara, Mohammad Mohaqiq) and had to share power and responsibilities with others. In late 2001, meetings were organized between the three leaders to divide the region's main infrastructures (e.g., the water system and the power plant) and sources of revenue (e.g., the fertilizer companies, customs, and gas) to better reflect the balance of power in northern Afghanistan: 50 percent to Dostum (Junbesh), about 30 percent to Ata (Jamiat), about 15 percent to Mohaqiq (Hezb-i Wahdat), and the rest to the smaller parties. Ata had the upper hand in Mazar-i Sharif, the capital of Balkh Province, and Dostum in his home-town of Sheberghan, the capital of Jowzjan Province. Mohaqiq and the others got the crumbs.

While Dostum had to compete for power in the North in general, he wielded uncontested authority in his own reduced fiefdom of Jowzjan Prov-ince in particular. "If one has to go, and has to go by road at night, the best way to travel is with a personal letter from Gen. Abdul Rashid Dostum guar-anteeing safe passage," wrote Andrew Bushell in the *Washington Post* on February 23, 2002. Reports indicate that the *junbeshi,* the Afghan currency in circulation in Dostum's territory in the 1990s, was still the preferred cur-rency of many northerners in late 2001 and early 2002. Dostum even oper-ated his own prison and appointed all officials in Jowzjan Province. Junbesh also controlled numerous administrations in Balkh Province, such as the local branches of the Ministry of Foreign Affairs and of the newly created National Directorate of Security (NDS), the municipality, and the local prosecutor's office. According to a UN diplomat, "In the period between September 2002 and January 2003, 21 senior appointments occurred in north Afghanistan, of which . . . fifteen [came] from Dostum."[43] In August 2002, Dostum even managed to get his brother Abdul Qader appointed as chargé d'affaires in Kyrgyzstan.

Dostum also got involved in economic and commercial activities, accu-mulating large revenues from oil and gas extraction as well as from taxing border trade. Former ambassador Robert Finn recalls trying to "turn [Dos-tum and Ata] into businessmen" and making sure that they would concen-trate on personal profit rather than becoming alternatives to the central state. In other words, the goal was to divert them from undertaking a *fonction to-tale* through the accumulation of all sources of power, in particular military power. He was unsuccessful, he believes, because they were fixated on the short term.[44] I would argue that he failed because it was wrong to assume that their commercial and economic activities would be strictly geared toward self-enrichment. Dostum indeed collected large revenues that should have filled the central government's coffers, but part of this economic capital was transformed into political power, through means of patronage (notably during the 2004 presidential campaign). Aware of the importance of reputation and perceptions, Dostum also invested part of these revenues to create his own television channel, Ayna TV, launched in 2004, which he has used as a tool for propaganda and power projection ever since.

During that period, Dostum continued to portray himself as the defender of northern Afghans and the patron of the Turkic community. In the words of a UN official, Dostum quickly "[understood] his future [was] in becoming the political representative of the Turkic groups in the north."[45] He liked to compare himself to Tamerlane, the mid-fourteenth-century leader, as a way to be associated with the "image of a powerful conqueror and major figure on the world stage."[46] His appearance matched this image: "With his long Uzbek robe and bulging physique, Dostum looks like a king on his throne. In many ways, Dostum is king," an NPR journalist described on December 2, 2001. Later that month, he was portrayed on CNN as spending endless hours meeting with people and holding court, while "long lines form[ed] outside his compound from early morning to late night." He also engaged in patronage relationships, distributing benefits to supporters as personal gifts. Part of this patronage also involved meeting with potential Turkish investors, discussing highway reconstruction projects with the head of the Asian Development Bank, receiving a Kazakh delegation for the development of commercial ties, and advocating for the reconstruction of factories.

Other displays of power played a major role in Dostum's ability to reestablish his authority. His return was accompanied by symbolic and external signs of wealth and power. For example, he soon refurbished and remodeled his Sheberghan headquarters, a walled-off compound that serves to accommodate guests, hold daily political meetings, and occasionally gather troops and followers. Inside the walls, which are plastered with giant posters of Dostum and his sons, the main gate leads to a large marble-paved court, surrounded by two scarlet buildings and a smaller blue one. A modest mosque stands on the opposite side of the garden. During my short stay there, in the winter of 2014, the little fountain that adorns the court was dry, and the fifty-foot-long pool inside the blue building was empty. I could not confirm the existence of the six swimming pools, the saunas, the whirlpool baths, and the massage tables suggested in some media reports.[47] That said, the compound did indeed contribute to Dostum's projection of power. "In Sheberghan and [Mazar-i Sharif]," wrote an American journalist in April 2002, "Dostum's portrait graces entrance archways of government buildings, schools, military installations and stores, similar to the way Iraqi leader Saddam Hussein use[d] his own ever-present portrait to remind his people exactly who [was] in charge."[48] In fact, the point was to remind not only his people but also the political elites at the national level and the international community at large.[49]

State Centralization and Shape-Shifting

Dostum was trapped in an ambiguous and precarious position as he attempted to navigate the new and complex political environment of post-9/11 Afghanistan. Trying to maximize his power while being constrained to pay allegiance to the new regime proved challenging. "In the early months of the Interim Authority," former US special envoy Khalilzad recalls, "Karzai was constantly at odds with various warlords. He vowed at times to arrest Dostum or demanded that we do so." According to Khalilzad, "No warlord irritated Karzai as much as Dostum."[50] Dostum, as leader of an ethnic minority, had long favored a federal system. This, combined with his reputation as a violent side-switcher, rendered his relationship with the center and the international community even more difficult. In this shifting international environment, he engaged in a constant bargaining, maximizing his authority for as long as he could.

As it became clear that ethnic Uzbeks were about to be sidelined in the new regime, Dostum started to alter the conciliatory discourse he had adopted in the immediate aftermath of 9/11, presumably a last-minute attempt to maximize his position and gauge his bargaining power. He reminded the international community of the six thousand Taliban prisoners in his custody and even made open threats against the future cabinet: "Now the whole world knows about ethnic minorities in Afghanistan, so no government in Kabul can ignore us. . . . But if they do not give us a place in a future government, I am ready to fight that government," he announced three days before the start of the Bonn conference.[51] Dostum coveted a prominent and prestigious government position (some say minister of foreign affairs, others minister of defense or chief of staff of the armed forces), but Junbesh obtained only the Ministry of Mines and Industries and the Ministry of Energy and Water, both minor ministries. Dostum started blaming the Panjshiris for not respecting their promises regarding the distribution of ministerial posts. He immediately announced that he would boycott the new government and would deny the government access to the country's oil and gas reserves located on *his* territory.

Yet, despite all his political posturing, Dostum had to comply with the new rules of the game. He gave no indication of planning to go to war against a US-backed government. "By no means should [the boycott] be understood as meaning that we are opposing the U.N. or other peace processes," he affirmed the day after the signing of the Bonn Agreement.[52] He reiterated his willingness to accept the new situation in a press conference held in Sheberghan a few days later: "People say General Dostum will again start bloodletting and war. This is not true. . . . The rule of law will return."[53] Dostum's statements clearly indicate his impotence in the face of shifting conditions. "The agreement on power sharing signed in Germany was not to my liking," he confessed, but "there is no need for conflict. . . . At the moment, it is impossible to share power by force."[54]

Dostum still found ways to express his defiance toward the new administration. He arrived late at Karzai's inauguration ceremony as chairman of the Afghan Interim Authority and, most significantly, at the head of his own delegation, in a very formal and state-like manner. His behavior gave the impression of a facade performance rather than an oath of allegiance to Karzai and the new Panjshiri-dominated political order—symbolized by the large portrait of Massoud hanging on the wall of the Ministry of Interior, in which the ceremony took place. Karzai appointed Dostum deputy defense minister two days later, in large part to appease the tensions between him and Fahim, the minister of defense and Northern Alliance leader. Emboldened both by his new position and by the success of his aggressive negotiating style, Dostum immediately announced that he had no intention of disarming his forces. Later that month, he claimed to a group of Sheberghan elders that his responsibilities would stretch across the North, where he "would take command of all the armed forces of the Northern Alliance."[55]

As a patron, Dostum remained consistent in his support to his men, always suggesting that those who had overthrown the Taliban ought to gain from the new political order: "These people fought to liberate their country. . . . There must be a plan to help them. Otherwise, I cannot send them back with nothing," he said in February 2002.[56] A month later, he was appointed as Karzai's special representative in the North, a "standard practice" aimed at co-opting him with "a meaningless title and a small budget."[57] When asked about these political appointments, the former president said to me: "I told him when we sat the first time. You are a senior leader, a senior elder. You have to be less military. You are now a political leader. You need political assignments."[58] Dostum kept making contradictory statements, always adapting the message to the audience. In March 2002, he was quoted on CNN International saying that "Warlordism must perish."[59] Yet, around the same time, he also asserted to a crowd of Mazari residents that "no one [but him] ha[d] the right to distribute new weapons to the villages and hamlets."[60]

Overall, Dostum seemed willing to play by the new rules of the game, in part because local elders were urging him to control his men and cooperate with the government and in part because of the shifting international environment, which made it impossible for him to take up arms against the new regime. Dostum repeatedly pledged his will to disarm illegal militias and create an integrated national force. "He had an understanding that he had to exert his power differently," a former European diplomat recalled.[61] Dostum started talking more about budgets and construction projects than military issues. He dropped his military fatigues for business suits and made efforts to secure good relations with both Karzai and former king Mohammad Zahir Shah, appearing next to the president at political rallies, "bow[ing] to US pressure to comply with the demands of the Karzai government."[62]

In the short term, Dostum's communication strategy seemed to bear fruit. On April 28, 2002, Carlotta Gall wrote in the *New York Times* that Dostum had "opted to fight the next round on the political front" and quoted a UN official who claimed that the Uzbek was "more of a politician than the other faction leaders." Dostum's public relations success did not last long, however. A Human Rights Watch report denouncing atrocities committed by his forces since the beginning of the US-led intervention was published shortly before the *loya jirga* of 2002 that was to elect the president of the Afghan Transitional Authority.[63] Around the same time, a UN delegation started to investigate the massacre of scores of surrendering Taliban troops by Dostum's soldiers. In this context, the Karzai administration quickly began to strip away Dostum's governmental responsibilities. The Uzbek leader was first deprived of his position of deputy defense minister with the formation of the first post–*loya jirga* cabinet in the summer of 2002. Less than a year later, in May 2003, he lost his title as Karzai's special representative in the North—which implied some executive power—and was "promoted" to adviser to the president for military and security affairs, "a consultative role to help with peace and security."[64] From that point on, Dostum changed his discourse entirely. While he had tried to portray himself as a political leader of national stature in the early days of the new regime, he stopped doing so and started to focus once again on his legitimacy as a military leader. A few days after his nomination, he declared that he was "not much of an expert in politics" but "the best and only expert in military affairs."[65]

In October 2003, the central government brokered a truce between Ata and Dostum, after their factions had started fighting again. The Karzai administration announced that it would collect the light and heavy weapons of Ata's Seventh Army Corps, "the military arm of the Jamiat party" in the North, and of the Junbesh-controlled Eighth Army Corps and would join their forces under a new neutral command.[66] Dostum agreed, gave his full backing to the process, and promised to implement the government's resolutions. In so doing, he took advantage of the rivalry between the president and Fahim, the minister of defense (who had long been supporting Ata in the North), and could potentially fall within Karzai's good graces. Still, Dostum was not eager to disarm. He in fact repeatedly argued that the war was still ongoing. After sitting down with Ata and Dostum, Donald Rumsfeld, then US secretary of defense, sympathized with (and hence legitimized) Dostum's reluctance to surrender his arsenal. "I don't think his position is unreasonable," he said, thus contradicting and undermining the US statebuilding project in Afghanistan.[67]

Dostum seemingly emerged from both the crisis with Ata and the disarmament process in a stronger political position. He finally agreed to hand over his heavy weaponry, in exchange, it was then reported, for a senior position in the government and millions of dollars of international aid to be allocated to his power base. It soon became clear that neither he nor anyone in his party would obtain the positions they were expecting. Dostum immediately stopped demobilizing.[68] He then resigned from his special adviser position in July 2004 to run in the presidential election and hence reaffirm his authority over his ethnic constituency while reassessing his position vis-à-vis the central government. With the warlords' political resources decreasing and the state's resources increasing, state centralization was under way and a change of political order (from regional authority to parallel authority) was taking place. To top it all, President Karzai had reacted to the announcement of his candidacy by appointing Ata as governor of Balkh Province. "At that time," said a resident of Mazar-i Sharif, "the central government wanted to use any tool to weaken Dostum, and [Ata] was a tool for Karzai."[69] Once deprived of most of his military might, Dostum had no choice but to adapt in order to survive. I explain below how he thoroughly turned into an ethnic entrepreneur in the years that followed.[70]

The Ethnic Entrepreneur (2004–2014)

Election and Co-optation

As a UN field officer perceptively noted, the 2004 election gave "a clear dictation of what political backing these factions ha[d]."[71] For Dostum, it was an opportunity to expand his power base, in particular among the Turkmen community. "By targeting the traditional notables," writes Giustozzi, "Dostum played a winning card, not least because despite state support the pro-Karzai elements had proved unable to deliver much to the Turkmen communities in terms of patronage or help."[72] The presidential election was a way for Dostum to reaffirm himself as the indisputable and uncontested leader of the North and of the Turkic community (that includes both Uzbeks and Turkmens). "For Dostum this time, it's not about winning but rather a posturing of support," said a Kabul-based researcher.[73] Getting as many votes as possible was a way to obtain a seat in the new government because, as a Western analyst put it, "it would be hard for Karzai to ignore that."[74]

Playing politics as a conventional candidate seeking election was compatible with Dostum's earlier strategies. The Uzbek leader could tap into his economic resources and his role as a patron and political champion of the North. He retained his popularity in his fiefdom of Sheberghan, where posters of him covered most storefronts, buildings, and windshields—which, as I witnessed myself, was still very much the case a decade later. He was also able to use money and violence to get votes. According to a former government official from northern Afghanistan, "Dostum has strongmen he can buy, and these strongmen can buy the votes."[75] On September 20, 2004, for example, Carol Harrington, in the *Toronto Star*, covered the story of a seventy-one-year-old farmer beaten because he and other elders had failed to attend a political meeting organized by Dostum's men: "After seeing the old man brutally pistol-whipped, more than 500 villagers fell in line and went to the meeting where they were ordered to vote for Gen. Abdul Rashid Dostum," she wrote.[76]

Dostum also made use of powerful symbols to promote his candidacy. "Wearing his trademark dark robe, Dostum ended Tuesday's rally by mounting a brown horse," wrote an observer, as campaign posters showed the Uzbek leader riding or posing with a stallion.[77] While Dostum had chosen the globe, a symbol of his new international face, to represent him on the ballot for the *loya jirga* representatives' election in 2002, this time he picked a horse, an image suitable to a traditional Afghan leader. The horse indeed has special importance in Central Asian cultures.[78] Likewise, Dostum has long been a sponsor of *buzkashi*, a traditional Afghan folk game that involves horse riders fighting over a calf carcass.[79] In fact, horses and *buzkashi*, a game in which "the cultural values of masculinity . . . [are] vividly embodied," have remained "front and center in Dostum's image management" throughout the years.[80] Addressing the press during his campaign, Dostum explained: "Remember, everyone knows the horse, likes the horse and I'm sure will vote for the horse." Pointing to one of the horses he keeps in his stables in Sheberghan, he told them: "If I were a horse, I would be this one. It's clever and courageous like me. That's why I should be president of Afghanistan."[81]

General Dostum received over eight hundred thousand votes (10 percent of the total and almost the entirety of the Uzbek vote), thus proving that he could still claim popular support, whether it was genuine, coerced, or bought. "If Turkic ethnicity finally conquered a position on the Afghan political scene," writes Giustozzi, "it was definitely due to Dostum's role in seizing the moment and adopting ethnicism as one of his key campaign platforms."[82] Yet, this did not fundamentally change his situation. Dostum's preferred candidates for the Ministry of Energy and Water and the Ministry of Light Industry in the new cabinet were rejected. The Karzai administration had started to find friends among Turkmens to limit Dostum's influence, while Junbesh remained underrepresented in the administration, cutting its leader's ability to reward followers through regular means of patronage.[83]

As members of the international community started to invest more heavily in the state-building project, it became clear after the election, that Dostum would have to become dormant to survive in the new political environment.

Yet, as a senior Afghan official once said of him, he was "a man of war . . . born in war and raised in war," a man who had "only lived in war and . . . can only survive in war."[84] And, as such, Dostum still relied on what had always constituted the backbone of his power, his military leadership and his ability to organize violence, as well as the followers and potential for disruption they provide. Taking care of and maintaining his relationships with his men thus became particularly important. For example, as a good military leader, Dostum had a cemetery built for the burial of Junbesh soldiers. This legitimization through "performances of heroism and martyrdom" resonates with his followers but also in part compensates for his lack of jihadist credentials.[85]

In January 2005, Dostum was the target of a failed suicide attack that created an image of vulnerability and relative weakness. Observers noted that he was subsequently eager to secure a position for himself in the state administration and capitalize on his government post to remunerate and reorganize his men. In the spring of 2005, Dostum was eventually appointed chief of staff of the high command of the armed forces, a symbolic position described as "fake," "completely unknown and meaningless," or, in the words of a former European diplomat, "a sinecure to associate him with the Kabul government without giving him executive power."[86] To Karzai, this political appointment provided additional benefits. It created rifts among the opposition and, under article 153 of the new Afghan constitution, required Dostum to resign as leader of Junbesh.[87]

For Dostum, this nomination also had other advantages. Being co-opted by the Karzai administration meant that he would be protected from human rights organizations and prosecution for past crimes. Most importantly, it allowed him to keep his men on payroll and maintain his military legitimacy by operating as a real patron vis-à-vis his followers. "Outside the government, you're nothing," reacted a Kabul-based analyst.[88] Hundreds of Dostum's men were integrated into the NDS Directorate 10—aimed at protecting important political personalities—operating as his bodyguards while being paid by the Afghan government. Others were integrated into the Afghan National Army or joined the Afghan National Police. As a former EU official once told me: "The [Ministry of Defense] is important to keep your men in jobs, but the police have more direct contacts with the population. It is also important for intelligence. Intelligence was helpful when Karzai was supporting all kinds of silly plots against him."[89] Dostum has multiple networks he can mobilize in the Afghan security apparatus, which has been essential for maintaining his ability to influence political events since 2001.[90]

Defeating Rivals

Armed followers provide Dostum with potential for disruption, and hence the ability to maximize his authority and defeat rivals to, in turn, remain indispensable. I provide two clear examples of this below.

The first example involves Juma Khan Hamdard, a Pashtun Hezbi with Junbesh sympathies who had been in charge of the Eighth Army Corps since the end of 2001 and sided with Hamid Karzai in the months preceding the 2004 presidential election. The election represented a great opportunity for him to "come out from behind the shadow of his former patron, General Dostum, and secure the support of a new patron."[91] His reward was to be appointed governor of Baghlan Province in the beginning of 2005. Faced with a wave of protests against Juma Khan's governorship, Karzai replaced him after a few months and appointed him governor of the neighboring Jowzjan Province. Juma Khan, originally from Balkh Province, had in fact become "a kind of henchman on behalf of the administration, ready to be deployed to do the president's bidding," in the North in particular.[92] His appointment as governor of Jowzjan Province, Dostum's backyard, was not only "part of a strategy on the president's part to diminish the already waning capacity of one of Afghanistan's most notorious strongmen" but also the "ultimate insult" to the general.[93]

Dostum did not remain idle in the face of explicit provocation and increasing state pressure. In May 2007, several hundred Jowzjanis violently protested to demand the removal of Juma Khan from his gubernatorial position. Things quickly deteriorated. Juma Khan's personal bodyguards opened fire on the crowd and killed a dozen protesters, making a peaceful resolution of the situation impossible. Dostum started making inflammatory declarations about Juma Khan's "organized fascist and autocratic programmes."[94] Juma Khan in turn blamed Dostum for escalating the violence. According to a former European diplomat, this was all part of Karzai's "systematic effort to shift the blame" and "trick NATO" into getting rid of General Dostum.[95] Yet, Karzai sacked Juma Khan after several pro-Dostum demonstrations took place in other northern provinces. It became clear that Dostum still dominated his hometown and enjoyed popular support throughout northern Afghanistan. As a former police chief of Jowzjan Province put it: "The reality is that for the time being, General Dostum is more powerful than the government [in the North]. He has more sovereignty."[96]

In the end, the crisis demonstrated Dostum's ability to control events in his home province, despite Kabul's attempts to limit his authority. A cable issued by the US embassy in Kabul indicated that "President Karzai [was] trying to find a candidate to fill the post who could help further erode Dostum's support in the predominantly Uzbek province, without provoking further disturbances by pro-Dostum Junbesh loyalists."[97] Such balance proved impossible to reach, and the next governor, Mohammad Hashim Zare, actually had to "dance to the general's tune," as predicted in a *Kabul Times* article of June 2007.[98] President Karzai replaced Zare with Mohammad Aleem Sayee, a Junbesh heavyweight in May 2010. Tensions with Dostum rose after he took over as leader of Junbesh's reformist wing. Incidents similar to what happened with Juma Khan eventually led Saee to flee. President Karzai officially sacked him in July 2013. He replaced him with a Turkmen governor, Baymorad Qoyunly who, on the very day of his inauguration, visited the Junbesh cemetery to pay his respects. Showing that he was indeed willing to abide by General Dostum's authority, he put a giant portrait of him on display on the roof of the governor's office. The portrait was still there during my 2014 visit to Sheberghan. A few hundred meters from the governor's office stood a large billboard portraying Dostum and the martyrs of the Juma Khan incident, like a symbol of the general's ability to shape political outcomes.[99]

A second example of Dostum's lasting ability to defeat his rivals and remain indispensable is provided by the Akbar Bai episode briefly mentioned in the introduction. In this instance, Dostum used his military power to prevent Akbar Bai, the head of the Turkmen Tribal Council of Afghanistan, from competing for the leadership of the Uzbeko-Turkmen community. Akbar Bai is a former Junbesh representative who was sacked in 2004 for not toeing the party line. In 2007, he began to vehemently accuse Dostum of killing Turkmens and Uzbeks, of possessing arms depots, and of entertaining close links with the ISI and the Taliban. A number of minor episodes followed these declarations, such as, according to a former European diplomat,

Dostum's dog being kidnapped and Akbar Bai's office being set on fire.[100] In November 2007, the Turkmen leader was briefly arrested by the NDS on charges of insurgency activities and plotting an attempt on the general's life.

The next round of this saga started during the night of February 2, 2008. As one observer relates, "the bizarre incident began, it's believed, when Dostum, well into the vodka, decided to invite Bai over for a conciliatory drink. The latter refused."[101] Dostum's men then reportedly beat Akbar Bai and members of his family, kidnapped him, and brought him back to Dostum's mansion in Kabul. "When police surrounded Dostum's own compound," wrote Conor Foley in the *Guardian* on the 21st of that month, "he appeared on the roof, allegedly drunk, to threaten and abuse them." According to the article, President Karzai did not give the police permission to arrest him, because he believed it would have provoked his guards to open fire. The Uzbek leader refused to turn himself in to the authorities but released Akbar Bai, who then demanded that Dostum be officially prosecuted.

After news of the police siege on Dostum's compound emerged, his men visited the governor of Jowzjan Province to pressure the central government while hundreds of protesters set up demonstrations in Maymana, the capital of Faryab Province, and in Taloqan, the capital of Takhar Province, threatening to take up weapons against the government if the police acted against their leader. A prominent member of Junbesh directly warned of unrest if police tried to arrest him: "If General Dostum is surrounded and anyone touches even one hair on Dostum's head, they must know that seven or eight northern provinces will turn against the government," he said.[102] The attorney general eventually concluded that bringing Dostum to court was too risky and would provoke factional fighting in northern Afghanistan, deploring that "even in those places where the rule of law does exist, sometimes we cannot enforce the law over some people."[103] As former US envoy to the Afghan resistance Peter Tomsen pointed out, Karzai "worrie[d] that arresting Dostum could destabilize the relatively stable northern provinces. . . . [He was] weak so he indulge[d] the warlords."[104]

Yet, despite the government's fear of Dostum's potential for disruption, an operation was designed to extract him from his compound—an operation during which "there was a high chance that Dostum would be killed," then NDS director Amrullah Saleh told me.[105] According to a Western diplomat, "Karzai was on and off on the plan. . . . The [Ministry of Interior], the [Ministry of Defense], and the NDS were on board, with [the NDS] supposed to lead. The US said they didn't want to have a direct role in it, be on the frontline, but they would support the government." But then, the Turkish minister of foreign affairs called President Karzai and "threatened to remove forces and cancel all aid projects if they went through with the plan."[106] The plan was dropped.

After Dostum refused to comply with the attorney general's summons for interrogation, he was placed under house arrest and suspended from all official positions. In December 2008, the Turkish Ministry of Foreign Affairs reached an agreement with Karzai to put an end to the Akbar Bai case, and a plane was chartered to bring Dostum to Turkey. All charges were dropped under the condition that Dostum would stay in exile indefinitely. Karzai warned Dostum that the army would march against him if he did not accept the offer. In a clear declaration of support, the spokesman for the Turkish Ministry of Foreign Affairs proclaimed: "[Dostum's] wife and children are also in Turkey. General Dostum is the honorary leader of [the Turkic] community in Afghanistan."[107] Fully embracing his relationship with and support from his Turkish patron, Dostum replied that he was "grateful to the Foreign Ministry and the Republic of Turkey."[108] While many had argued that Turkey was no longer supporting Dostum, the Akbar Bai episode clearly showed that Turkish protection was still a valuable asset, even in the context of renewed US pressure.[109]

Dostum's Comeback

In the spring of 2009, Karzai took a secret trip to Ankara, during which he was allegedly pressured to let Dostum return. The latter indeed remained instrumental to Turkish foreign policy. Turkey had invested in him to exert influence in northern Afghanistan and had no intention of losing its asset short of an alternative client. It was in Karzai's interest to comply with the demands of a government that played an increasingly important role (both militarily and economically) in Afghanistan and the region. Amrullah Saleh, NDS director at the time, even claims that it was in fact Karzai who urged the Turkish government to bring Dostum back to Afghanistan, first personally paying a visit to the Turkish ambassador in Kabul, and only then taking a trip to Ankara.[110]

Karzai, up for reelection, had reasons for bringing Dostum back, first of which was to secure the Uzbek vote. Building a broad electoral coalition was all the more crucial to his reelection given that his personal relationship with the United States had quickly deteriorated since the election of Barack Obama. Karzai could no longer count on US political support on the domestic scene. Warlords had in fact become "voting banks," so Karzai promised Dostum that the charges against him would be dropped in exchange for his support in the upcoming presidential election.[111] Dostum's return also provided the president with an alternative to Ata in the North, who had grown increasingly autonomous since becoming governor of Balkh Province in 2004. Overall, as a Kabul-based analyst aptly noted, "Dostum's arrival show[ed] how worried Karzai [was]."[112]

About a month before the election—a timing that was certainly not coincidental—old reports resurfaced exposing Dostum's role in the alleged murder of over 2,000 Taliban prisoners of war during the opening days of the US-led intervention, further straining Karzai's relationship with the Obama administration. "We're obviously going to be encouraging Karzai not to let Dostum have a formal role in the government," revealed a US bureaucrat.[113] The pressure intensified after US government officials blamed the Bush administration for not investigating those deaths, and after President Obama ordered his national security team to look into those reports. John Dempsey, of the United States Institute of Peace, explains: "[Obama was sending] a strong signal that accountability and the rule of law matter. . . . Until very recently, top officials ha[d] argued that security trumps justice, saying it [was] better to bring these guys into the government's tent rather than hold them accountable for the serious crimes they've committed."[114]

Dostum's return also disgruntled many within his own party. Before his exile, the Uzbek leader had accepted to be replaced as party chair by one of his loyalists, Sayed Noorullah Sadat, and was appointed instead as both founding father of Junbesh and honorary chairman. It is highly unlikely that Dostum ever intended to give up control of the party, but Karzai had made promises to others during his absence. With Dostum's return, their "dreams of assuming ministerial offices [were] now up in smoke."[115] A group of dissidents who had grown tired of Dostum's ways started to emerge. Najibullah Salimi, founder of the Junbesh youth council, announced that he would back Abdullah Abdullah, the front-runner in the presidential election, hence going against Dostum's call to support Karzai. The general reacted vehemently

in a message read in his name at a political gathering: "A number of opportunist elements using [the] name of Dostum and [Junbesh] are leaping about
here and there to obtain personal benefits as they have voiced support for another candidate. . . . Whatever I have ordered, the movement is following and
whoever follows the movement's orders is following Gen Dostum's order."[116]

Three days before the election, Dostum made a triumphant comeback to
Sheberghan. He gave a brief statement thanking Karzai for allowing him to
return and addressed a crowd of ten thousand people on behalf of the Turkish
government, hence presenting himself as the representative of the Turkic
community in Afghanistan: "I would like to convey greetings of the Turkish government and the Turkish president, prime minister, foreign minister,
members of parliament and the entire heroic nation of Turkey to you."[117] A
few days later, under US pressure, Dostum was transferred to Kabul in Turkish armored vehicles and then flown back to Turkey in a Turkish military
plane. The US Department of State was indeed fiercely opposed to Dostum's
comeback. "They didn't want his vote bank to be used in my favor," Karzai
told me.[118]

Dostum definitively returned to Afghanistan the day Karzai's victory was
made official, and was reinstated as chief of staff of the high command of
the armed forces shortly thereafter. The move was heavily criticized by Western bureaucrats. "Dostum came back to cash in," professed a US defense
official.[119] British foreign secretary David Miliband raised the issue with President Karzai during his visit to Afghanistan, while Karl Eikenberry, then
US ambassador in Kabul, clearly targeting Dostum, condemned the appointment of human rights violators to senior government posts. "My coming
back," Dostum declared, "will help peace and stability. . . . I want to sit with
my American friends and make a plan so that within two or three years, we
will secure all of Afghanistan."[120]

Reaffirming Power

Once reelected, however, Hamid Karzai never delivered on his alleged promises to Dostum, namely five provincial governorships, four ministries, and
four ambassadorships. "Dostum didn't ask for anything and I didn't offer him
anything. There was no deal then," Karzai told me.[121] It is hard to know
where the truth lies in such cases. According to former NDS director

Amrullah Saleh, "Karzai promised too many things. . . . He distributed fake bonds, bonds which did not exist. . . . He sold shares of a fictional company . . . created his own bitcoin, a crypto-currency. . . . When people came to him with their vouchers, they were all invalid."[122] Interviewed years later, Abdul Qader Dostum, the general's brother (and vice president of Junbesh), talked of a "conspiracy" against Junbesh and its leader. "In 2009," he complained to me, "Karzai promised a lot of things but he cheated us."[123] From his perspective, the Afghan president clearly tried to scatter the party to divide and rule.

Dostum still had to face internal dissension in his own party. Most problematic for him was the emergence of a younger generation, educated in Turkey, who had returned with reformist agendas and political ambitions and wished to replace the old guard to turn Junbesh into a modern political party. Yet, Dostum eventually managed to progressively reassert his leadership up to forcefully removing Sayed Noorullah Sadat, the party chair who had led the reformists, in February 2013. Dostum was back at the helm, if not yet officially, at least in practice. He could now reorganize the party as he pleased, methodically restaffing all Junbesh offices in the North with people he trusted.

Dostum also had to reassert his political influence in the North beyond Junbesh. In 2010, he established the Dostum Foundation (emulating the already existing Massoud Foundation), which finances and implements aid and cultural projects for the benefit of the Turkic population. The foundation, under the management of his eldest son (and designated heir), explicitly portrays Dostum as the latest in the line of Tamerlane's successors and serves as a clear tool of patronage.[124] In the spring of 2012, he organized a pilgrimage to Mecca for him, his son, and around two hundred followers.[125] Pictures of him and his son praying in the holy city were still scattered on large billboards throughout Sheberghan when I went there two years later. In the beginning of 2013, Dostum started to hold local party meetings that gathered thousands of people, in the hope of regaining seats in the 2014 provincial elections.

Finally, Dostum's comeback could not have been complete without reestablishing his military power, still the backbone of his authority, which he also did with great success. Dostum's intent to build on his military legitimacy and reaffirm the support of his former commanders can be traced back to September 2009, when he made the following declaration: "I don't want to be a minister, not even the defense minister. I need to be with my soldiers. Give me the task and I will do it."[126] In the years that followed, he remobi-

Billboard of General Dostum and his son Batur in Mecca, Sheberghan
(photograph by the author).

lized his commanders, distributed weapons, and rearmed his followers in
Jowzjan, rekindling his relationships with his commanders and those between the commanders and the subcommanders in charge of securing some
roads, districts, and villages against the Taliban's strengthening insurgency.
In the year leading to the presidential election, Dostum's men captured multiple ammunition depots. His willingness to prepare for a potential change
in the international environment (and a full-blown civil war) following the
withdrawal of foreign forces is further underscored by the construction of
many two-story concrete towers, "old fashion fortifications" with slits for
shooting weapons that I saw all around Sheberghan, and in particular on
the main roads going to his compound. "It's general hedging on the lead up

to the election," a Western diplomat told me. "He wants to be able to fend for himself if things go south."[127]

Dostum's success in these difficult times is reflected in his ability to project authority and portray himself as a leader able to deliver the votes of the Uzbek community in the 2014 presidential election (as he did for Karzai in 2009). In the end, Dostum's support may well have been indispensable for Ashraf Ghani's electoral victory and what really distinguished him from the other Pashtun candidates. Former president Karzai at least seems to believe so. "He got him elected," he told me.[128] Dostum did not deliver the entirety of the Turkic vote. It would have been unrealistic to expect him to do so. But he still managed to convey the impression that he could. He projected authority in a fashion that persuaded Ghani to appoint him as his running mate in the presidential election, making him first vice president of the Islamic Republic of Afghanistan. Once again, Dostum had become indispensable.[129]

Post-2014: Toward a Fonction Totale?

General Dostum, the secular Uzbek, the high school dropout, the ultimate marginal, was officially sworn in as first vice president of the Islamic Republic of Afghanistan on September 29, 2014. Not only did he survive the exile and political marginalization of the previous years, but he returned in a stronger position. This new status was accompanied by an attempt to normalize and institutionalize his authority. Interviewed a little over a year after the election, Dostum's media adviser bluntly acknowledged that the vice president had had the image of being a "controversial warlord" and that his first objective when he joined Dostum's team had been to "remove this . . . find [him] a new face, a new image."[130]

This was done (successfully, if we believe Dostum's adviser) through a number of public relations initiatives aimed at turning General Dostum into a more conventional and likable political leader in the eyes of both Afghans and the international community: a campaign promoting physical activity that was supplemented with remarkable, if unflattering, billboards depicting the sixty-year-old warlord in a track suit, blood donations organized at the vice presidency, hospital visits, and even the inauguration of a hotline for people to share their problems.[131] All of this is of course being advertised, embellished, and narrated through his two television channels but it is also

Billboard of General Dostum leading a campaign for physical activity,
vice presidential palace, Kabul (photograph by the author).

accompanied by an increased presence on (and an active monitoring of) social media (particularly Facebook and Twitter), with several accounts related to the vice president's activities directly administered by his media adviser.

Changing a warlord's image is an extremely difficult, if not impossible, endeavor, especially when that warlord remains militarily active through repeated attempts to coordinate all anti-Taliban war efforts in the North.[132] From a Western perspective, it is inconceivable for a vice president to lead men into battle.

Yet, what could seem paradoxical for a "regular" political leader and ill-advised for a warlord trying to launder his reputation is in fact entirely consistent with Dostum's effort to accumulate and combine all sources of power

Posters of General Dostum leading the fight against the Taliban in northern Afghanistan, vice presidential palace, Kabul (photograph by the author).

simultaneously. This is especially relevant for military might, which is particularly useful in times of increasing uncertainty. On the one hand, Dostum is trying to affirm his prominence over Ata, his main rival in the North, and bring some of the commanders he had lost to him during his absence back under his wing; on the other hand, he is attempting to get closer to Russia and the Central Asian countries, using the specter of groups like the so-called Islamic State, the Islamic Movement of Uzbekistan, and the Islamic Jihad Union as justification.[133] As a Kabul-based analyst put it: "He wants to show the government that he is still a strong commander, the only one able to lead in the North."[134]

Improving Dostum's image was made even more challenging after he was accused of publicly beating up a political rival, Ahmad Ishchi, in November 2016, before ordering his guards to abduct him and to sexually abuse him with their weapons. The vice president was then put under investigation and several of his guards sentenced to five years in prison, in a case highly reminiscent of that of Akbar Bai discussed above. The following May,

Dostum flew to Turkey, officially for medical reasons. Over a year later, in July 2018, President Ghani faced large antigovernment protests across several northern provinces after the violent arrest of one of Dostum's commanders, Nizamuddin Qaisari, and the physical abuse of his bodyguards by government forces. Northerners continued to protest and demanded the release of Qaisari and the return of the vice president. Under increasing pressure, Ghani eventually allowed Dostum to come back. The Uzbek warlord, welcomed by a government delegation at Kabul's international airport, made a triumphant homecoming that summer, once again proving his ability to survive even the most dire circumstances. "Lined up behind the general," wrote Mujib Mashal in the *New York Times* on August 7, 2018, "were several of the bodyguards who had been convicted—and who should have been in jail, not on television." General Dostum has since been replaced by Amrullah Saleh, a Panjshiri, on Ghani's ticket for the 2019 presidential election. Yet, his return showed once again that Ghani (like Karzai before him), up for reelection, could not afford to antagonize Dostum and lose the Uzbek vote.[135]

Dostum rose as a pro-government militia leader in the 1980s and, after the collapse of the regime he worked for (and to which he largely contributed), became an active warlord undertaking a *fonction totale* over northern Afghanistan in the 1990s. He established his own warlord polity, which he managed to rule independently from the rest of the country until it was captured by the Taliban and he had to leave Afghanistan. Since 2001 and the beginning of the US-led intervention, Dostum has experienced many ups and downs, from active warlord to political pariah to vice president, rising again after each fall, but also always struggling to be accepted by those in central institutions.

In fact, Dostum spent the past forty years trying to gain acceptance from the political elites in Kabul. His attempts have been hindered by his ethnic identity, combined, after the end of the Soviet-Afghan war, with his lack of jihadist credentials and associated secularism.[136] This, for example, explains why Dostum has at times tried to reach out beyond his core ethnic constituency (such as in the early days of Junbesh) and striven to develop his religious credentials (for instance, by taking highly publicized pilgrimages to Mecca).[137] But Dostum has remained constricted by Afghanistan's brand of ethnic politics in which Tajik and Pashtun elites forge alliances with compliant minority partners. Dostum's lifelong effort to combine local autonomy with a share of power in the center has regularly clashed with the logics of an overly centralized Afghan state that strongly resists any form of decentralized authority. As a result, he and his followers have regularly complained about the Uzbek community not getting the respect they deserve from Kabul. Many Uzbeks in Afghanistan consider themselves to be the victims of social injustice and feel constantly let down by their political partners, who often fail to keep their promises. In fact, Kabul's political elites never accepted Dostum as one of their own, even after he became first vice president of the Islamic Republic of Afghanistan. In their eyes, he has always been and will always be an Uzbek warlord above all.

And yet, as Hamida Ghafour wrote in the *Telegraph* on October 8, 2004, Dostum is "the survivor of Afghan politics." He has survived many different regimes and political orders precisely *because* he has remained an Uzbek warlord. His political actions are grounded in ethnic politics. Dostum is an ethnic entrepreneur who has the "ability both to speak to and *on behalf of*" a marginalized and fragmented community that has always been kept out of the decision-making process.[138] As a prominent member of the Afghan parliament once explained to me, Dostum "supports his people to stay in power" and provides "livelihood and survival" to his commanders. In return, they protect him and "would obviously react" if he were to be removed or contested in the North.[139] This we witnessed during the Akbar Bai and Ahmad Ishchi episodes. And the large gatherings of followers he regularly holds in the Afghan capital serve as a reminder. In the words of former US ambassador Robert Finn, Dostum can "deliver the votes and can create trouble."[140] He delivered the votes in 2004, 2009, and 2014. And he has been creating trouble for the post-Taliban regime on a regular basis since 2001. In the summer of 2016, for example, some of his followers engaged in a gun battle with Tajik demonstrators who planned to rebury Habibullah Kalakani, a Tajik insurgent who had briefly seized power in 1929, on a hill of high symbolic value to the Uzbek community.[141] Dostum also regularly threatens the government: "I don't need a coup d'état or anything," he declared in October 2016, "but if the day comes, I will gather my people, I will unburden my heart to them. And after that . . ."[142]

The tensions within Junbesh show that Dostum may no longer control "all things Uzbek" (if he ever did) in Afghanistan. But, as long as Dostum can exert violence to prevent would-be political rivals from emerging and prospering, there will be no credible alternatives. According to an Afghan scholar, Dostum has in fact become the symbol of "Uzbek bitterness . . . a symbolic thug, a thuggish leader [who] can kill people if he wants to. . . . If you remove Dostum, nothing keeps them together. . . . [He] has become a fluid concept, the embodiment of nationalistic feelings."[143] Yet, Dostum remains the cement of that community. He embodies Uzbek pride and loyalty, "shap[es] the Uzbek mentality" through his two television channels, and has developed his own "brand" of ethnic warlordism.[144] As a former European diplomat once told me, "He still is *the* strongest Uzbek in the political apparatus. . . . He retains his appeal as *the* single most renowned Uzbek personality . . . [and that] gives him street power and sway in the traditional society among Uzbek leaders."[145] In Dostum's own words, expressed on the eve of the 2009 election: "If you mess with Dostum, you mess with a million people."[146]

Chapter 5

Massoud and Fahim

The Mujahid and the Violent Entrepreneur

I first set foot in Afghanistan on September 9, 2007, on what, I realized later, was the sixth anniversary of Ahmad Shah Massoud's assassination. The streets of Kabul were conspicuously quiet, almost entirely deserted, roamed only by pickup trucks packed with unidentified armed men (former Massoud supporters, it turned out). Not what I had imagined. This sudden immersion into the realities of Afghan politics was my first introduction to something I already suspected but would fully understand only much later: for most Afghans, Massoud was not the "national hero" that Hamid Karzai had once deemed him to be.[1]

Above all, Massoud was a warlord with great diplomatic skills and a rare ability for shaping his own image, from mujahideen to pro-Western and anti-Taliban resistance leader. His assassination by members of al-Qaeda disguised as journalists, on September 9, 2001, only two days before the attacks on New York and Washington, made him a legend. But in fact, as Azoy put it, "[Massoud]'s legacy of charismatic leadership, so powerful among his eth-

Portrait of Ahmad Shah Massoud with inscription "national hero"
(graffiti adding "of Pakistan"), Kabul (photograph by the author).

nic kin and so celebrated among expatriate admirers, is regarded with equal suspicion and even enmity by other groups, especially [Pashtuns]."[2]

Ahmad Shah Massoud was not the typical warlord. He was "a mix" between a purely patrimonial leader and a purely ideological one: he "hijacked" a community when joining the jihad, progressively becoming one of the main commanders of the Jamiat-i Islami (henceforth Jamiat), but he still enjoyed a high level of legitimacy and operated as a community leader, eventually earning his nickname of lion of Panjshir.[3] After establishing control over the small Panjshir Valley, northeast of Kabul, Massoud extended his power even farther toward the northeast and created the Shura-i Nazar, a protostate structure to rule over the region. However, for Massoud, a more ideologically driven warlord than the other cases covered in this book, central power was always the issue at stake. He reached his goal when his forces captured Kabul in April 1992, but then, in 1996, he was pushed away by the Taliban, which he fought until his assassination on September 9, 2001.

Mohammad Qasim Fahim stands in sharp contrast. After Massoud's death, he inherited the leadership of the Shura-i Nazar, the politico-military structure that Massoud had established in the 1980s (even though it was no longer officially in existence by the time Fahim reached the helm), and of the Northern Alliance, the military alliance Massoud had created in the 1990s, after the fall of Kabul to the Taliban. Fahim, however, never mustered the same level of legitimacy as his predecessor, either locally in Panjshir or externally among the international community. Unlike Massoud, Fahim also never had the opportunity to become an active warlord who could combine all sources of power simultaneously, apart from the very early days of the US-led intervention. He did not possess Massoud's diplomatic skills and failed to adapt to the post-2001 changes in the international system. These changes created new rules of the game that constrained Fahim's behavior but also generated new opportunities for him to transform his newly acquired military power into other forms of capital (mostly economic). Yet, in the short term, he failed to remain indispensable to either foreigners or domestic actors and was politically marginalized after he lost the Ministry of Defense and the Vice Presidency in 2004.

On May 4, 2009, President Hamid Karzai announced that he had chosen Fahim as his running mate in the upcoming election. Karzai's selection took external observers aback, for Fahim had received almost no international media attention since 2004. To most, he was a remnant of Afghanistan's darkest times. A Western diplomat perfectly summed up the international community's reaction: "I want to move to a situation where leaders and people who have a reputation for being involved in serious human rights violations disappear from the political landscape, and not the opposite."[4] Nevertheless, by 2009, the international environment had changed, and Fahim had proved indispensable to President Karzai. Fahim may have experienced a temporary demise between 2004 and 2009, but he was in fact a political phoenix, once again serving as Afghanistan's first vice president from November 2009 until his death in March 2014.

Ahmad Shah Massoud: The Lion of Panjshir

Genesis and Rise

Ahmad Shah Massoud was born in Jangalak, a village located in the lower Panjshir Valley, in the early 1950s, to an esteemed Tajik family. On his father's side, they belonged to the prestigious Sarkarda clan. His father, Dost Mohammad Khan, a former colonel in the Royal Afghan Army of King Zahir Shah, was employed by the Ministry of Interior. His paternal grandfather, Yahya Khan, was a well-respected elder who had worked for King Amanullah Khan. His maternal grandfather, an attorney from the neighboring town of Rukha, also came from a prominent Panjshiri clan, the Bakhshi. Although he was born in Panjshir, the young Ahmad Shah—who would adopt "Massoud" (the fortunate one) as a nom de guerre years later—spent most of his childhood and teenage years in Kabul, where he learned French at the Lycée Estiqlal. In the early 1970s, he enrolled at the Kabul Polytechnic Institute for Engineering and Architecture, where he was involved in Jamiat's student branch, Sazman-i Jawanan-i Musulman, which was becoming increasingly popular among university students.

After Daoud came to power in the 1973 coup d'état and started cracking down on the Islamists, Massoud went into hiding for a few months in Panjshir while others left for Pakistan. He briefly came back to Kabul to partake in a coup attempt led by Gulbuddin Hekmatyar, one of the leaders of the Islamist movement, and flew to Peshawar, Pakistan, after their plan was discovered by the government. Yet again, in 1975, Massoud joined Hekmatyar in another effort to topple the regime of Mohammad Daoud Khan. This time, the rebellion was to combine a military coup in the capital with simultaneous uprisings in various provinces. Massoud was charged with starting the uprising in Panjshir, but his efforts failed, in part due to strong popular resistance that he did not expect. About half of his men were killed or wounded, while Massoud and nearly twenty others from his group hid in the mountains. In Kabul, the coup never took place. Massoud blamed Hekmatyar, who, he believed, had never intended to implement the plan. Infuriated, Massoud returned to exile in Pakistan, where he and other members of the Islamist movement started secret military training under the authority of the Inter-Services Intelligence (ISI). Before long, Hekmatyar left to create his own party, Hezb-i Islami (henceforth Hezb), as explained in chapter 1. When the People's Democratic Party of Afghanistan came to power in 1978, Massoud first left Pakistan to join the uprising that had started in Nuristan—the province between Panjshir and the Afghanistan-Pakistan border. There he learned a great deal about war and adopted the *pakol*, a traditional Nuristani top-rounded woolen hat that would become his men's signature apparel.

In the summer of 1979, Massoud followed the Nuristani example and drew on the networks he had acquired on the eastern front to return to Panjshir, upward of two dozen men, this time all from the valley, to stir up a revolt against the new communist regime.[5] At that time, he was only in his mid-twenties and mostly unknown to the local population. He had never lived in Panjshir except for a few months in hiding in the early 1970s and summer holidays as a child. Learning from the failure of the 1975 uprising, Massoud put forward a significant effort to gain local support before entering Panjshir. First, he met with a delegation of Panjshiris at the edge of the valley and built a partnership with Pahlawan Ahmad Jan, a prestigious wrestler and *buzkashi* rider who would provide legitimacy to Massoud's enterprise—especially in the upper Panjshir, where the famed wrestler originated. Massoud then sent missives and dispatched messengers throughout the valley to secure the support of local khans and mullahs while trying to unite the different clan leaders around a shared notion of political Islam.

Despite his efforts to rally influential Panjshiris (such as Pahlawan Ahmad Jan) and build on their legitimacy, Massoud initially struggled to establish his authority in the valley. This was the case in particular in the valley's lower section, where a large portion of the population worked in Kabul, either in the private sector (shopkeepers, housekeepers, etc.) or directly for the government (soldiers, bureaucrats, etc.). In retrospect, Massoud considered late 1979 as one of the most challenging periods of his life, along with 1975. In fact, the Panjshir rebellion almost failed when government forces, supported by communist sympathizers, regained control of the lower valley temporarily. Nevertheless, Massoud's authority gradually increased, in particular due to his charisma and military prowess. For the most part, opposition was overcome, albeit through the occasional use of threats and direct violence. Spies and traitors were threatened or (later) liquidated; Hezbis and Maoists already present in the valley were rallied, killed, or captured; and defectors were sentenced—Pahlawan Ahmad Jan, for example, was later executed for attempting to start a pro-government rebellion in Panjshir. In the words of a former Shura-i Nazar commander, the valley was "cleaned up."[6]

To further affirm and legitimize his authority, Massoud also engaged in considerable efforts to vilify the enemy, starting very early on by having his men inscribe anti-Soviet slogans on rocks and publish newspapers to be used by mullahs in their Friday prayers. Such tactics were an effective way, for him, "not only to create solidarity but also to present [his group] and its violent actions as necessary, appropriate and comparatively less destructive."[7] Once he had made himself known and had gathered support from influential members of Panjshiri society, Massoud could finally build on his existing social capital (his family's prestige, reputation, and contacts) in the lower part of the valley. In the long run, his family background was in fact essential to his personal legitimacy and to his ability to provide governance while waging a war (hence relying on mutually reinforcing sources of legitimacy). According to one of his former commanders: "If [Massoud] had not belonged to this family, Panjshiris would not have obeyed him . . . [Support from the tribes was] key to his war."[8]

In 1980, Massoud supervised the creation of a nonmilitary governing body in every military base under his men's control. These bodies oversaw the recruitment of young mujahideen, engaged in propaganda efforts, printed newspapers, ran radio channels, and educated local children, cadres, and fighters about the necessity of the jihad against the Soviet Union, hence building a common symbolic repertoire to "bring together the disparate agendas at the local level with the central cleavage."[9] Additional classes were organized around disciplines such as international politics and Islamic ideology. Massoud, a fervent reader of Mao, Che Guevara, Régis Debray, and others, even taught guerrilla warfare.

The small and sparsely populated Panjshir Valley was of vital importance to Moscow. Indeed, it neighbored the main and only reliable overland supply route from the Soviet Union to Kabul, the Salang highway (and two-kilometer-long tunnel), which passed through the Hindu Kush mountains that traverse Afghanistan from the northeast to the southwest. Once Massoud had established his authority in the valley, he and his men started raiding and looting Soviet convoys on the highway, the adjacent mountains enabling hit-and-run tactics. Moscow reacted to Massoud's attacks

Soviet tank remnant, Panjshir Valley (photograph by the author).

by launching six consecutive assaults on the Panjshir Valley between 1980 and 1982. Massoud received early warnings about aerial bombings from his intelligence networks inside the Afghan Army (in part acquired through family connections). His forces could therefore disappear into the mountains before the bombings began, only to subsequently reappear and surprise Soviet tanks entering Panjshir. By targeting the first and last tanks going through the narrow valley, Massoud's forces could stop entire columns, forcing the enemy to abandon their vehicles.

Over the years, Massoud also became increasingly independent from Burhanuddin Rabbani and the rest of the Jamiat leadership in Peshawar. In the summer of 1982, the Soviet command in Afghanistan reached out to Massoud to negotiate a temporary cease-fire with him directly. A Soviet officer eventually flew to Panjshir in the beginning of 1983 to present Massoud with a letter from the general secretary of the Communist Party, Yuri Andropov himself. In the valley, multiple carpet-bombing campaigns, coupled with a blockade organized by the rival Hezb, had left the population weary and nearly famished. Massoud saw the truce offer as a welcome opportunity to give the population of Panjshir some temporary relief. Without consulting with the Jamiat leadership, he accepted a six-month cease-fire, which was renewed for another six months the following summer. Until then, Massoud had not been able to exert his own high-level diplomacy. Signing a truce with the Soviet Union "raise[d] his stature by placing him on an equal footing with a superpower."[10] It established him as a major diplomatic player, thus affirming his independence from Pakistan and the Jamiat leadership.

All Soviet troops left Panjshir (except for one battalion located at the southern entrance of the valley), and both parties agreed to stop all military activities for the duration of the cease-fire. Temporarily liberated from Soviet pressure (the bombings would indeed start again in April 1984), Massoud and his men moved north to the province of Takhar. The move had mutually reinforcing objectives: to defeat rival organizations (in particular, Hezb) in the North and hence further secure Panjshir; to bring law and order to an extended fiefdom; to keep his men active (and hence maintain his military legitimacy); and to further establish his autonomy vis-à-vis Jamiat.

Massoud used that time to create the Shura-i Nazar (supervisory council), a protostate structure aimed at governing most of northeastern Afghanistan. At a time when the activities of most Afghan commanders were limited to classic guerrilla tactics, he formed a civilian shadow government, separate from the military, while institutionalizing consultation with influential members of society. Various committees, such as the health committee, the education committee, and the reconstruction committee, were created within the Shura-i Nazar to provide services (and charity) to the population, along with the creation of a military police, courts, a bank, and other state-like institutions. Although these committees were not always fully functional, they were the commencement of rebel governance—"the production of government for civilians during the protracted violence and high levels of coercion produced by civil war."[11] Massoud and his men also implemented a taxation system, taxing the export of lapis lazuli and emeralds (10 percent of all sales) and collecting taxes from the local population as well as from the Panjshiris living and working in Kabul (5 percent of their salaries). By 1984, Massoud had truly become an active warlord, operating across all different realms of authority simultaneously.[12]

Rebel Diplomacy

During that period, in the early 1980s, Massoud also developed his own warlord diplomacy, then a form of rebel diplomacy aimed at building his personal authority. Initially, he interacted mainly with foreign journalists, a critical component of the international arena, especially for rebels with limited outside access. As Bridget Coggins perceptively notes: "Using media outlets and personal contacts to spread the insurgents' ideology, propagandize, and inform may win the favor or neutrality of key constituencies."[13] Western journalists started to provide detailed reports of Massoud's war in Panjshir as early as 1981. Foreigners established close relationships with Massoud, spread his message of resistance to the Soviets throughout Europe, and contributed to his fame, which only attracted more media attention.

Massoud's men in Peshawar began organizing trips to Panjshir for foreign journalists. Once they were in the valley, Massoud would have a person of trust take care of (and control) them. He even had a guesthouse built to make sure they would be hosted according to his dictates. Journalists were Massoud's primary means of reaching people outside Afghanistan during the Soviet-Afghan war. "The way he treated them and shared his views with them was very important," relayed the former Shura-i Nazar representative in Washington. "They fell in love with him," he said.[14] According to Massoud's former head of intelligence, bringing journalists to Panjshir was in fact a strategy to bypass Jamiat and the ISI in making international connections.[15] All in all, Massoud was well aware of the importance of good public relations. He knew the role the media could play in shaping his image and portraying him as *the* main resistance leader against the Soviets to the outside world.

Massoud's relations with NGO workers followed a similar pattern. In fact, they often traveled with journalists.[16] NGOs played an important role in the functioning of Massoud's complex administration. The Shura-i Nazar depended on them for most nonmilitary matters, such as health, reconstruction, and education. Massoud also harnessed NGOs and international organizations working in his fiefdom as a way of legitimizing his rule through service provision. As Dorronsoro explains, "The commanders profited . . . directly and indirectly [from the presence of NGOs] through its influence on their prestige or legitimacy."[17] Hence the importance, for Massoud, of boosting his image internationally, claiming a monopoly over diplomatic channels, and portraying himself as a good leader that NGOs would be willing to support.

Yet, in the 1980s, Massoud's ability to connect with foreign countries was still limited. Officially, the Panjshiri remained a commander working under the Jamiat leadership. To lobby in his favor, Massoud soon started to personally recruit or send people abroad to staff the party's offices or open their own. In addition to bringing journalists to Panjshir, his men in Peshawar were in charge of establishing direct (and at times secret) links to foreign services and powerful individuals, as well as to buyers for the gems of the Panjshir Valley.[18] People and offices in Washington, New York, London, or Paris had similar, though less covert, activities, such as organizing meetings with journalists, state officials, and members of parliament, publishing newspapers, or seeking additional support from the Afghan Tajik diaspora. These offices played an increasingly important role after the Soviets started attacking the Panjshir again in 1984, and Massoud began to staff them with the people he trusted most. He sent his own brothers, among others, to London and Peshawar, the two most important offices.

Yet, for a long time, the only external military support Massoud received came in the form of military training (both inside and outside Afghanistan) and matériel (e.g., radios, explosives, rifles, and night-vision goggles) provided by the French and British intelligence services.[19] Many, among European spy agencies, particularly in France, liked to portray Massoud as an Afghan liberator, in part because he spoke some rudimentary French. Within the CIA, however, most officers had a very different opinion of Massoud. They became suspicious of him after he signed the truce with the Soviet Union in 1983, and then blamed him for refusing to destroy the Salang tunnel, which was vital both to him and to the supply of Soviet military matériel. Nevertheless, in 1984, the CIA started providing Massoud with cash and weapons through his Peshawar office. According to an American journalist, the funding reached $200,000 a month in 1989, with two additional payments of $900,000 and $500,000 made to one of his brothers between May 1989 and January 1990. In exchange for the second payment, Massoud was required to close the Salang highway until the end of the winter of 1990–91, which he failed to do. The CIA cut his monthly stipend and eventually stopped supporting him entirely shortly after the collapse of the Soviet Union.

While attempting (with mixed success) to court the Western world, Massoud was also struggling to establish contacts in the Arab world. He was joined by individual Arab fighters, who had their own guesthouse in Panjshir, but his rivalry with Hekmatyar and the Hezb propaganda against him had made him widely unpopular among jihadist networks. Things changed toward the end of the Soviet-Afghan war, after Massoud received a visit from Abdullah Azzam, the well-respected father of global jihad, who, until then, had been very critical of him. Upon his return from Panjshir, the Palestinian ideologue started praising Massoud's leadership, prompting a push in financial aid from his networks throughout the Arab world. Azzam was killed shortly thereafter, in the fall of 1989. The following year, Massoud sent a representative to Riyadh to persuade Prince Turki al-Faisal, the chief of Saudi intelligence, to initiate a rapprochement with the Pakistani intelligence services. Massoud himself then took a trip to Islamabad to meet with the ISI director and the CIA station chief. This trip led to increased shipments from Pakistan's main intelligence agency, hence making Massoud less dependent on Jamiat for weapons and ammunition.[20]

From Rebel to Quasi-State Leader

On April 14, 1988, on the brink of collapse, the Soviet Union signed the Geneva Accords, by which it committed to withdraw its troops from Afghanistan between May 1988 and February 1989. Contrary to US expectations, the Afghan government remained firmly in place for another three years. To save the regime, Mohammad Najibullah offered Massoud the position of defense minister, as well as the leadership of an autonomous northeastern region to be created. The Panjshiri declined both offers. Unlike Dostum and Ismail Khan, who prioritized their regionalist agendas, Massoud always had a national ambition. His aim was to capture and centralize power. For him more than for anyone else, the state had become the principal objective. Seizing it would provide international recognition, legitimacy, and resources.

After Moscow's supplies to the regime got cut off with the collapse of the Soviet Union in December 1991, Massoud started approaching the most powerful pro-government commanders of the North to plan the capture of Kabul and all ensuing power-sharing arrangements. In parallel, Massoud was named minister of defense through the Peshawar Accords, a power-sharing agreement signed by the main political leaders exiled in Pakistan on April 24, 1992. Hekmatyar was made prime minister. The following day, Massoud and his northern allies entered the capital and pushed back Hekmatyar's forces, thanks in part to the networks of loyalties the Panjshiri had developed among regime military forces (which would later join his ranks). The end of the communist regime had resulted in shifting alliances and violent power struggles between the different armed groups, some of which had participated in the highly fragmented anti-Soviet resistance (such as Jamiat and Hezb), and others led by former militia commanders who fought alongside the communist regime.[21]

The new mujahideen government, still under attack from the prime minister's forces, now ruled over a quasi state, a state that is recognized as such by the international community but lacks the capacity to exert de facto sovereignty.[22] In accordance with the Peshawar Accords, Rabbani officially became president of the Islamic State of Afghanistan at the end of June 1992 (a position he was supposed to hold for four months but did not relinquish until December 2001). Yet, it was Massoud who controlled the main state institutions in the capital—in no small part thanks to Panjshir's proximity to Kabul. An acute observer of Afghan politics once compared the Rabbani-Massoud relationship to the one between the seventeenth-century king of France Louis the XIII and his chief minister, Cardinal Richelieu: Rabbani was the legitimate monarch (with the advantage of printing money, receiving hard currency, and making official appointments) to whom Massoud paid allegiance, but the Panjshiri was the one in command—especially as he spent most of his time inside the country, whereas Rabbani was spending a significant portion of his time abroad.[23]

At the time Massoud took Kabul, Rabbani had pressured him to end the Shura-i Nazar, which had already become largely independent of Jamiat during the Soviet-Afghan war. While Massoud accepted and announced the dissolution of the protostate structure, he never took concrete actions to end it. He instead maintained his own separate structure as a way to build his personal authority, in parallel to both the state and the party (and I will therefore keep referring to the Shura-i Nazar, both for continuity purposes and because it continued to exist de facto, if not officially). According to the American reporter Steve Coll: "By 1994 the Panjshiris were seen by many

Pashtuns in Kabul as a kind of battle-fighting mafia. United by a decade of continuous war under Massoud's charismatic leadership, the Panjshiris were close-knit, tough, secretive, and a government within the government."[24]

Rabbani's government was further undermined by the creation of the Taliban in 1994. This Islamic fundamentalist militant movement took control of most of the country (with the exception of a northeastern corner made of parts or all of the provinces of Takhar, Badakhshan, Kapisa, and Parwan) and eventually seized Kabul in 1996.[25] While Massoud and Rabbani had gained international recognition by capturing the capital and toppling the government in 1992, the same did not apply to the Taliban. Only three countries recognized the Taliban as the official regime in Afghanistan: Pakistan, Saudi Arabia, and the United Arab Emirates.[26] Rabbani's government remained the official representative of the Islamic State of Afghanistan throughout the war, even though it no longer controlled Kabul and had to move to the northeast of the country, still controlled by Massoud and his men, in 1996. It first moved to Mazar-i Sharif, then to Taloqan (Takhar Province), and, finally, to Fayzabad (Badakhshan Province) as the Taliban advanced farther east. Massoud reacted to this forced exile by creating and leading the Northern Alliance, a loose coalition of warlords and commanders who had fought against each other throughout the 1990s but together opposed Taliban rule.

Tajikistan, then engaged in a civil war of its own, suddenly became of tremendous strategic value as a potential safe haven. Massoud, who had hosted the Tajik Islamist opposition on the government-controlled Afghan territory since the beginning of the 1990s, compelled the Tajik Islamists into mediation with the president of Tajikistan Emomali Rahmonov (nowadays known as Emomali Rahmon) that culminated in the signing of a peace agreement in June 1997. In exchange, the mujahideen government was given access to Tajik airports as well as permission to enter Tajik territory without visas, which provided Massoud with both a safe haven (where he could hold his diplomatic meetings, including those with the CIA) and a direct access road for Russia and Iran to deliver military supplies (see below). Dushanbe, Tajikistan's capital, eventually became the center of the Afghan resistance.[27] This was a milestone for Massoud: "It was the first time Massoud played such a positive role in the region," said a former Afghan military attaché in Tajikistan. "Before he was only seen as a big commander, he proved to be a leader."[28] Central Asian Republics and Russia stopped seeing the Panjshiri leader as a threatening Islamist and started cooperating more closely with him. In this sense, the Tajik reconciliation process really launched Massoud's diplomatic campaign.[29]

Quasi-State Diplomacy

While the mujahideen government was in Kabul, between 1992 and 1996, "Rabbani compensated for Massoud's relatively weak international connections."[30] International interest in Afghanistan had largely faded with the end of the Cold War. Yet, belonging to the internationally recognized government of Afghanistan gave Massoud the means to develop a more formal diplomatic campaign and become a real "wartime diplomat."[31] Massoud started to build a more formal diplomatic corps. He continued to dispatch representatives abroad and to delegate diplomatic tasks to his most trusted lieutenants but this time as official representatives of the Afghan government. Abdullah Abdullah, then deputy minister of foreign affairs, explains that the main offices abroad (in particular those in the United Kingdom and the United States), staffed mostly with Massoud's and Rabbani's aides, worked "like branches of the Foreign Affairs Ministry more than as mere embassies."[32] After Kabul fell to the Taliban, Massoud tried to rally the Afghan diaspora to the resistance by spreading his message through embassies, newspapers, and radio. "He wanted to make a bridge between the mujahideen inside and the intellectuals outside Afghanistan," recalled Ahmad Wali Massoud, who represented his brother in London.[33]

Massoud's discourse shifted with the emergence of the Taliban. An American CIA operative recounts a meeting in the summer of 2000 during which, "[as] always when he had an American audience, [Massoud] talked about the broader threat that the Taliban posed to the Islamic world and to the West."[34] The Panjshiri continued to search for potential backers and asked his representatives to establish contact with specific people who could offer him support. Ahmad Wali, for example, remembers meeting with Benazir Bhutto, Pakistan's prime minister, or the Aga Khan, at his brother's request.[35] Massoud also sent his most trusted lieutenants on diplomatic trips, in particular Abdullah, who eventually became minister of foreign affairs in 2000, giving

Massoud the country's most potent international platform. Abdullah began attending conferences and multilateral events (e.g., the Economic Organization Conference, the UN Millennium Summit) and joined Massoud on diplomatic trips (e.g., to Iran, India, and Uzbekistan) aimed to raise awareness and prompt concrete aid.[36]

The Russian government became concerned about the Taliban after they took Kabul and advanced north toward Mazar-i Sharif. Massoud's involvement in the Tajik peace process also curried Moscow's favor, especially with his contacts in the Russian administration lobbying on his behalf. In 1997, Massoud met with Russian officials in Moscow to open negotiations about arms supplies and airfield access. He later met with the Russian minister of defense in Dushanbe, took another trip to Moscow to meet with President Putin in 2000, and eventually started buying weapons and ammunition from the former occupying power he had spent a decade fighting against.

Massoud's relations with Tehran, cold at best, also changed drastically after a dozen Iranian diplomats were killed in the attack of Iran's Mazar-i Sharif consulate in the summer of 1998. Massoud requested an urgent meeting with the Iranian authorities, who held the Taliban responsible for the attack and, as part of a military exercise, had sent two hundred thousand soldiers (and seventy thousand members of the Revolutionary Guard) to the border with Afghanistan. An Iranian plane picked him up in Dushanbe and flew him to Tehran to meet with Iran's minister of foreign affairs and his deputy. Massoud, now the uncontested leader of the Afghan resistance, persuaded the Iranians to go through him and to give him the monopoly over arms and ammunition distribution instead of confronting the Taliban directly. From there on, Massoud received regular deliveries of ammunition and logistical support from Iran through Dushanbe, with the support of the Tajik government.

Massoud also took steps to strengthen his connections in Europe. The French intelligence services supplied hardware, radio equipment, and weapons to Massoud, who in turn provided the French with intelligence on Arab jihadist networks operating in Afghanistan. In September 1999, a couple of French politicians visited Massoud in Panjshir as part of a public relations operation. A group of European deputies made a similar visit in the spring of 2000, and a resolution condemning the Taliban regime was adopted by the European Parliament in March 2001. Massoud was invited to Strasbourg shortly thereafter, as vice president of Afghanistan—a title he had recently acquired to boost his international legitimacy—to give a speech before the European Parliament. A trip was organized by his team in Paris (helped by his brother Ahmad Wali and Abdullah, his minister of foreign affairs) in April 2001. In Strasbourg, Massoud gave a speech that was very well received and met with a number of European officials, deputies, and political groups. Although Massoud's visit failed to spark interest from the French government, it marked an important turn for Massoud's image. Not only did it boost his international stature, but it also greatly improved his legitimacy vis-à-vis the Afghan diaspora.

Public relations operations and a Tajik safe haven, though vital to the survival of the Afghan resistance, would not be sufficient for Massoud and his allies to defeat the Taliban. He needed US support.[37] CIA officers, worried about the rise of the Taliban, reestablished contacts with Massoud in the mid-1990s. Gary Schroen, the CIA station chief in Islamabad, flew to Kabul in September 1996, right before the mujahideen government vacated the city, to discuss a Stinger missile recovery program. Massoud was strongly opposed to the program at first and wanted to keep the missiles. However, after the loss of Kabul to the Taliban, the collaboration seemed like a good opportunity to rebuild a strong relationship with the United States. "We wanted to use it as a means of getting our message—the message of resistance and the message of the cause—back to Washington," said one of Massoud's senior intelligence aides.[38] CIA officers, while doubting Massoud's ability to defeat al-Qaeda, held meetings in Dushanbe and even sent teams to Panjshir to provide him with cash—up to $250,000 per trip—and electronic equipment, and to establish direct secure communication lines between him and the CIA headquarters to pass along information on Osama bin Laden and al-Qaeda.

However, at the time, almost no one in Washington was really interested in hearing about Massoud. State Department officials retained a negative opinion of the Panjshiri leader and were strongly opposed to the CIA's push for a stronger collaboration. Secretary of State Madeleine Albright (and the rest of the Clinton administration) remained deeply skeptical of Massoud and his allies in the Northern Alliance. Robin Raphel, assistant secretary for South Asia, and Tom Simons, ambassador to Pakistan, "dismissed [Massoud's] 'rosy scenario' [of a bottom-up democracy]" and denounced the "'self-righteousness' of Massoud's besieged government."[39] The US ambassador to Pakistan believed that supplying arms to Massoud would only fuel the conflict along ethnic lines. Others, in the CIA in particular, were concerned about alleged drug-related activities undertaken by the Shura-i Nazar.[40] The situation changed with al-Qaeda's bombings of US embassies in Kenya and Tanzania in 1998. A more nuanced policy toward Massoud emerged from the State Department in the summer of 1999. President Clinton declared a policy of strict neutrality in the Afghan civil war but stated that his administration would be willing to cooperate with him on intelligence operations. At the same time, the US government made clear to its Iranian and Russian counterparts that Washington did not oppose their arms deliveries to Massoud.

The Panjshiri later tried to persuade the new Bush administration to do more for the Afghan resistance. He wrote a letter to Vice President Cheney, dispatched Abdullah to Washington, and even hired a lobbyist: "Massoud invited his new Washington advocate, Otilie English, a lobbyist who had worked for the Committee for a Free Afghanistan during the 1980s, to meet with him in northern Afghanistan. With his chief CIA liaison, Amrullah Saleh, providing translation, Massoud recorded a videotaped seminar for English about the changing landscape inside Afghanistan, al Qaeda's strengths and weaknesses, foreign involvement in the war, and his own strategy. Massoud and his aides hoped English would use the commander's ideas to change minds in Congress or the State Department."[41] These efforts were to no avail. State Department policy toward the Northern Alliance changed only after Massoud's death and the attacks on the World Trade Center and the Pentagon that followed.

Massoud always had a good understanding of the importance of good public relations, and he indeed received great exposure. This was certainly the case after the end of the Soviet-Afghan war, and maybe even more so after the capture of Kabul by the Taliban. Among others, Christophe de Ponfilly came back to Panjshir to film *Massoud l'Afghan*, and *National Geographic* sent Reza Deghati and Sebastian Junger to profile him. Massoud understood the benefits of media exposure and so did his enemies, who took advantage of his desire to improve his image in the Arab world. On September 9, 2001, two days before the terrorist attacks on the World Trade Center and the Pentagon, two al-Qaeda agents disguised as journalists blew themselves up and killed the lion of Panjshir. They had "emphasized that they

Massoud Mausoleum, Panjshir Valley (photograph by the author).

intended to portray the Northern Alliance in a positive light, to help reha-
bilitate and promote Massoud's reputation before Arab audiences."[42]

Massoud's diplomatic activities showed that he could represent his military prowess and charismatic leadership capabilities to a variety of foreign
governments. These governments were acting on their national interests and
may have preferred cooperation with Massoud because he controlled strategic territory. Yet, they became more eager to work with him as a consequence
of his self-representation. Massoud then used the resources that these foreigners provided to assert his domestic authority. In sum, the warlord's international diplomacy gave him the autonomy to rule as he saw fit.[43]

Marshal Fahim: Rise and Fall of an Afghan Phoenix

A Warlord by Inheritance

Mohammad Qasim Fahim only inherited the leadership of the Shura-i Nazar—which Massoud had created during the Soviet-Afghan war (but by then no longer *officially* existed)—and of the Northern Alliance—the anti-Taliban military alliance that Massoud had launched after being ousted from Kabul—because of Massoud's assassination. Born in the village of Omarz, in the Panjshir Valley, in 1957, Fahim, the son of a local mullah from northern Afghanistan (but outside Panjshir), grew up in a humble home. Like President Rabbani, he studied Islamic law and theology at Abu Hanifa, a prestigious religious school in the Afghan capital. Associated with Gulbuddin Hekmatyar at first, he eventually left Hezb to join Rabbani's Jamiat and follow Massoud in Panjshir.

Although he had been continually involved in the successive Afghan wars, Fahim was not an accomplished military leader. He had started as a *mutaharek*, a soldier in Massoud's elite mobile units, but was not particularly recognized for his bravery in combat. A former Shura-i Nazar commander even told me that Fahim had "never shot a bullet."[44] While this is probably an exaggeration, Fahim did not draw his authority from his ability to fight, but rather from the inheritance of an already functioning (but fragmented) organization. During the Soviet-Afghan war, Fahim worked as an intermediary between Massoud and other domestic actors, acting as his "mobile ambassador," participating in talks and meetings with commanders all over northern Afghanistan, "often journeying beyond the Panjshir to meet with other resistance factions on his behalf."[45] He eventually became Massoud's de facto deputy. After the collapse of Najibullah's pro-Soviet regime in 1992, Fahim was appointed head of Afghanistan's intelligence services, a position he kept for four years, until Kabul fell under Taliban rule. In reality, Fahim was mostly in charge of dealing with logistical issues, such as distributing money and ammunition to the commanders—a role he played throughout the resistance against the Taliban—and led his own paramilitary unit in the fight against the Taliban in Kabul. A former head of intelligence explained to me: "When state institutions are not formed, when people are under the stress of violence . . . , the roles become blurred, personalities matter more than offices."[46]

Contrary to what has been reported by AFP on October 3, 2001, Fahim was not a "close friend and hand-picked successor to Massoud." Their relationship was complicated and at times very tense. The Shura-i Nazar had a very fluid structure that relied heavily on Massoud's personality, authority, and charisma. His assassination, therefore, presented a major threat to the very existence of the organization. In this context, the decision made by a restricted group of Shura-i Nazar leaders to appoint Fahim as his successor in the immediate aftermath of Massoud's death owed much to contingency. An aide to Massoud who was present at the time explains: "It was a military situation. Politics was not our first priority. Survival was our first priority. We needed someone with a military experience."[47] Fahim, a senior Shura-i Nazar leader with a military background and authority among the commanders, not only fit the profile but also happened to be posted nearby when the assassination took place. His position was then confirmed by a larger group of Shura-i Nazar leaders gathered in Panjshir and made official by decree of President Rabbani (to whom Fahim was allegedly closer than to Massoud).

Massoud's death, however, transformed the Shura-i Nazar into an atypical organization, in which the burden of decision making was shared by its main leaders: Fahim and Bismullah Khan, the commander overseeing all operations on the Shamali Plain (the plain that separates Kabul from Panjshir) were the main military figures; Mohammad Yunus Qanooni and Abdullah Abdullah, both close friends of Massoud's, had the political experience; and Ahmad Zia and Ahmad Wali Massoud, who had adopted their brother's nom de guerre as their family name, had legitimacy by virtue of the Massoud name. To this day, the Shura-i Nazar is a collection of individuals connected by patronage networks and interpersonal solidarities more than an organization with specific rules and structures. In the words of the former head of Afghan intelligence services, Amrullah Saleh: "The sentiment is there, but the organization is not."[48] This peculiarity played against Fahim, in the sense that he never concentrated all sources of power within the organization. His political leadership was contested by Qanooni and Abdullah before he was even appointed. A week after 9/11, Abdullah named a representative in Washington to become "the voice of Massoud in

DC," a way to claim Massoud's legitimacy abroad as well.[49] Yet, despite real disagreements and occasional tension between them, Panjshiris (and members of the Shura-i Nazar) have remained united in times of uncertainty. "When there is a problem," a former Shura-i Nazar commander told me in 2011, "there is no Abdullah or Fahim, they are the same group."[50] It is in fact not rare to hear Panjshiris refer to *us* or *our people*.[51] Following Ahmad Shah Massoud's death, Fahim had become the first among equals, "the unofficial leader of the 'shadow' [Shura-i Nazar]," and the most powerful military leader in Afghanistan.[52]

Fahim's newly acquired position, combined with the United States's decision to rely on local ground forces to overthrow the Taliban regime, gave him the opportunity to interact with CIA operatives and US Special Forces through Operation Jawbreaker—an operation through which US Special Forces intended to build a partnership with the Northern Alliance and prepare the Panjshir Valley as a "base of operations" in the fight against the Taliban and al-Qaeda.[53] Fahim received millions of dollars from the United States for his cooperation, but this did not prevent him from defying the Bush administration's order not to move his men into Kabul. The "Panjshiri Troika"—Fahim, Qanooni, and Abdullah—captured three of the most important state institutions (the Ministry of Defense, the Ministry of Interior, and the Ministry of Foreign Affairs, respectively) and doled out positions to their men.[54] Controlling the Ministry of Defense allowed Fahim to turn his military power into political power and shape the state-building process to suit his interests, in particular in its economic dimension.

Fahim's institutional control over the security apparatus also allowed him to maintain his military might. In mid-2003, he allegedly commanded over fifteen thousand well-equipped troops in Kabul alone, and about one hundred thousand men altogether. An estimate in July 2004 counted five thousand troops loyal to Fahim in Kabul and the abutting Shamali Plain, north of the capital. Another report describes the fields of the Panjshir Valley as "lined with rows of new Russian military tanks and rocket launchers," with a force of fifty thousand men "under the thumb of the Afghan minister of defense."[55] Fahim claimed that these weapons were property of the ministry rather than a personal armory. Nevertheless, it makes no doubt that his men were his "ace in the hole, a backup option easily activated for a march on Kabul if his political ambitions [were] thwarted."[56]

The warlord strategy (discussed in chapter 1) posed a major dilemma to US policymakers, as relying on warlord forces, and Fahim's in particular, not only shored up nonstate power but also undermined their efforts to support the Afghan president, who controlled no armed forces of his own.[57] This resulted in a "Karzai-fronted but Fahim-dominated government."[58] In April 2002, Fahim was made Marshal. "They forced [Karzai] to do it," confessed one of the president's advisers.[59] The American journalist Joshua Partlow even reports that Fahim, emboldened by his military superiority, would sometimes sit in Karzai's chair (even in his presence) as if it were his own.[60] "Who is Karzai? This is my country," he allegedly bragged in 2003.[61]

The New Rules of the Game

For Fahim, being considered as Massoud's heir was not enough to be accepted by the international community. His inability to charm Western interveners strongly contrasted with Hamid Karzai's manners and diplomatic skills. Fahim "tried to give himself a modern face, and appear as a modern leader [after 2001], but he couldn't," said a Kabul-based analyst.[62] Although he had some success leading the Shura-i Nazar after Massoud's death, he was still seen as the organization's military arm only. His reluctance to disarm and lack of talent for public relations exposed him to local and Western complaints about his human rights record and undemocratic methods.

It soon became manifest that the international community would not permit Fahim to keep his newly acquired military power in the post-Bonn political environment. Fahim first refused to comply with the Bonn Agreement's call for the withdrawal of all Afghan factions from Kabul. "The heavily armed units of the Northern Alliance soldiers who swept into Kabul will be withdrawn from the streets, but they will not leave Kabul," he declared.[63] Likely aware that the presence of international peacekeepers would limit his influence over the new institutions, Fahim took steps to make sure that the international security force would not outnumber his own men in the Afghan capital. He announced that no more than three thousand international peacekeepers would be deployed in Afghanistan over the following six months, with only one thousand in the capital. He also proclaimed

that their role would be "largely symbolic," that they would have no authority to disarm anyone, and that their duties would be limited to protecting
government buildings.[64] "Our people can handle that on their own," he told
the press in December 2001, making clear that foreigners should not get involved in domestic affairs.[65] Yet, only a few weeks later, Fahim declared that
"the military struggle [was] over in Afghanistan and the political struggle
[had] begun."[66]

While the Americans still relied heavily on Afghan warlords to fight the
Taliban and al-Qaeda, they also tried to limit their power to strengthen the
authority of the central government. After Karzai was elected president of
the Afghan Transitional Authority in June 2002, he faced strong pressure to
revamp his cabinet to limit the Panjshiris's stranglehold on the most consequential ministries. Qanooni was moved from the Ministry of Interior to the
Ministry of Education, and Karzai tried to persuade Fahim to give up either
the Vice Presidency or the Ministry of Defense. Fahim refused to do so.
Under strong international pressure, and after US Deputy Defense Secretary Paul Wolfowitz expressed concerns about Fahim's reluctance to build a
truly multiethnic national army, Karzai ordered Fahim to reduce the number of Panjshiris in the Ministry of Defense by 60 percent and to replace them
with members of other ethnic groups, which would cut one of Fahim's most
important sources of patronage. According to a US official, "Fahim [was] saying all the right things, and Karzai [said] Fahim [was] doing all the right
things," by adopting a more positive attitude toward building a multiethnic
national army.[67]

Suspicions were still high. An Afghan official close to the president reckoned: "For six months Fahim dictated to Karzai, and he was the most
powerful man in Afghanistan. Now he is worried that may change. . . . The
president has gotten [foreign] protection now, but I still think he is in danger.
Fahim and his friends are warlords, and you cannot make peaceful men out
of them."[68] In his memoirs, Zalmay Khalilzad, then president Bush's special
envoy in Afghanistan, also recalls that, by August, his office was "seeing a
number of reports suggesting that Fahim might indeed be planning a coup."[69]
Under Khalilzad's pressure, Fahim gave a press conference in which he announced that he and Karzai had "joined hands for national unity and
peace."[70] He denounced the "propaganda" depicting him as someone "who
would like to keep power to himself" and developed his vision of a "united
Afghanistan . . . where the rule of law and legality prevail."[71] At a different

venue he declared: "It is now in our interest to give up some positions, because everybody is propagandizing that Panjshiris have too much."[72]

The formal disarmament, demobilization, and reintegration process started in October 2003, with the implementation of the Afghanistan New Beginnings Programme. The program targeted 100,000 of the Afghan Militia Forces, the forces under the nominal command of the Ministry of Defense. This number accounted for less than half of the 250,000 men claimed by the ministry, although the official count was most certainly inflated in order to collect additional salaries. International pressure to disarm was strong since the process was considered to be linked to the success of the 2004 presidential election and US political credibility. Yet, AFP reported that, as of July 27, 2004, only "11,770 troops out of an estimated 40,000 to 60,000 private militiamen [had] laid down their guns."[73] Fahim's early capture (and enduring political control) of the Ministry of Defense gave him the ability to resist international pressure to disarm his men and recruit them into the Afghan National Army. This in turn allowed him to maintain one of his most prominent sources of patronage, not least by controlling the disarmament, demobilization, and reintegration process and the benefit packages that came with it.[74]

Political Downfall

The 2004 presidential election was a turning point for Fahim, who had been expected to be on Karzai's ticket. "He thought he would always stay in power," said a former aide to Ahmad Shah Massoud.[75] It would have forced him to resign from all cabinet positions, as all candidates except for the president were required to do under the newly introduced electoral laws. If nominated, his deputy, General Rahim Wardak, a Pashtun supporting the disarmament process, would have taken over as minister of defense. Fahim, however, tried to install a member of the Shura-i Nazar, Bismullah Khan, as his replacement, which Karzai declined. Fahim refused to resign; he was then dropped from the ticket and replaced by Massoud's brother Ahmad Zia. Some interpreted this move as Karzai's attempt to weaken Fahim while fragmenting the Shura-i Nazar by turning its main leaders against one another. According to a prominent Panjshiri, Ahmad Zia Massoud was chosen "because he was a non-entity."[76]

While it was a snub for Fahim, Ahmad Zia Massoud's decision to join Karzai was actually acceptable from a Shura-i Nazar perspective. It resulted from a kind of political hedging through which the leaders of the Shura-i Nazar not only cornered the state institutions and the security apparatus but also managed to place their men both inside and outside the government. "It's good to have one in and one out," an Afghan scholar told me. "It's not a comprehensive strategy but an instinct of survival. They can't cut themselves entirely from Karzai. They would lose. . . . This is Afghan politics. They are hedging their bets."[77] In the words of a former aide to Ahmad Shah Massoud: "It was not so important [to us] whether it was Fahim or Zia, as long as it was a Tajik."[78] Karzai's decision, in turn, strengthened his popularity among Pashtuns. It was a good opportunity to "shake off a reputation for using kid gloves with the warlords who dominate much of the country."[79]

Fahim's refusal to comply with the new electoral laws was not the only reason for Karzai's decision. The Afghan president was facing significant pressures from foreigners eager to put an end to the warlord strategy. Prior to nominating his running mates, Karzai held numerous meetings with foreign diplomats and Afghan leaders, during which he was strongly encouraged to cut Fahim loose.[80] Military officials and foreign diplomats were concerned at the time that Fahim would react negatively to this decision and destabilize the security situation in Kabul. Karzai postponed a visit to Pakistan; the troops from the International Security Assistance Force (ISAF) stationed in the capital were put on heightened alert, and additional night patrols were conducted. When nothing happened, Canadian Lieutenant General Rick Hillier, the ISAF commander, declared that it demonstrated "an amount of maturity that one would not have dreamt possible even six months [earlier]."[81]

While the US-led intervention and the accompanying warlord strategy had allowed Fahim to accumulate power from the end of 2001 to July 2004 as minister of defense and vice president, the disarmament process and the loss of all official positions weakened his status.[82] Fahim's (temporary) downfall offers a glimpse at warlord demise that is consistent with the book's argument. In the short term, he had failed to convince actors at all levels of politics that he was indispensable. His failure to build on Massoud's charisma and concentrate all sources of power simultaneously had made him vulnerable to international pressure. Not only did he suffer from a lack of foreign support, but influential members of the international community actively pushed for his demise. Domestically, Fahim still suffered from a lack of local and military legitimacy. In the years that led to the 2004 presidential election he had already become a violent entrepreneur (see below). He had overexploited (and privatized) his political position, hence further weakening his legitimacy. In other words, he had failed to reach a balanced distribution of his sources of power, which had damaged his authority in Panjshir and among the wider Tajik community, and jeopardized his survival. Some predicted that 2004 was to mark the end of Fahim's political career.[83] In reality, his downfall would only be temporary.[84]

From Warlord to Violent Entrepreneur

Even though Fahim had been progressively marginalized politically between 2001 and 2004, he had also very effectively shifted his power bases (his military might in particular). Through a variety of power conversion mechanisms (state infiltration, land grabbing, private protection, and extortion, for example), he had become the quintessential violent entrepreneur, using personal means of coercion and institutional resources (such as control of the military airport through the Ministry of Defense) to accumulate economic capital (for example, through unregulated import-export). This metamorphosis in turn gave him the ability to maintain his patronage networks, and hence some of his local political authority—which later allowed his comeback.

It is not easy to gather hard evidence of personal involvement for the kind of trades and practices in which Marshal Fahim was engaged. Volkov explains: "In legal practice, the charge of extortion is rather difficult to prove, since threats may often be indirect or veiled. The target may not necessarily experience victimization, especially when those who practice extortion manage to present themselves in a friendly manner and refrain from any explicit hostility. It would also be difficult to call a case an episode of extortion when threats or damage come from someone who is not the direct beneficiary, that is, when the transaction is made with another, seemingly unconnected person."[85] Fahim and his men clearly fell under Volkov's description.

Fahim was also suspected of involvement in cases of institutional extortion, of which the 2003 Sherpur scandal probably constitutes the best example.[86] As Pamela Constable noted in a *Washington Post* article on October 10, 2003:

A growing scandal over the tiny community known as Sherpur, spurred by two sharply critical reports from a U.N. housing expert and the Afghan Independent Human Rights Commission, has deeply embarrassed the U.S.-backed government. According to the reports, seven cabinet ministers and Kabul's mayor received plots in Sherpur, which abuts the capital's most exclusive neighborhood, for nominal fees.

The dispute has thrown a spotlight on the widely rumored but previously undocumented practices of high-level grabbing, corrupt municipal real estate dealings and forcible occupation of properties in the capital, where half the population of 3.2 million does not have adequate housing.

In a desperate attempt to justify his actions (and those of the other Shura-i Nazar leaders), Yunus Qanooni, then minister of education, pointed out that this land grab was actually legal. "There is a difference between those who are given land by the current rulers under current laws and those who take land by force," he said.[87] Qanooni's statement has far-reaching theoretical consequences. It stresses a fundamental difference between private extortion, which requires the mobilization of private means of coercion, and institutional extortion (the one he calls legal), which requires institutional resources.

Both of these mechanisms served at least two purposes: first, to commodify land and accumulate economic resources (by developing and reallocating said land); and second, to reward followers and develop patronage networks. The construction of Goldpoint, a high-rise building in downtown Kabul that houses jewelry shops, is a clear example of the first purpose, as it was built on land that Fahim's forces had grabbed and was financed by his own brother. The wide redistribution of the Sherpur plots to cabinet members illustrates the role that extortion plays in the development of patronage networks.

The story of Hasin Fahim, Marshal Fahim's half brother, is also particularly telling. For the journalist Pratap Chatterjee, the two brothers "offer a perfect exemplar of the new business elite."[88] It was right after Fahim's nomination as vice president (in 2002) that his brother Hasin "started to build a business empire" and that "good fortune began to rain down on the family in the form of lucrative 'reconstruction' contracts."[89] Zahid Walid Group Fuel and Gas Services Company Ltd (ZWG), a conglomerate owned by Hasin Fahim focusing on construction, equipment, and fuel and gas services, was formed in November 2001. Over the years, its client list has included (among others) the US Army, the US Agency for International Development (USAID), the US State Department, ISAF, and the Canadian Armed Forces, as well as several Afghan ministries (the Ministry of Public Health, the Ministry of Public Works, the Ministry of Interior, and the Ministry of Commerce). ZWG has won a series of contracts to work on buildings such as a NATO base, the US embassy, and the Kabul international airport. It also began importing Russian gas. Gas Group, which specializes in the distribution of gas and fuel to private households and small businesses, was created in 2006. That same year, ZWG reportedly won a $12 million contract from the Afghan Ministry of Energy and Water to supply fuel to an old diesel plant in Kabul's northern outskirts. The following year, ZWG allegedly won another $40 million contract to supply diesel, followed by a $22 million contract less than two years later. And, during a visit Chatterjee paid to ZWG's headquarters in the fall of 2009, the managing director of the diesel-import division informed the journalist that the company had just won a $17 million contract "to supply fuel to the 100-megawatt diesel power plant being built by Black & Veatch, a Kansas construction company, with money from USAID."[90]

Fahim was also active in the private military sector—hence also operating as a job provider—through his brother Hasin and his company, Strategic Security Solutions International (SSSI). According to a *Business Wire* article of June 21, 2004, SSSI "provides strategic and tactical security services to major and newly organized governments, militaries, multi-nationals and high-profile governments and business clients in every corner of the world. SSSI specializes in high-risk markets and the inherent security challenges of those environments requiring the highest level of expertise and performance." Most notably, SSSI was hired as a security provider at the US embassy in Kabul.[91] While not much is known about this private security firm, it is clear that it was especially well suited to acquire economic capital (while keeping Fahim's men on the payroll) within the context of the Afghan state's and NATO's war efforts.

During the 2004–9 period, Fahim privatized much of his authority at the expense of his already fragmented local base. He became more of a politician and a businessman focused on short-term economic gains than a community leader, and hence failed to monopolize all sources of authority within his own constituency, offering a glimpse at warlord demise. Yet, his exploitation of public office also allowed him to build a strong private sector network and acquire huge financial reserves.

Political Comeback

On May 4, 2009, Karzai announced that he had picked Marshal Fahim as one of his running mates in the upcoming presidential election. As a vice presidential candidate, Fahim presented multiple advantages. If Karzai's attempt to fragment the Shura-i Nazar may in part explain his decision to replace Fahim with Ahmad Zia Massoud in 2004, it also accounts for the 2009 reversal. By choosing Fahim, a heavier political weight than Ahmad Zia, Karzai automatically diverted some of the Tajik vote from Abdullah, his main opponent in the election. "Fahim was the boss, it didn't matter what Abdullah did," a former member of the Shura-i Nazar told me.[92] Given the chorus of disapproval that it engendered from the international community, Karzai's decision may also be interpreted as a provocation, or at least a signal of independence. In 2004, Karzai had bowed to US pressure to drop Fahim from the presidential ticket. By 2009, he was no longer inclined do so. "That was a mistake," he told me, "not having Marshal Fahim [in 2004]. We were misled by Western diplomatic activities and media. Within three or four months I realized it was a major mistake and I had decided to bring him back for 2009."[93] By then, Karzai's relationship with the US administration had largely deteriorated and he was willing to risk antagonizing his main financial backer. It "was a decision that I made for the good of the country, for the unity of the country, for the strength of Afghanistan, in which it has a government that is Afghan and not influenced from outside," Karzai said about choosing Marshal Fahim.[94]

Another reason for picking Fahim was financial. Karzai's brother Mahmood had strong commercial ties with Fahim's brother Hasin, whose commercial allies were reported to have contributed to financing Karzai's 2009 presidential campaign.[95] Fahim's 2009 comeback was in large part due to his incredibly successful conversion of power (especially through the accumulation of economic power), his phoenix-like ability to accumulate wealth and riches he could rely on in times of adversity. Fahim also proved indispensable to a president in need of political muscle in the North, which

Ahmad Zia Massoud had failed to provide between 2004 and 2009. As a vice president, Fahim would allow Karzai to "divide labor" and extend his authority (or at least his political patronage) to the North. And, in fact, Fahim essentially became in charge of "all things North" from 2009 till 2014, especially political appointments. "The only door that gave access to power," said a former aide to Ahmad Shah Massoud, "was Fahim's house."[96]

Of all the cases considered in this book, Fahim was the least geographically rooted. He also exerted his authority differently. Partially rejected in Panjshir, Fahim "[did not] have a region, but he ha[d] influence among rural people in the North," even among the Uzbeks (although he is a Tajik).[97] "His power comes from being a khan," explained a political observer a year before Fahim's death. "He has the ability to offer, distribute, and solve disputes. . . . First, he takes care of his family, then his cousins, then his village, etc. He has a power base among a class. It is not geographical per se. . . . He represents a multi-ethnic class (in the North) and that's why Karzai likes him."[98] In fact, Fahim exerted authority as a notable only within a certain fringe of the population, protecting, patronizing and entertaining landowners (khans) throughout northern Afghanistan.

Since 2004, Fahim's economic capital had allowed him to grease and maintain his patronage networks and operate as a community leader—for example, through sponsoring *buzkashi* (the Afghan horse riding game discussed in chapter 4), which became Fahim's preferential way of asserting social power after 2001. Not only is it perceived locally as a sign of wealth and generosity, but, in the words of Fahim himself: "buzkashi revolves around relationships" (and hence patronage networks).[99] As Azoy put it: "Whatever transpires in the course of a buzkashi is . . . imbued with special importance. On account of its links with the past, buzkashi in the present is symbolically larger than life. . . . [It] acts as a metaphor for the particular sort of unbridled competition—chaotic, uninhibited, and uncontrollable—which lurks below the apparent cooperative surface."[100] In line with this metaphor and with regard to the broader Afghan political environment, critics of Fahim claim that he was systematically using coercion to acquire the best *buzkashi* horses as well as to ensure that his team would always win.[101]

Fahim's combination of brute force and diffused authority made his power hard to fathom, in particular for Western observers. Former US ambassador to Afghanistan Robert Finn captured Fahim's paradoxical nature in a few simple words: "He looks like an ogre, but . . . people love him."[102] Yet, compared with other warlords (and especially with Massoud), in the short term, Fahim failed to reach a balance between the different sources of power, overly relying on his military might and economic capital, without ever acquiring enough local legitimacy. For a while, he had become an irresponsible warlord, a violent entrepreneur more than a good patron. This, combined with his inability to convince the international community that he was still indispensable, explains his temporary demise. Fahim never managed to go beyond the fragmentation of the Shura-i Nazar to truly become the one and only successor to Ahmad Shah Massoud. He remained the most powerful, the richest, and the most warlord-like to follow in Massoud's footsteps, but he never acquired all the sources of power that his predecessor had developed in the previous decade. In the view of one Afghan scholar, "Fahim is just a khan. He failed to transform his patronage system into something modern. There is no substance. It's just a shaky pyramid. It's money driven. His power will collapse as soon as there is a hint of alternative."[103] And yet, Fahim remained powerful until he died, on March 9, 2014.[104]

Although Fahim was the direct successor of Massoud, these two warlords followed very different trajectories. Massoud's rise to power may be explained by numerous factors: among others, "his genuine tactical skills, his capabilities as a speaker and in inter-personal relations, and the failure of the Soviets to subdue him despite the concentration of overwhelming military force."[105] His bourgeois upbringing, urban youth, and Western-style education certainly account for the relative ease with which Massoud interacted with Western countries in general, and France in particular. Even though he later failed to become a unifying force when he had the opportunity, Massoud managed to concentrate most sources of power in the territory under his control in the 1980s. Eventually, in the 1990s, he partly ruled over an internationally recognized quasi state with embassies and ministries. Throughout this whole time, he maintained authority over his core constituency in Panjshir. He possessed unmatched diplomatic skills and a nose for good public relations. He was telegenic, media savvy, and articulate and had developed a great romantic image that charmed the international community, with his *pakol* hat eventually becoming a symbol of resistance first to the Soviet Union and then to the Taliban.[106] Massoud always exercised great "mastery of the international zeitgeist."[107] For example, when he was in dire need of Western support after the fall of Kabul to the Taliban, he positioned himself as a supporter of democracy and the emancipation of women and portrayed himself as a bulwark against Islamic fundamentalist terrorism.[108] In the end, Massoud ended up "inventing an icon."[109]

The Panjshiris from the Shura-i Nazar use forums such as the media outlets they control and the Massoud Foundation—whose mission is to "keep [Massoud's] vision and memory alive"—to claim his inheritance.[110] "[Massoud] is regarded as a prophet by his fellow Tajiks," writes Azoy.[111] Even though Massoud had started as a community leader "in his reliance on a single group (the Panjshiris) as the core of fighting forces and as the leadership of his military-political organization" (and never quite played the same role vis-à-vis the northeastern population as he did in his home valley), his leadership in the resistance and his diplomatic efforts eventually gave him a unique national dimension.[112] But, when Massoud died, the Panjshiris lost their national reach and became more communitarian, especially as they successfully sidelined former president Rabbani (a fellow Tajik from Badakhshan, in the northeast), the only person who "connects a Tajik from Badghis [Province] with a guy from the Shamali Plain and a Herati."[113]

Fahim inherited an organization fragmented by the death of its leader, but lacked the ideological capital and local legitimacy of his glorious predecessor to keep it together and maintain his authority across all different realms. His lack of diplomatic skills and failure to convince international actors that he was indispensable eventually led to his temporary demise in 2004. After he failed to be reappointed as minister of defense and was replaced by one of Ahmad Shah Massoud's brothers, Ahmad Zia, Fahim declared that "Karzai ha[d] made a mistake by distancing himself from [them]."[114] Fahim's extremely successful conversion of power (in large part due to the capture of state institutions), however, allowed him to maintain his patronage networks and accumulate enough economic resources to wait for a more favorable environment. The opportunity to retake center stage presented itself when Karzai chose him to be his running mate in the 2009 presidential election. Fahim had political, social, and economic assets that Karzai could use to get elected and run the country. If Fahim failed to convince the international community that he could play a positive role in a peaceful post-Taliban environment, the uncertainty that started to surround

Afghanistan in the years before his death had made him relevant once again. "He was a formidable counterpart . . . a pillar of stability," Karzai told me.[115] Yet, his potential for disruption was undeniable, especially considering the political and military weight of the Shura-i Nazar as a whole. "If they want to remove Karzai," a former Shura-i Nazar commander told me in 2011, "they can. Most ANA [Afghan National Army] and ANP [Afghan National Police] are our people."[116]

Conclusion

Beyond Warlord Survival

Most international actors involved in Afghanistan and other war-torn countries would prefer that warlords fall into insignificance to favor the construction of a rule-based Weberian bureaucracy. And yet, I show throughout this book that most warlords manage to remain influential despite the pressure that some international and state actors exert to marginalize them. Warlord survival is a story of shrewd individuals who develop creative political strategies to survive in hostile environments, in which international and state actors attempt to homogenize the exercise of power. This work explains how these men maintain authority.

Afghan Warlords: A Comparison

Like the warlords of Republican China before them, Ismail Khan, General Dostum, Ahmad Shah Massoud, and Marshal Fahim all "understood they were caught up in a complex balance of power and responded with certain distinctive modes of calculation."[1] In the 1990s, Ismail Khan, Dostum, and Massoud controlled territories and populations and attempted to concentrate all sources of power to impose their own political order in their respective fiefdoms (*fonction totale*). In post-2001 Afghanistan, Ismail Khan, Dostum, and Fahim all projected and converted power to adapt to their new environment; they all used violence (or, at a minimum, the threat thereof) to rein in their rivals; they all infiltrated the state's institutions, in one way or another; and they all operated as patrons, providing jobs and security to their followers. In short, they all became armed notables, leaders who mediate between their communities and the outside world, including state and international actors, and have the ability to coerce and provide security. Yet, due to their respective social backgrounds, existing capital, and personal trajectories, they all projected and transformed power in different ways, adopted different faces, developed different strategies, and used different power resources to achieve their objectives. These different positionings in turn led to different outcomes in the post-2001 era.

Ismail Khan is certainly the most typical warlord presented in this book. In the post-Taliban period, he is the one who has developed the most balanced set of resources. As a result, he has become a typical armed notable, building his authority on his roles as notable and security provider. He has relied on his jihadist credentials and portrayed himself as a pious and conservative Muslim through the promotion of a harsh version of Islam. It should come as no surprise that these two aspects of his persona were further emphasized each time we met: his jihadist credentials by inviting me to attend gatherings of former mujahideen and, as mentioned earlier, by shaming me for not mentioning *his* Jihad Museum as my favorite monument in the city; his religiosity by interrupting both interviews to go pray, although this is not uncommon in Afghanistan. Ismail Khan has created his own quasi-mythical persona: the amir of western Afghanistan, a religious nonsectarian community leader and security provider; the only man able to fulfill a *fonction totale* in western Afghanistan.

Dostum's past as a pro-government militia leader during the Soviet-Afghan war has always meant that, unlike Ismail Khan, for instance, he would never hold any jihadist or religious credentials. This, in Afghan politics, is a serious disadvantage. Dostum has instead built his authority on his ethnic identity, using and maintaining his status as the sole Turkic leader able to promote his community's interests. He "gave the Uzbeks a national political importance they had not had in 150 years," wrote Barfield.[2] Yet, rejected by political elites in Kabul, he has been torn, throughout his political carrier, between ethnicizing his political and military movement and adopting an inclusive approach toward ethnicity aimed at broadening his support base.[3] Dostum has positioned himself as a traditional Central Asian leader, developing his own brand of ethnic warlord. It was in this spirit that his eldest son and heir apparent offered me a *chapan* (a traditional coat worn throughout Central Asia) and a *doppi* (an Uzbek rug cap) after our first meeting.[4] Dostum has long portrayed himself as the one and only successor to Tamerlane, the great leader of Central Asia who has now become a "symbol of Uzbek identity."[5]

Fahim, finally, followed a different path. His trajectory illustrates the limits of a warlord's actions and highlights variables critical to success. Unlike the other cases covered in this book, he did not exert a *fonction totale* in the 1990s; he inherited the Shura-i Nazar after Ahmad Shah Massoud was killed on September 9, 2001. However, he crucially lacked the social and ideological capital of his predecessor. In Panjshir, he had much less local legitimacy than Ismail Khan has in Herat, for example. And he was never able to operate as an ethnic entrepreneur vis-à-vis the Tajik population the way Dostum does with the Uzbeks and, to a lesser extent, the Turkmens. Fahim instead prioritized the accumulation of economic capital (at the expense of other sources of power), hence further weakening his standing within the Tajik community and losing his local power base in Panjshir, eventually becoming more of a violent entrepreneur than an armed notable. Yet, in the context of increased insecurity and instability of post-2009 Afghanistan, he was able to put his very successful conversion of power to good use and become the country's first vice president once again.

Resilience Post-2014

All post-2001 cases discussed in this book offer a glimpse at warlord demise. Ismail Khan risked losing his power base when he was repatriated to the capital in 2004. Dostum's lack of political capital in Kabul meant he was on the verge of political demise for most of the 2001–14 period. And Fahim, who never managed to overcome the divisions within the Shura-i Nazar, privatized most of his authority and ended up jeopardizing his position in the

Tajik community. Yet, all three managed to compensate and bounce back, eventually acquiring new resources to remain relevant. I show throughout this work that warlords are in fact here to stay because they have the ability to transform their power to resist pressure and ensure their political survival. In other words, warlords demonstrate strong signs of resilience: they have the "ability to recover from or adjust easily to misfortune or change."[6] One way they did so, in the first years of the US-led intervention, was by recycling their military power into sources of authority that would be more useful in the new environment. This process is reversible too. Dormant warlords will switch back to being active warlords if given the opportunity. They will further develop their military capital and eventually undertake a *fonction totale*, if they can.

If my theory is correct, we would expect warlords to react to a sharp decline in state resources (accompanied by a weakening of the state's ability to control its territory) by attempting to reacquire military power. This is precisely what happened after December 2009, when President Obama announced a military surge, to be followed, eighteen months later, by the gradual withdrawal of US forces from Afghanistan and the complete handover of security operations to the Afghan authorities (to be completed by 2014).[7] "That's our responsibility to defend Afghanistan," Ismail Khan proclaimed before the gathering of former mujahideen I attended in Herat in March 2011.[8] And the warlords' rearmament and remobilization process only accelerated after 2014: "Commanders are trying to assert themselves, to become the person in charge in case something happens," a Kabul-based researcher told me in the fall of 2015. "It's a time of arming," she insisted.[9] After 2014, warlords started getting ready to make the transition from dormant to active warlords. Dostum, for example, took the initiative to lead the fight against the Taliban himself in his home region (even though he remained the first vice president of the Islamic Republic of Afghanistan), while, as of my last visit in the summer of 2018, Ismail Khan was still hosting commanders in his guest house on a weekly basis. "In a short time," he told me then, "we can gather 1,000 mujahideen."[10]

With the end of NATO combat operations and the negotiations with the Taliban gaining momentum, the demand for protection, trust, and security has strongly increased. "As when the Najibullah government was collapsing and the Taliban government was ousted," wrote Martin in 2014, "the Helmandis are looking to their tribal leadership to provide stability into the next era."[11] Indeed, people tend to stand by their leaders in times of uncertainty. "We promise our brother Ismail Khan that we will be ready for his call," said one of Ismail Khan's lieutenants during the above-mentioned gathering.[12] The same phenomenon was seen in Republican China, where, "with the decrease in the possibilities of making effective predictions as to future eventualities, the military officials tended more and more to gravitate toward those leaders with whom they had the closest associations."[13]

A Kabul-based analyst observed: "Jihadist credentials are becoming more important as technocrats reveal [themselves to be] ineffective and for those who consider that the Taliban are no alternative. [What people hear is:] 'I fought and I will fight again if I need to. . . . I remained here and I'm able to remain here.'"[14] International actors are also increasingly in need of what warlords can provide. As a former Shura-i Nazar commander told me as early as March 2011: "After 2002 the West described the Jihadist fighters as warlords, criminals, etc. Now the West says that mujahideen are good people, etc. because of the Taliban insurrection. They need to use these people." In fact, the United States "has realized that it was a mistake" to sideline and ostracize the mujahideen in the early years of the intervention.[15]

Indeed, in Afghanistan, warlords represent important elements of political continuity. In the coming years, should the United States continue on the path of disengagement initiated by the Obama administration—for example, by withdrawing all forces (a possibility that cannot be ruled out)—ordinary Afghans will tend to rely on those who can protect them, leaders whom they can count on to fight the Taliban and other groups. On the contrary, if current and future US administrations increase the number of troops in Afghanistan, warlords will more likely remain dormant and oscillate between rearming and switching back their power sources, depending on the specific circumstances.

A New Generation?

In this book, I show that warlords develop complex survival strategies and have the ability to rise again after each fall. For that reason, they remain relevant until they die, at which point their immaterial sources of authority might well vanish with them if they fail to institutionalize their power. Giustozzi reaches the conclusion that warlord polities are "subject to quickly foundering once the charismatic leader at their centre disappears or loses his abilities. . . . [Their] 'empires of mud' can disappear without leaving a trace."[16] In other words, warlords do not build perpetually lived organizations, "whose existence is independent of the lives of their members."[17] The warlords' mortality might in fact be their main weakness.[18] Warlords attempt to prevent and overcome this by preparing this progeny and transmitting their sources of authority to them.

Ismail Khan "seemed intent on establishing a succession line, grooming his son Mirwais [Sadeq] as future leader."[19] Mirwais Sadeq indeed attended the 2001 Bonn conference and served as minister of labor and social affairs under the Afghan Interim Authority from December 2001 till June 2002, and then as minister of civil aviation and tourism under the Afghan Transitional Administration, until he was killed in 2004. Another of Ismail Khan's sons, Mohammad Yaser Sadeq, is a diplomat. A third, Taha Sadeq, was using his father's *shura* to campaign during the gathering of former commanders I attended in 2018. He was subsequently elected as a representative of Herat Province in parliament.

General Dostum's eldest son, Batur, has been groomed to take over after his father for years. Educated in Turkey, Batur Dostum, born in 1987, has been president of the Dostum Foundation and B-TV (the television channel named after him) since their creation, in 2011 and 2013, respectively. When his father was in exile in Turkey, between March 2017 and July 2018 (following the Ahmad Ishchi events), Batur was running Junbesh-i Mili (at least officially) as the acting head of the party.[20] And, like Ismail Khan's son, he was voted to parliament in the 2018 election.

Ahmad Shah Massoud's only son, Ahmad, was educated in the West and groomed to play a role in Afghan politics. After studying at the Royal Military Academy Sandhurst, King's College, and the University College London, Ahmad Massoud returned to Afghanistan and was appointed president of the Massoud Foundation in November 2016, at age twenty-seven. In his words: "I was raised with one goal and one goal only: continue on the path traced by my father. I am going to spend my life preparing myself to be a leader, in the hope that the people will want me."[21]

Finally, Marshal Fahim's eldest son, Adib, holds a bachelor's degree in International Relations from the American University of Sharjah and a master's degree in public administration and policy from New York University.

Posters of Ahmad Shah Massoud and Marshal Fahim on a police
checkpoint, published by the Massoud Foundation and the Marshal
Fahim Foundation, respectively, Kabul (photograph by the author).

"When my father passed away," he said to me, "naturally I had to take over."
Former mujahideen and prominent politicians gave him his blessing in a ceremony organized by then president Karzai himself. "It had a very important symbolic significance," Adib Fahim told me.[22] A year later, in 2015, the
year of his thirtieth birthday, he was appointed NDS deputy director. "Adib
Fahim belongs to the family of jihad and the mujahideen," Abdullah, the
country's chief executive officer, declared during his introduction ceremony.[23]
And, like Ahmad Massoud, he heads the foundation set up to honor his
father's memory.[24]

However, it is doubtful, considering the importance of military legitimacy in a warlord's power, that the next generation will ever manage to replace their fathers (even though Dostum tried to overcome this by having his three other sons appointed in the Afghan Army).[25] "The second generation has softened. The first generation was fighters," a former aide to Massoud told me. "Power is magnetic, wealth is magnetic, but charisma is ultra-magnetic," he said. "People with power and wealth will attract followers. But they lack charisma, devotion, the drive. . . . Massoud's magnetism was because of who he was, not what he had. He had nothing." I asked: "Are there people with that amount of charisma today?" The former aide answered: "No. No pope or priest, even if crucified, will become Jesus. No fat man drinking whisky at 2 o'clock in the afternoon saying great things will become Churchill. . . . Green glass is so beautiful, but emerald is so valuable. It's because emerald has lived for million years, under pressure. It has cooked, it has ripened. Green glass is made in factories. Massoud was the product of a high, high pressure. Hundreds of thousands of bombs dropped, trillion tons of ammunition, and it produced Massoud."[26]

Implications for State Formation and State Building

In this work, I adopt a microlevel perspective, carefully tracing the trajectories of four Afghan warlords, to conduct an empirical study of macrolevel processes. I address the role of warlords in state formation and state building and uncover a process of warlord survival that challenges the universality of the Western state formation process (and the Western state) and shows that there is in fact no teleological endpoint to state consolidation. By linking microlevel analyses of warlord strategies and behaviors with macrolevel processes of state formation and state building, I posit the existence of multiple pathways to state formation. The kind of state one sees in Afghanistan, where political authority is extremely fragmented, dramatically differs from the Weberian state that the international community uses as the universal benchmark to build states through intrusive social engineering interventions.

Conventional notions of historical state formation and contemporary state building often assume hierarchies of authority and clear delineations of tasks.

While a state is never "a coherent, fairly unified actor, set apart from, or above, other social organizations," it is even less the case in fragmented societies, where warlords and other nonstate armed actors are in fact integral to the state.[27] Reflecting on his experience in the market town of Istalif, Coburn explains the inability of outside interveners to comprehend the "ambiguity of the state's role" in Afghanistan: "[The international community] acted as if Afghanistan followed the bounded, Westphalian model, with certain figures representing state institutions and all others threatening the state's power. In accounts that describe the state as Westphalian, complaints of corruption come from the idealistic notion that corruption resulted from government officials not performing their duties correctly, as opposed to the reality that corruption reflected the state's lack of clear borders and the ways local patronage networks connected to government officials."[28] Afghanistan must in fact be seen as a kind of mini-empire in which sources of authority overlap (with people "often pay[ing] their dues to several authorities at the same time") and the lines between these sources of authority are often blurred.[29]

These findings should in turn encourage us to question the relevance of applying a universal model of external state building as the ultimate tool for peace building. While policymakers have developed ambitious state-building agendas in places as varied as Nicaragua, Angola, and Timor Leste, with the hope that the reestablishment of functioning statehood will foster sustainable and durable peace, attempts to build strong, legitimate, and democratic states have often proved illusory. International actors seem incapable of stabilizing failed states and establishing political order in places like Iraq, Somalia, and the Democratic Republic of the Congo, where alternative forms of governance persist. If my theory is correct, international efforts to consolidate states might in fact be futile, as political arrangements between state and nonstate actors always remain in flux.[30] The persistence of alternative forms of governance points to the inconsistencies and limits of contemporary state-building and counterinsurgency strategies conceived as zero-sum situations in which either the state or the rebels rule. It creates a dilemma that policymakers seriously need to acknowledge.

The book's findings also invite us to question the nature of power and authority in the international system. In *Warlord Survival*, I investigate the nature of international society in light of continuing efforts to homogenize the exercise of power within it, through state building in particular. I reject

Arnold Wolfers's realist vision of the state as a "billiard ball" whose individual properties have little effect on its behavior in the international system.[31] Following Hendrik Spruyt, I posit that "unit type influences international relations [and that a] change in the constitutive elements of the system means a change in the structure of the system."[32] Hence, I conclude that the nature of the Afghan state impacts the nature of the international system itself. In sum, the international environment that warlords have to face is not strictly determined by the structure of the international system, as often assumed, but also by the warlords' actions, as they figure out how to adapt and shape their state to suit their interests.[33] Warlords are not subjects but actors of the international system. They have the ability to conduct international relations and can benefit from and manipulate interactions with foreign actors. This gives them the ability to craft new bases for their authority and reinvent themselves once they lose control over their territories. All in all, this should hint at a bright future for Afghan warlords in the more flexible post-2014 environment.

How to Deal with Warlords?

These findings have important policy implications. The "paper tiger" argument discussed in the book's introduction suggests that warlords are created by states and that the international community should just "punch these guys in the face."[34] I show throughout this work that, no matter how hard one punches them, they always come back. Warlords and other nonstate armed actors cannot be disregarded, nor can they be circumvented, until a generational change actually takes place. Once foreign governments decide to intervene, they have no choice but to engage with them. As the journalist Aryn Baker said back in 2009: "The warlords are not our kind of guys, especially for our public opinion, but we have to work with what we've got. . . . We need to stop focusing on getting the Dostums out."[35]

In fact, there is no reason to believe that contemporary warlords, whether in Afghanistan or elsewhere, will simply disappear under accrued state pressure. While the development of the absolutist state in Western Europe is often cited as the ultimate case of state domination over societal forces—against which to assess all state formation processes—even that case is not so clear-cut. The British historian Perry Anderson notes that "absolutism was essentially just this: *a redeployed and recharged apparatus of feudal domination*, designed to clamp the peasant masses back into their traditional social position."[36] In the end, "the ruling class remained the same."[37] This also goes for contemporary warlords. In spite of all their struggles and fighting, they often constitute a "political class" tied together by the solidarity of its members.[38]

Afghan warlords formed alliances in the past, both in times of war—for instance, when Dostum pledged allegiance to Massoud in the fight against the Taliban—and in times of peace. In March 2007, several warlords, including Ismail Khan, Dostum, and Fahim, formed the United National Front (UNF), a political alliance aimed at promoting a general amnesty for war crimes and protecting its members against the Karzai government. In the words of one Afghan source, as reported in *Jane's Intelligence Digest*: "These men are preparing to defend themselves against Karzai, the Taliban or anyone else. If the centre weakens, they are aligning themselves for another civil war."[39] In 2008, following the Akbar Bai episode and the criticisms voiced against Dostum, Fahim, then first vice president, called the siege of the Uzbek general's house "intolerable" and the UNF spokesman warned that the government's actions could harm stability in the country.[40] Given the confusion surrounding post-2014 Afghanistan, warlords will undoubtedly unite again if and when needed.

Adib Fahim explains: "Generally speaking, a broad political identification of the country post-2001 is that people who served during the jihad and were important to topple the Taliban [form] one political camp. Another camp is made of people coming from the West (who were out of the country when the country needed them most)." Asked whether the members of this first camp would come together if needed, he replied: "That's what the past seventeen years has shown. That's what they do."[41] And indeed, in the summer of 2017, amid continued criticism of President Ashraf Ghani, Dostum (first vice president), Ata (governor of Balkh Province), Mohaqiq (deputy chief executive officer), and Salahuddin Rabbani (minister of foreign affairs, head of Jamiat-i Islami, and son of late Burhanuddin Rabbani), some of whom are longtime rivals and have fought on opposite sides of battles, formed a new political alliance to oppose the very government they belonged to.[42]

Rather than developing highly ambitious and intrusive social engineering projects aimed at neutralizing alternative forms of governance, Western policymakers should question their conceptions of states and governance and revise their state-building agendas.[43] They need to accept that external state building aimed at establishing Weberian institutions, as currently conceived, is doomed to fail, at least in the short term. States need to develop more inclusionary forms of governance to give warlords and their constituencies just enough incentives to "play the state-building game" while trying not to build them up unnecessarily.[44] They should encourage warlords to provide goods and services to their communities while developing new forms of accountability. In practice, this balancing act is extremely difficult to perform. Identifying, training, and supporting local nonstate armed actors that exercise capacities to control populations and collect information almost always has unanticipated long-term consequences. Policymakers should carefully weigh the pros and cons before they adopt strategies of indirect irregular warfare aimed at building up local militias to defeat the so-called Islamic State and other radical Islamist groups in Somalia, Nigeria, Mali, and elsewhere—a lesson that applies equally to non-Western counterinsurgents operating in places like Syria and Iraq.

Can warlords be integrated into twenty-first-century state building? The warlords' phoenix-like tendencies suppose that state building can be successful only if it actually involves the incorporation and absorption of their social capital and networks on terms useful to states rather than their simple defeat and replacement by state authority.[45] State builders should acknowledge this not only because they have to but also because "embeddedness provides sources of intelligence and channels of implementation that enhance the competence of the state."[46] This is even more the case if one agrees with Haruhiro Fukui that "an important function of informal politics is to fill in lacunae in the reach of formal politics" and that "[this] function is particularly critical in organizations with a weak tradition of the rule of law," such as the Afghan state.[47]

All these challenges and pitfalls should encourage foreign governments and international agencies to consider the possibility that "under some circumstances, less international intervention may actually lead to more stable political arrangements and state structures."[48] Jeremy Weinstein calls this a process of *"autonomous recovery* in which states achieve a lasting peace, a systematic reduction in violence, and post-war political and economic development in the absence of international intervention."[49] In fact, external military intervention often leads to political instability and in most cases fails to foster state consolidation, instead empowering and creating ties with the ones it aims to weaken. When the international community finds it necessary to intervene, it should not aim to build institutions and empower specific decision-making bodies. Rather, it must foster virtuous mechanisms of nonviolent dispute resolution and take steps to empower local populations (that both warlords and state elites need to be accountable to) so that they can engage in genuine and indigenous processes of state formation.

NOTES

Introduction

1. As Barfield notes: "No one has ever really agreed on Afghanistan's population." Thomas Barfield, *Afghanistan: A Cultural and Political History* (Princeton, NJ: Princeton University Press, 2010), 23. One usually distinguishes among four main (ethnic) groups: the Pashtuns, historically and politically dominant, make up about 40 percent of the country's population; the Tajiks form a Persian-speaking group that composes about 30 percent of the population; the Hazaras, unlike the other Afghan groups, are predominantly Shia Muslims and constitute about 15 percent of the population; and the Uzbeks and Turkmens are two Turkic groups that, together, make up about 10 percent of the population. Other smaller groups include the Aimaqs, the Nuristanis, the Baluch, and the Kirghiz (Barfield, 23–31). In this book, *Tajik*, *Turkmen*, and *Uzbek* are not used to designate people from Tajikistan, Turkmenistan, and Uzbekistan, respectively, unless specifically indicated.

2. Paul Jackson, "Warlords as Alternative Forms of Governance," *Small Wars & Insurgencies* 14, no. 2 (Summer 2003): 131–50. For a critical view of warlords and governance, see Kimberly Marten, "Warlords and Governance," in *The Transnational Governance of Violence and Crime: Non-State Actors in Security*, ed. Anja P. Jakobi and Klaus Dieter Wolf (Basingstoke, UK: Palgrave Macmillan, 2013), 22–39.

3. Quoted in David Blair, "SAS Peace Deal Helps Tame the Warlords," *Telegraph*, July 9, 2002.

4. Keith Stanski, "'So These Folks Are Aggressive': An Orientalist Reading of 'Afghan Warlords,'" *Security Dialogue* 40, no. 1 (2009): 73.

5. In this book, I tried to use the English spelling of Persian names used by the actors themselves or, when non-applicable, the spelling most commonly used. For Persian names, I followed the transliteration guide of the *International Journal of Middle East Studies* for general guidelines, albeit in simplified and modified form.

6. Conversation with Afghan scholar 1, 2007. Several interviewees mentioned that, to their knowledge, the word *jangsalar* had not been used (or used so rarely that they were not aware of it) before 2001, if not before the 1990s.

7. John MacKinlay, "Defining Warlords," in *Peacekeeping and Conflict Resolution*, ed. Tom Woodhouse and Oliver Ramsbotham (London: Frank Cass, 2000), 55, 59.

8. On spoilers, see Stephen J. Stedman, "Spoiler Problems in Peace Processes," *International Security* 22, no. 2 (Autumn 1997): 5–53; Ken Menkhaus, "Governance without Government in Somalia: Spoilers, State Building, and the Politics of Coping," *International Security* 31, no. 3 (Winter 2006/07): 74–106; Edward Newman and Oliver Richmond, "Obstacles to Peace Processes: Understanding Spoiling," in *Challenges to Peacebuilding: Managing Spoilers during Conflict Resolution*, ed. Edward Newman and Oliver Richmond (New York: United Nations University Press, 2006), 1–19.

9. Stanski, "'So These Folks Are Aggressive,'" 91. For a similar approach, see Ariel I. Ahram and Charles King, "The Warlord as Arbitrageur," *Theory and Society* 41, no. 2 (2012): 169–86.

10. Kimberly Marten, *Warlords: Strong-Arm Brokers in Weak States* (Ithaca, NY: Cornell University Press, 2012), 4. For a typology of Afghan armed groups, see Michael Bhatia, "Armed Groups in Afghanistan," in *Afghanistan, Arms and Conflict: Armed Groups, Disarmament and Security in a Post-War Society*, ed. Michael Bhatia and Mark Sedra (New York: Routledge, 2008), 77.

11. Referring to warlords as violent political entrepreneurs is not to say that they are necessarily engaged in violence themselves, but that (the threat of) violence by them or their supporters is a key component of their exercise of authority.

12. Michael Weiss and Hassan Hassan, *ISIS: Inside the Army of Terror*, 2nd ed. (New York: Regan Arts, 2016), 53–54.

13. William Reno, *Corruption and State Politics in Sierra Leone* (New York: Cambridge University Press, 1995), 178. On Taylor and "Taylorland," see also William Reno, *Warlord Politics and African States* (Boulder, CO: Lynne Rienner, 1998), chap. 3.

14. On unstable environments and short-term interests, see Lucian Pye, *Warlord Politics: Conflict and Coalition in the Modernization of Republican China* (New York: Praeger, 1971), 10, 77–112. On side switching in civil war, see, for example, Fotini Christia, *Alliance Formation in Civil Wars* (New York: Cambridge University Press, 2012); Lee J. M. Seymour, "Why Factions Switch Sides in Civil Wars: Rivalry, Patronage, and Realignment in Sudan," *International Security* 39, no. 2 (Fall 2014): 92–131; Sabine Otto, "The Grass Is Always Greener? Armed Group Side Switching in Civil Wars," *Journal of Conflict Resolution* 62, no. 7 (2018): 1459–88.

15. John Lee Anderson, "The Unravelling: In a Failing State, an Anti-Islamist General Mounts a Divisive Campaign," *New Yorker*, February 23, 2015. Accessed online.

16. Mike Martin, *An Intimate War: An Oral History of the Helmand Conflict* (New York: Oxford University Press, 2014), 54–55.

17. Robert I. Rotberg, "Failed States in a World of Terror," *Foreign Affairs* 81, no. 4 (2002): 128. For the purpose of this book, I use the terms *failed* and *collapsed states* interchangeably, the latter being usually considered "a rare and extreme version" of the former (Rotberg, 133). For critiques and further conceptualization of "failed state" and "state failure," see Jennifer Milliken and Keith Krause, "State Failure, State Collapse, and State Reconstruction: Concepts, Lessons and Strategies," *Development and Change* 33, no. 5 (2002): 753–74; Michael J. Mazarr, "The Rise and Fall of the Failed-State Paradigm: Requiem for a Decade of Distraction," *Foreign Affairs* 93, no. 1 (2014): 113–21; Susan L. Woodward, *The Ideology of Failed States: Why Intervention Fails* (New York: Cambridge University Press, 2017). Here I also build on the concept of limited statehood to distinguish between states and areas of statehood, rather than assuming the homogenous exercise of state authority across territories. See Thomas Risse, *Governance without a State? Policies and Politics in Areas of Limited Statehood* (New York: Columbia University Press, 2011).

18. Marten, *Warlords*, 7. See also Sasha Lezhnev, *Crafting Peace: Strategies to Deal with Warlords in Collapsing States* (Lanham, MD: Lexington Books, 2005); Laura Freeman, "The African Warlord Revisited," *Small Wars & Insurgencies* 26, no. 5 (2015): 790–810.

19. Reno, *Warlord Politics*, 2. See also Joel S. Migdal, *Strong Societies and Weak States: State-Society Relations and State Capabilities in the Third World* (Princeton, NJ: Princeton University Press, 1988).

20. Interview with resident of Hargeisa, Somaliland, 2014. A Kabul-based analyst used the same image for Dostum, describing him as "more skillful than many warlords because he is changing his colours." Quoted in Hamida Ghafour, "Warlord with Shifting Loyalties 'Hero of Peace' in Afghan Vote," *Globe and Mail*, October 7, 2004.

21. Marten, *Warlords*, 4.

22. Patrick Chabal and Jean-Pascal Daloz, *Africa Works: Disorder as Political Instrument* (Bloomington: Indiana University Press, 1999); Bertrand Badie, *Le diplomate et l'intrus: L'entrée des sociétés dans l'arène internationale* (Paris: Fayard, 2008).

23. Stathis N. Kalyvas, *The Logic of Violence in Civil War* (New York: Cambridge University Press, 2006), 111.

24. Stephen D. Krasner, *Sovereignty: Organized Hypocrisy* (Princeton, NJ: Princeton University Press, 1999), 3–4.

25. Joel S. Migdal, *State in Society: Studying How States and Societies Transform and Constitute One Another* (Cambridge, UK: Cambridge University Press, 2001), 16.

26. Jean-François Médard, "L'État patrimonialisé," *Politique africaine* 39 (1990): 27 (translated by the author). It should be noted that Médard makes this argument in the context of African states, not of the Afghan state. For similar arguments, see also James Ferguson and Akil Gupta, "Spatializing States: Toward an Ethnography of Neoliberal Governmentality," *American Ethnologist* 29, no. 4 (2002): 981–1002; Joel S. Migdal and Klaus Schlichte, "Rethinking the State," in *The Dynamics of States: The Formation and Crises of State Domination*, ed. Klaus Schlichte (Aldershot, UK: Ashgate, 2005), 1–40.

Coburn observes that, in certain contexts, the Afghan state is not a symbolic reality but a "useful fiction" that people purposely maintain. See Noah Coburn, *Bazaar Politics: Power and Pottery in an Afghan Market Town* (Stanford, CA: Stanford University Press, 2011), chap. 8.

27. Michael Semple, "The Revival of the Afghan Taliban 2001–2011," *Orient* 2 (2012): 58.

28. Timothy Earle, *How Chiefs Come to Power: The Political Economy in Prehistory* (Stanford, CA: Stanford University Press, 1997), 3 (first quote); Robert A. Dahl, *Modern Political Analysis* (Englewood Cliffs, NJ: Prentice-Hall, 1963), 40 (second quote); Alex Weingrod, "Patronage and Power," in *Patrons and Clients in Mediterranean Societies*, ed. Ernest Gellner and John Waterbury (London: Duckworth, 1977), 43 (third quote).

29. Zachariah Cherian Mampilly, *Rebel Rulers: Insurgent Governance and Civilian Life during War* (Ithaca, NY: Cornell University Press, 2011), 52.

30. G. Whitney Azoy, *Buzkashi: Game and Power in Afghanistan* (Philadelphia: University of Pennsylvania Press, 1982), 23, 35, 23, 22, 25, 25. This circular definition of power in Afghanistan is also identified by Coburn: "Power, for a malik or an elder, was circular; such a figure's ability to wield influence came from his ability to perform these duties and to mobilize the resources and the respect of his community. The more honor a man had, the more men and resources he could mobilize" (*Bazaar Politics*, 112).

31. For examples of the "paper tiger" argument, see Sarah Chayes, *The Punishment of Virtue: Inside Afghanistan after the Taliban* (New York: Penguin, 2006), 227; Marten, *Warlords*, 2.

32. Ahram and King, "The Warlord as Arbitrageur," 174.

33. Marten, *Warlords*, 3, 2.

34. Interview with Thomas Barfield, Afghanistan scholar, October 27, 2011.

35. Abdulkader H. Sinno, *Organizations at War: In Afghanistan and Beyond* (Ithaca, NY: Cornell University Press, 2008).

36. Paul Staniland, *Networks of Rebellion: Explaining Insurgent Cohesion and Collapse* (Ithaca, NY: Cornell University Press, 2014); Sarah Zukerman Daly, *Organized Violence after Civil War: The Geography of Recruitment in Latin America* (New York: Cambridge University Press, 2016); Christopher Day, *The Fates of African Rebels: Victory, Defeat, and the Politics of Civil War* (Boulder, CO: Lynne Rienner, 2019).

37. Day, *Fates of African Rebels*.

38. For an excellent review and critical discussion of organizational approaches in the civil war literature, see Sarah E. Parkinson and Sherry Zaks, "Militant and Rebel Organization(s)," *Comparative Politics* 50, no. 2 (2018): 271–90.

39. Staniland, for example, acknowledges that his theory is not well suited to explain complex warlord politics and the fluidity of collapsed states: "The book's claims are less likely to apply to armed groups emerging from state collapse in a situation where parts of the state itself become non-state armed groups (they usually become 'warlords'). . . . My analysis ends when insurgent groups sign a peace deal that demobilizes them as fighting forces; when they abandon violence in favor of party politics, crime, or collusive arrangements with the state; or when they are wiped out" (*Networks of Rebellion*, 10–11).

40. Marielle Debos, *Living by the Gun in Chad: Combatants, Impunity and State Formation* (London: Zed Books, 2016), 9.

41. See Migdal, *Strong Societies and Weak States*.

42. Azoy, *Buzkashi*, 1982, 30.

43. Ashraf Ghani and Clare Lockhart, *Fixing Failed States: A Framework for Rebuilding a Fractured World* (New York: Oxford University Press, 2009), 133.

44. Martine van Bijlert, "Imaginary Institutions: State-Building in Afghanistan," in *Doing Good or Doing Better: Development Policies in a Globalizing World*, ed. Monique Kremer, Peter van Lieshout, and Robert Went (The Hague: Amsterdam University Press, 2009), 159. For a counterargument, see Bermeo and Bhatia's study of leadership preferences in Afghanistan, which suggests that, "contrary to scholarship arguing in favor of public support for traditional warlord candidates, voters across a range of age and socioeconomic groups prefer highly educated younger leaders," regardless of the circumstances. Nancy Bermeo and Jasmine Bhatia, "Strongmen or Technocrats? Experimental Evidence Testing Leadership Preferences in Afghanistan" (International Growth Centre Report, London, 2017), 16.

45. Quoted in Sinno, *Organizations at War*, 267.

46. Habibullah Khan, district governor of Nad-i Ali, Helmand Province, quoted in Martin, *An Intimate War*, 178. On Mir Wali, see Martin, 141. For another example of similar practices, see Jean-Christophe Notin, *La guerre de l'ombre des Français en Afghanistan 1979–2011* (Paris: Fayard, 2011), 772–73. Chayes argues that warlords do not provide security but are "actually the source of *in*security." She goes as far as to claim that Gul Agha Sherzai was "carefully regulating the flow of extremism" in Kandahar, "never fully cutting it off," for it enabled him to exploit his relationships with Pakistan and the United States simultaneously (Chayes, *Punishment of Virtue*, 268). These strategies are similar to the creation of protection rackets described by Tilly (Charles Tilly, "War Making and State Making as Organized Crime," in *Bringing the State Back In*, ed. Peter Evans, Dietrich Rueschemeyer, and Theda Skocpol [Cambridge, UK: Cambridge University Press, 1985], 169–91) and to the practices of "orchestrated blackmail" identified by Badie (Bertrand Badie, *L'impuissance de la puissance: Essai sur les nouvelles relations internationales* [Paris: Fayard, 2004], 173, translated by the author).

47. Alex de Waal, *The Real Politics of the Horn of Africa: Money, War and the Business of Power* (Cambridge, UK: Polity, 2015).

48. Van Bijlert, "Imaginary Institutions," 160.

49. Martin, *An Intimate War*, 129, 134.

50. Azoy, *Buzkashi*, 1982, 28. Here Azoy does not describe warlords but khans. I explain in chap. 2 how warlords have come to replace khans in post-2001 Afghanistan.

51. Antonio Giustozzi, *Empires of Mud: Wars and Warlords in Afghanistan* (New York: Columbia University Press, 2009), 5.

52. Van Bijlert, "Imaginary Institutions," 162.

53. James C. Scott, "Prestige as the Public Discourse of Domination," *Cultural Critique* 12 (Spring 1989): 146.

54. Bruce Berman and John Lonsdale, *Unhappy Valley: Conflict in Kenya and Africa* (London: James Currey, 1992), 15. Here I diverge from Berman and Lonsdale's definition of state building as "a deliberate means to contain and direct power for the benefit of the few" (Berman and Lonsdale, 15). I adopt instead Migdal's perspective with regard to the creation of an "overpowering" organization (Migdal, *Strong Societies and Weak States*, 24).

55. Jackson, "Warlords as Alternative Forms of Governance," 147. See also Pye, *Warlord Politics*, 3–4. Although the term *warlord* is subject to controversy and used as a political and normative label, its familiarity, resonance, and theoretical utility are particularly valuable for the study of state-building and state formation processes. The term designates a specific category of actors whose relationships with the state remain largely underresearched. See Antonio Giustozzi, "Don't Call That Warlord a Warlord," *Foreign Policy*, February 25, 2010; Marten, *Warlords*, 3–7.

56. On state formation in Western Europe, see Charles Tilly, *Coercion, Capital, and European States, AD 990–1990* (Malden, MA: Blackwell, 1990); Philippe Contamine, "The Growth of State Control. Practices of War, 1300–1800: Ransom and Booty," in *War and Competition between States*, ed. Philippe Contamine (New York: Oxford University Press, 2000), 163–93.

57. Dipali Mukhopadhyay, *Warlords, Strongman Governors, and the State in Afghanistan* (New York: Cambridge University Press, 2014).

58. On related topics, see the concepts of vulgarization of power (Berman and Lonsdale, *Unhappy Valley*, 5), reciprocal assimilation of elites (Jean-François Bayart, *The State in Africa: The Politics of the Belly* [London: Longman, 1993], 150–79), and imported state (Bertrand Badie, *The Imported State: The Westernization of the Political Order* [Stanford, CA: Stanford University Press, 2000]). See also Jean-François Bayart, ed., *La greffe de l'État: Les trajectoires du politique, 2* (Paris: Karthala, 1996).

59. Chabal and Daloz, *Africa Works*, 155. In the Afghan political context, see also van Bijlert, "Imaginary Institutions"; Haseeb Humayoon, *The Re-election of Hamid Karzai* (Washington, DC: Institute for the Study of War, 2010).

60. Bayart, *The State in Africa*, 220. On political networks in Afghanistan, see Timor Sharan, "The Dynamics of Elite Networks and Patron-Client Relations in Afghanistan," *Europe-Asia Studies* 63, no. 6 (2011): 1109–27; Timor Sharan, "The Network Politics of International Statebuilding: Intervention and Statehood in Post-2001 Afghanistan" (PhD diss., University of Exeter, UK, 2013); Timor Sharan and Srinjoy Bose, "Political Networks and the 2014 Afghan Presidential Election: Power Restructuring, Ethnicity and State Stability," *Conflict, Security & Development* 16, no. 6 (2016): 613–33.

61. Due to the sensitivity of the research topic, I anonymized most of the interviews (even when the interviewees gave me permission to mention their names). I provided the names of the interviewees and the dates I conducted the interviews on only when the names of the interviewees were important for context, and only if these actors were high-ranking officials or political elites who would not have to worry about the consequences of their names appearing in this book (and, of course, only when given permission to do so). To further limit the possibility of identifying the interviewees, I also bundled all sources of background information together at the end of each section, and mentioned specific interviews only when these were used for quotes. Finally, I did not specify whether the quotes were translated and did not provide any indication of which language they were translated from. In addition to field research and interviews, I used LexisNexis to build a broad database of news reports related to Ismail Khan, Dostum, Massoud, and Fahim. These reports were all consulted in English, even though they were often origi-

nally in other languages. All foreign titles and names of foreign television and radio channels are referenced as they appear on LexisNexis.

62. For more on the challenges of conducting such research, see Romain Malejacq and Dipali Mukhopadhyay, "The 'Tribal Politics' of Field Research: A Reflection on Power and Partiality in 21st-Century Warzones," *Perspectives on Politics* 14, no. 4 (2016): 1011–28.

63. Jesse Driscoll, *Warlords and Coalition Politics in Post-Soviet States* (New York: Cambridge University Press, 2015), 86. See also Driscoll, 159–66. For a critical discussion of Driscoll's model, see Jennifer Brick Murtazashvili, Anastasia Shesterinina, Suzanne Levi-Sanchez, Timothy Blauvelt, and Jesse Driscoll, "Warlords and Coalition Politics in Post-Soviet States, by Jesse Driscoll," *Caucasus Survey* 6, no. 2 (2018): 163–81. For other formal game theoretic approaches of warlord politics, see Stergios Skaperdas, "Warlord Competition," *Journal of Peace Research* 39, no. 4 (2002): 435–46; Gordon H. Mccormick and Lindsay Fritz, "The Logic of Warlord Politics," *Third World Quarterly* 30, no. 1 (2009): 81–112.

64. As Simmons and Smith point out, "Researchers can take *the process* through which a given outcome is produced as the object of inquiry . . . rather than explaining a given outcome." Erica S. Simmons and Nicholas Rush Smith, "Comparison with an Ethnographic Sensibility," *PS: Political Science & Politics* 50, no. 1 (2017): 128.

65. See Alexander L. George and Andrew Bennett, *Case Studies and Theory Development in the Social Sciences* (Cambridge: MIT Press, 2005). Antonio Giustozzi and Noor Ullah explain the lack of strong warlords in southern Afghanistan as follows: "In this area, throughout the years of *jihad* and civil war, few warlords emerged, and few of those who did lasted very long. Since the general conditions brought about by the war in this area were similar to those of the rest of the country it appears obvious that the weak presence of warlords must be due to local factors. Even when former military commanders of the government became autonomous and seized local political power, their military structures could not be sustained in the long term." Antonio Giustozzi and Noor Ullah, "'Tribes' and Warlords in Southern Afghanistan, 1980–2005" (Crisis States Working Paper 7 [Series 2], London, 2006), 2. According to the authors, "The experience of southern Afghanistan suggests that warlords can only prosper in social environments that allow them to easily acquire political control over a territory. It is the intrinsic political role of the tribes that prevented warlordism from finding a fertile ground" (Giustozzi and Ullah, 17). Malkasian's analysis of Garmser District, in the southern province of Helmand, confirms their argument: "The power of a tribal leader tended to end within the tribe, if not within his cluster of villages. Few tribal leaders succeeded in having influence beyond their tribe, let alone reaching across the people of Garmser and uniting them behind him." Carter Malkasian, *War Comes to Garmser: Thirty Years of Conflict on the Afghan Frontier* (New York: Oxford University Press, 2016), 9.

66. Interview with Antonio Giustozzi, Afghanistan scholar, October 11, 2008; see also Antonio Giustozzi, "Respectable Warlords? The Politics of State-Building in Post-Taleban Afghanistan" (Crisis States Working Paper 33 [Series 1], London, 2003).

1. Warlords, States, and Political Orders

1. Interview with international relations adviser to the first vice president of Afghanistan, 2015.

2. Joel S. Migdal, *Strong Societies and Weak States: State-Society Relations and State Capabilities in the Third World* (Princeton, NJ: Princeton University Press, 1988), 34. See also Joel S. Migdal, *State in Society: Studying How States and Societies Transform and Constitute One Another* (Cambridge, UK: Cambridge University Press, 2001). Brick Murtazashvili's in-depth work on Afghanistan's customary governance further challenges "assumptions of the 'state and society' approach, which posit an inherent conflict between modernizing states and customary order." Jennifer Brick Murtazashvili, *Informal Order and the State in Afghanistan* (New York: Cambridge University Press, 2016), 17.

3. On Chinese warlords, see James E. Sheridan, *Chinese Warlord: The Career of Feng Yü-Hsiang* (Stanford, CA: Stanford University Press, 1966); Lucian Pye, *Warlord Politics: Conflict and Coalition in the Modernization of Republican China* (New York: Praeger, 1971); Hsi-Sheng Chi, *Warlord Politics in China, 1916–1928* (Stanford, CA: Stanford University Press, 1976); Diana Lary, "Warlord Studies," *Modern China* 6, no. 4 (1980): 439–70; Prasenjit Duara, "State Involution: A Study of Local Finances in North China, 1911–1935," *Comparative Studies of Society and History* 29, no. 1 (1987): 132–61; J. A. G. Roberts, "Warlordism in China," *Review of African Political Economy* 45/46 (1989): 26–33; Arthur Waldron, "The Warlord: Twentieth-Century Chinese Understandings of Violence, Militarism, and Imperialism," *American Historical Review* 96, no. 4 (2011): 1073–1100.

4. Kimberly Marten, "Warlordism in Comparative Perspective," *International Security* 31, no. 3 (Winter 2006/07): 48. For the first approach, see, for example, Roger Charlton and Roy May, "Warlordism and Militarism in Chad," *Review of African Political Economy* 45/46 (1989): 12–25; William Reno, *Warlord Politics and African States* (Boulder, CO: Lynne Rienner, 1998).

5. Ariel I. Ahram and Charles King, "The Warlord as Arbitrageur," *Theory and Society* 41, no. 2 (2012): 171. On variation in types of warlordism and a reconceptualization of the term *warlord*, see Laura Freeman, "The African Warlord Revisited," *Small Wars & Insurgencies* 26, no. 5 (2015): 790–810.

6. Freeman, 796.

7. Roy argues that these men's ultimate goal, in the post-2001 context, is not to destroy their enemies or force the coalition forces to leave, but to push for a new, more favorable balance of power, under state authority, and state mediation, when required. See Olivier Roy, "Afghanistan: La difficile reconstruction d'un Etat," *Cahier de Chaillot* 73, no. 1 (2004): 37–38. In an interview conducted on October 5, 2011, former US ambassador to Afghanistan Robert Finn also argued that warlords did not want the United States to leave, because then "the money would run out."

8. This does not mean that they are necessarily rebels. Some warlords have tried to overthrow or break away from the regime; they are former rebels (which does not imply that all rebels have the ability to become warlords). Others have not; they have never rebelled.

9. On Russian warlords, see Adam B. Ulam, *A History of Soviet Russia* (New York: Praeger, 1976), 36–43; Alexandre Skirda, *Nestor Makhno: Anarchy's Cossack* (Chico, CA:

AK, 2004); Evan Mawdsley, *The Russian Civil War* (Edinburgh: Birlinn, 2008), 143–48; Jamie Bisher, *White Terror: Cossack Warlords of the Trans-Siberian* (London: Routledge, 2009).

10. John Lee Anderson, "The Unravelling: In a Failing State, an Anti-Islamist General Mounts a Divisive Campaign," *New Yorker*, February 23, 2015. Accessed online.

11. Antonio Giustozzi, "The Debate on Warlordism" (Crisis States Discussion Paper 13, London, 2005), 8.

12. Christopher Clapham, *Africa and the International System: The Politics of State Survival* (Cambridge, UK: Cambridge University Press, 1996), 19. On the politics of international recognition, see Bridget Coggins, "Friends in High Places: International Politics and the Emergence of States from Secessionism," *International Organization* 65, no. 3 (Summer 2011): 433–67. Krasner defines international legal sovereignty as "the practices associated with mutual recognition, usually between territorial entities that have formal juridical independence." Stephen D. Krasner, *Sovereignty: Organized Hypocrisy* (Princeton, NJ: Princeton University Press, 1999), 3. For a definition of domestic sovereignty, see this book's introduction.

13. Phillip Liu, "Cross-Strait Scramble for Africa: A Hidden Agenda in China-Africa Cooperation Forum," *Harvard Asia Quarterly* 5, no. 2 (2001): 1–9.

14. On the importance of controlling Kabul, see Gilles Dorronsoro, "Kabul at War (1992–1996): State, Ethnicity and Social Classes," *South Asia Multidisciplinary Academic Journal*, 2007. Accessed online.

15. Kimberly Marten, *Warlords: Strong-Arm Brokers in Weak States* (Ithaca, NY: Cornell University Press, 2012), 3.

16. Marten, 103.

17. John Waterbury, "An Attempt to Put Patrons and Clients in Their Place," in *Patrons and Clients in Mediterranean Societies*, ed. Ernest Gellner and John Waterbury (London: Duckworth, 1977), 332. "The desired good may simply be to be left alone or protected from a worse fate than is one's own already, or it may be of a more positive nature consisting in material rewards or strategic resources" (Waterbury, 332). It should be noted that Waterbury writes here of patronage networks in general, not specifically of those of warlords.

18. Jean-François Médard, "Le 'big man' en Afrique: Esquisse d'analyse du politicien entrepreneur," *Année sociologique* 42 (1992): 167–92; Jean-François Médard, "Le système politique bordelais (le 'système Chaban')," *Revue internationale de politique comparée* 13, no. 4 (2006): 657–79.

19. Ernest Gellner, "Patrons and Clients," in *Patrons and Clients in Mediterranean Societies*, ed. Ernest Gellner and John Waterbury (London: Duckworth, 1977), 6.

20. Ahram and King, "The Warlord as Arbitrageur," 172.

21. Reno, *Warlord Politics*, 79–80.

22. On the US intervention in Afghanistan as an interaction process, see Yama Torabi, "State-, Nation- et Peace-Building comme processus de transactions: L'interaction des intervenants et des acteurs locaux sur le théâtre de l'intervention en Afghanistan, 2001–08" (PhD diss., Institut d'Études Politiques de Paris, 2009).

23. Ken Menkhaus, "The Rise of a Mediated State in Northern Kenya: The Wajir Story and Its Implications for State-Building," *Afrika* 21, no. 2 (2008): 30.

24. Jesse Driscoll, *Warlords and Coalition Politics in Post-Soviet States* (New York: Cambridge University Press, 2015), 10.

25. Daniel Chirot, "Concluding Talk" (talk given at the Empire and Nation Conference, University of California San Diego, December 5–7, 2003). Quoted in Karen Barkey, *Empire of Difference: The Ottomans in Comparative Perspective* (New York: Cambridge University Press, 2008), 12–13.

26. On the territorial logic of states, see Danny Hoffman, *The War Machines: Young Men and Violence in Sierra Leone and Liberia* (Durham, NC: Duke University Press, 2011). In Hoffman's words: "States dig trenches and plot straight lines. . . . States undertake projects of distinguishing the legal from the illegal, the legitimate from the illegitimate, the licit from the illicit. States territorialize" (8).

27. Hendrik Spruyt, "The Origins, Development, and Possible Decline of the Modern State," *Annual Review of Political Science* 5 (2002): 133.

28. Karen Barkey, *Bandits and Bureaucrats: The Ottoman Route to State Centralization* (Ithaca, NY: Cornell University Press, 1994), 10.

29. Barkey, *Empire of Difference*, 2.

30. Mark Duffield, "Post-Modern Conflict: Warlords, Post-Adjustment States and Private Protection," *Civil Wars* 1, no. 1 (Spring 1998): 89.

31. Cristian Cantir and Philip A. Schrodt, "Neomedievalism in the Twenty-First Century: Warlords, Gangs and Transnational Militarized Actors as a Challenge to Sovereign Preeminence" (paper presented at the Annual Convention of the International Studies Association, New Orleans, February 17–20, 2010), 35–36. See also Arnold Wolfers, *Discord and Collaboration: Essays on International Politics* (Baltimore: Johns Hopkins University Press, 1962), 242; Hedley Bull, *The Anarchical Society: A Study of Order in World Politics* (Basingstoke, UK: Macmillan, 1977), 245–46; Duffield, "Post-Modern Conflict," 69–71.

32. Edward Shils, *Political Development in the New States* (The Hague: Mouton, 1968), 10. According to Shils, "Modernity entails democracy and democracy in the new states must above all be equalitarian. To be modern is to be scientific. . . . Modernity requires national sovereignty. Modern means being Western without the onus of dependence on the West" (8–10).

33. Philippe Contamine, "The Growth of State Control. Practices of War, 1300–1800: Ransom and Booty," in *War and Competition between States*, ed. Philippe Contamine (New York: Oxford University Press, 2000), 164.

34. Quoted in Elaine Sciolino, "Afghan 'Dictator' Proposed in Leaked Cable," *New York Times*, October 3, 2008. Tilly already noted how the involvement of external actors in contemporary state making has altered the "state making by war making" process he described for Western Europe: "To a larger degree, states that have come into being recently through decolonization or through reallocations of territory by dominant states have acquired their military organization from outside, without the same internal forging of mutual constraints between rulers and ruled. To the extent that outside states continue to supply military goods and expertise in return for commodities, military alliance or both, the new states harbor powerful, unconstrained organisations that easily overshadow all other organizations within their territories. To the extent that outside states guarantee their boundaries, the managers of those military organisations exercise

extraordinary power within them. The advantages of military power become enormous, the incentives to seize power over the state as a whole by means of that advantage very strong." Charles Tilly, "War Making and State Making as Organized Crime," in *Bringing the State Back In*, ed. Peter Evans, Dietrich Rueschemeyer, and Theda Skocpol (New York: Cambridge University Press, 1985), 186.

35. For a comparison of warlords in medieval Europe, Republican China, Somalia, and Afghanistan, see Marten, "Warlordism in Comparative Perspective."

36. Perry Anderson, *Lineages of the Absolutist State* (London: NLB, 1974); Jean-François Bayart, "L'historicité de l' État importé," in *La greffe de l' État: Les trajectoires du politique, 2*, ed. Jean-François Bayart (Paris: Karthala, 1996), 11–39.

37. Thomas Barfield, *Afghanistan: A Cultural and Political History* (Princeton, NJ: Princeton University Press, 2010), 5.

38. According to Marcel Merle, an actor in the international system can be "any authority, body, group and even person likely to 'play a part' in social life—the international scene in the case in point." Marcel Merle, *The Sociology of International Relations* (New York: Berg, 1987), 253.

39. Stephen Chan, "The Warlord and Global Order," in *Warlords in International Relations*, ed. Paul B. Rich (Basingstoke, UK: Macmillan, 1999), 165; Paul B. Rich, "The Emergence and Significance of Warlordism in International Politics," in *Warlords in International Relations*, 1.

40. See, for example, Duffield, "Post-Modern Conflict"; Reno, *Warlord Politics*.

41. Bridget Coggins, "Rebel Diplomacy: Theorizing Violent Non-State Actors' Strategic Use of Talk," in *Rebel Governance in Civil War*, ed. Ana M. Arjona, Nelson Kasfir, and Zachariah Mampilly (New York: Cambridge University Press, 2015), 101.

42. Duffield, "Post-Modern Conflict," 81.

43. Paul Jackson, "Warlords as Alternative Forms of Governance," *Small Wars & Insurgencies* 14, no. 2 (Summer 2003): 132.

44. Jean-François Bayart, Stephen Ellis, and Béatrice Hibou, "From Kleptocracy to the Felonious State?," in *The Criminalization of the State in Africa*, ed. Jean-François Bayart, Stephen Ellis, and Béatrice Hibou (Oxford: James Currey, 1999), 1–31.

45. Mike Martin, *An Intimate War: An Oral History of the Helmand Conflict* (New York: Oxford University Press, 2014), 23, 120.

46. Sarah Chayes, *The Punishment of Virtue: Inside Afghanistan after the Taliban* (New York: Penguin, 2006), 181, 279.

47. For similar dynamics, see, for example, Béatrice Pouligny, *Ils nous avaient promis la paix: Opérations de l'ONU et populations locales* (Paris: Presses de Sciences Po, 2004); Michael Barnett and Christoph Zürcher, "The Peacebuilder's Contract: How External Statebuilding Reinforces Weak Statehood," in *The Dilemmas of Statebuilding: Confronting the Contradictions of Postwar Peace Operations*, ed. Roland Paris and Timothy D. Sisk (Abingdon, UK: Routledge, 2009), 23–52; Pierre Englebert and Denis M. Tull, "Post-conflict Reconstruction in Africa: Flawed Ideas about Failed States," *International Security* 32, no. 4 (Spring 2008): 106–39.

48. For similar descriptions, see Tobias Hagmann and Markus V. Höhne, "Failures of the State Failure Debate: Evidence from the Somali Territories," *Journal of International Development* 21 (2009): 46; James D. Fearon and David D. Laitin, "Neotrusteeship

and the Problem of Weak States," *International Security* 28, no. 4 (Spring 2014): 7. Reciprocally, states are more likely to consolidate in the absence of multiple competing actors. As Driscoll notes, "One can safely generalize that it was not simply a strong outside intervener tipping the military balance that cauterized the wars that broke out as the USSR collapsed—it was the *absence of multiple competing interveners*" (*Warlords and Coalition Politics*, 10).

49. Interview with former Western diplomat, 2011.

50. Paul Staniland, "States, Insurgents, and Wartime Political Orders," *Perspectives on Politics* 10, no. 2 (2012): 247.

51. Paul Staniland, *Networks of Rebellion: Explaining Insurgent Cohesion and Collapse* (Ithaca, NY: Cornell University Press, 2014), 139.

52. This definition is adapted from Jean-Patrice Lacam, "Le politicien investisseur: Un modèle d'interprétation de la gestion des ressources politiques," *Revue française de science politique* 38, no. 1 (1988): 27. On political resources, see also Robert A. Dahl, *Modern Political Analysis* (Englewood Cliffs, NJ: Prentice-Hall, 1963), 35.

53. For a detailed analysis of divide and rule as coup-proofing, see Driscoll, *Warlords and Coalition Politics*, chap. 5.

54. This is somehow similar to v* in Driscoll's game-theoretic model, which amounts to the lootable wealth in the state (v), increased by an influx of international assistance (*Warlords and Coalition Politics*, chap. 2). However, my typology also accounts for all symbolic and immaterial resources that come with control of the state apparatus.

55. Robert I. Rotberg, "Failed States in a World of Terror," *Foreign Affairs* 81, no. 4 (2002): 132.

56. Colin Elman, "Explanatory Typologies in Qualitative Studies of International Politics," *International Organization* 59, no. 2 (Spring 2005): 293–326.

57. Mancur Olson, "Dictatorship, Democracy, and Development," *American Political Science Review* 87, no. 3 (1993): 567.

58. Stathis N. Kalyvas, "The Changing Character of Civil Wars, 1800–2009," in *The Changing Character of War*, ed. Hew Strachan and Sibylle Scheipers (Oxford: Oxford University Press, 2011), 205.

59. On the fragmentation of political authority in Somalia and the abrupt loss of state resources that caused it at the end of the Cold War, see Aisha Ahmad, *Jihad & Co.: Black Markets and Islamist Power* (New York: Oxford University Press, 2017), chap. 5.

60. On the fragmentation of political authority and state failure, see William Reno, *Corruption and State Politics in Sierra Leone* (New York: Cambridge University Press, 1995); Robert H. Bates, "State Failure," *Annual Review of Political Science* 11 (2008): 1–12. On armed group fragmentation more specifically, see, for example, Victor Asal, Mitchell Brown, and Angela Dalton, "Why Split? Organizational Splits among Ethnopolitical Organizations in the Middle East," *Journal of Conflict Resolution* 56, no. 1 (2012): 94–117; Kristin M. Bakke, Kathleen Gallagher Cunningham, and Lee J. M. Seymour, "A Plague of Initials: Fragmentation, Cohesion, and Infighting in Civil Wars," *Perspectives on Politics* 10, no. 2 (2012): 265–83; Michael Findley and Peter J. Rudloff, "Combatant Fragmentation and the Dynamics of Civil War," *British Journal of Political Science* 42, no. 4 (2012): 879–901.

61. Freeman, "The African Warlord Revisited," 796. See also Charles Tilly, *Coercion, Capital, and European States, AD 990–1990* (Malden, MA: Blackwell, 1990); Dipali Mukhopadhyay, *Warlords, Strongman Governors, and the State in Afghanistan* (New York: Cambridge University Press, 2014).

62. On rebel governance, see, for example, Zachariah Cherian Mampilly, *Rebel Rulers: Insurgent Governance and Civilian Life during War* (Ithaca, NY: Cornell University Press, 2011); Isabelle Duyvesteyn, Georg Frerks, Boukje Kistemaker, Nora Stel, and Niels Terpstra, "Reconsidering Rebel Governance," in *African Frontiers: Insurgency, Governance and Peacebuilding in Postcolonial States*, ed. John Idriss Lahai and Tanya Lyons (Farnham, UK: Ashgate, 2015), 31–41; Ana Arjona, *Rebelocracy: Social Order in the Colombian Civil War* (New York: Cambridge University Press, 2016); Jeroen Adam, Bert Suykens, and Koen Vlassenroot, eds., *De Alledaagse Rebel: Tien Rebellengroepen in Het Zuiden* (Gent, Belgium: Academia, 2017).

63. Mancur Olson, *Power and Prosperity: Outgrowing Communist and Capitalist Dictatorships* (New York: Basic Books, 2000).

64. It should be noted that there is no consensus in the literature regarding the mechanisms connecting resource flows and armed group organizations. My theory is in line with Staniland's argument that armed groups with "strong preexisting ties can rapidly absorb and use large resource endowments without losing discipline." Paul Staniland, "Organizing Insurgency: Networks, Resources, and Rebellion in South Asia," *International Security* 37, no. 1 (Summer 2012): 174. I adopt a broad definition of resources and argue that warlords need not only external, commercial, and monetizable resources but also social and symbolic ones to avoid "[falling] prey to military ineffectiveness and internal conflict" (Staniland, 174).

65. Robert H. Jackson, *Quasi-states: Sovereignty, International Relations and the Third World* (Cambridge, UK: Cambridge University Press, 1990); Tilly, *Coercion, Capital, and European States*; Clapham, *Africa and the International System*.

66. Interview with Western diplomat 1, 2014.

67. Thomas Risse, "Governance in Areas of Limited Statehood: Introduction and Overview," in *Governance without a State? Policies and Politics in Areas of Limited Statehood*, ed. Thomas Risse (New York: Columbia University Press, 2011), 5.

68. Driscoll, *Warlords and Coalition Politics*, 1. Driscoll notes that in the case of Georgia and Tajikistan, it is not the actual influx of state resources but the promise of future rewards that led warlords to form ruling coalitions and engage in the state-building process. There, "the warlords became the state" (2). However, the state consolidation process that Driscoll describes is not a bureaucratization of state authority but a coup-proofing enterprise in which state leaders have successfully insulated themselves from militias that have "become *explicitly* part of the state, well positioned to contest their share of the rents of statehood" (181). Driscoll also stresses that, unlike the cases considered in this book, "even the most disadvantaged states on the Soviet periphery were 'born strong' in important respects" (4).

69. This is consistent with Barnett, Fang, and Zürcher's finding that "increasing resources is unlikely to produce a more liberal outcome unless the lack of resources is the principal constraint (which it rarely is)." Michael Barnett, Songying Fang, and

Christoph Zürcher, "Compromised Peacebuilding," *International Studies Quarterly* 58, no. 3 (2014): 610.

70. See Driscoll, *Warlords and Coalition Politics*.

71. Alex de Waal, "Dollarised: Alex de Waal Writes about the Political Marketplace," *London Review of Books* 32, no. 12 (2010): 41.

72. On process tracing, see Alexander L. George and Andrew Bennett, *Case Studies and Theory Development in the Social Sciences* (Cambridge: MIT Press, 2005), chap. 10; Jason Lyall, "Process Tracing, Causal Inference, and Civil War," in *Process Tracing: From Metaphor to Analytic Tool*, ed. Andrew Bennett and Jeffrey T. Checkel (Cambridge, UK: Cambridge University Press, 2014), 186–208.

73. The term *Pashtunistan* is used to describe the Pashtun tribal areas located astride Afghanistan and Pakistan. At the time of the partition of British India, in 1947, the government of Afghanistan argued that the Pashtun population, separated since the creation of the contested Durand line in 1893, should either be reattached to the Afghan state or given the opportunity to declare independence the same way India and Pakistan were, two potential outcomes that did not align with Pakistan's interest. Pakistan reacted to Daoud's Pashtunistan policy by backing the Afghan Islamists against the regime from 1975 onward. Worried that a pro-Soviet government would still want to claim Pashtunistan as its rightful territory, Pakistan continued to support Afghan Islamist parties throughout the 1980s. See Michael Barry, *Massoud: De l'islamisme à la liberté* (Paris: Audibert, 2002), 246–67; Barnett R. Rubin, *The Fragmentation of Afghanistan: State Formation and Collapse in the International System*, 2nd ed. (New Haven, CT: Yale University Press, 2002), 62, 88, 100; Barfield, *Afghanistan*, 48. The fragmentation of the Afghan resistance was made even more acute by the fact that Iran, predominantly Shia (as opposed to Afghanistan, where roughly 85 percent of the population is Sunni and 15 percent Shia), similarly recognized and supported eight Shia parties.

74. In the context of the Cold War, the United States launched a covert action program to support the Afghan mujahideen indirectly, through the Pakistani regime, which oversaw the money distribution. The United States increased its aid from $30 million in 1980 to $630 million in 1987, which was matched by Saudi Arabia for a total of about $1 billion. Rubin, *The Fragmentation of Afghanistan*, 179–83.

75. Fahim also belonged to Jamiat. He is not included here, because he did not operate as an active warlord.

76. Antonio Giustozzi, *Empires of Mud: Wars and Warlords in Afghanistan* (New York: Columbia University Press, 2009), 16.

77. On the Soviet withdrawal, see Artemy M. Kalinovsky, *A Long Goodbye: The Soviet Withdrawal from Afghanistan* (Cambridge: Harvard University Press, 2011). On the Soviet involvement in Afghanistan more generally, see Rodric Braithwaite, *Afgantsy: The Russians in Afghanistan 1979–89* (New York: Oxford University Press, 2011).

78. Rubin, *The Fragmentation of Afghanistan*.

79. Interview with former mujahideen government official, 2008. In his memoirs, Khalilzad recalls something similar: "Years later, Fahim told me a story that helped me understand his mindset. Well before 9/11, he and Massoud were discussing the future of Afghanistan. Massoud asked Fahim what kind of political arrangement would create a stable Afghanistan. Fahim waved off the question. When pressed, Fahim finally said,

'The reason we are not going anywhere is that you want to be the leader of Afghanistan. Tajiks, Uzbeks, and Hazaras might accept you, but we need the Pashtuns to buy in. That means that a Pashtun will have to be the number-one leader. Only then will they join forces and share power. However, you don't want to do that—you don't want to be the number two.' Massoud conceded that he wanted to be the top leader." Zalmay Khalilzad, *The Envoy: From Kabul to the White House, My Journey through a Turbulent World* (New York: St Martin's, 2016), 183. For further criticism of Massoud's treatment and perception of other ethnic groups, see Barry, *Massoud*, 47; Jean-Christophe Notin, *La guerre de l'ombre des Français en Afghanistan 1979–2011* (Paris: Fayard, 2011), 280, 387–88.

80. Among other authors belonging to this school of thought, see John Mearsheimer, "Back to the Future: Instability in Europe after the Cold War," *International Security* 15, no. 1 (Summer 1990): 5–56; Martin van Creveld, *The Transformation of War* (New York: Free Press, 1991); Robert Kaplan, "The Coming Anarchy," *Atlantic Monthly* 273, no. 2 (1994): 44–76. For a more detailed literature review on these authors, see Didier Bigo, "Nouveaux regards sur les conflits?," in *Les nouvelles relations internationales: Pratiques et théories*, ed. Marie Claude Smouts (Paris: Presses de Sciences Po, 1998), 309–54. The misunderstanding of violent conflicts by outsiders is nothing new. In 1971, Pye noted that Chinese warlords were already being depicted as irrational: "To Westerners, the scene was bizarre and could only make sense if treated as empty sound and fury" (*Warlord Politics*, 13).

81. On the concentration of power, see Gilles Dorronsoro, "Afghanistan: Des réseaux de solidarité aux espaces régionaux," in *Économie des guerres civiles*, ed. François Jean and Jean-Christophe Rufin (Paris: Hachette, 1996), 147–88.

82. William Reno, *Warfare in Independent Africa* (New York: Cambridge University Press, 2011), 30. See also Tilly, "War Making and State Making."

83. Martin, *An Intimate War*, 51, 79. For background information conveyed in this section, see Anthony Davis, "The Battleground of Northern Afghanistan," *Jane's Intelligence Review* 6, no. 7 (1994): 323–26; Assem Akram, *Histoire de la guerre d'Afghanistan* (Paris: Balland, 1996), 418; William Maley, *The Afghanistan Wars* (Basingstoke, UK: Palgrave Macmillan, 2002), 176; Rubin, *The Fragmentation of Afghanistan*, 271–74; Willem Vogelsang, *The Afghans* (Malden, MA: Wiley-Blackwell, 2002), 324–25; Steve Coll, *Ghost Wars: The Secret History of the CIA, Afghanistan and Bin Laden, from the Soviet Invasion to September 10, 2001* (London: Penguin Books, 2004), 237; Gilles Dorronsoro, *Revolution Unending: Afghanistan, 1979 to the Present* (New York: Columbia University Press, 2005), 239–43; Human Rights Watch, *Blood-Stained Hands: Past Atrocities in Kabul and Afghanistan's Legacy of Impunity* (New York: Human Rights Watch, 2005); Giustozzi, *Empires of Mud*, 11; Peter Tomsen, *The Wars of Afghanistan: Messianic Terrorism, Tribal Conflicts, and the Failures of Great Powers* (New York: Public Affairs, 2011), 487–91. See also Edward A. Gargan, "Afghan President Agrees to Step Down," *New York Times*, March 19, 1992; "Afghan Council Announced Rebels Chosen for Kabul Posts," *Globe and Mail*, April 25, 1992.

84. On side switching and group fractionalization during the Taliban era, see Fotini Christia, *Alliance Formation in Civil Wars* (New York: Cambridge University Press, 2012), 88–100; Martin, *An Intimate War*, 77–109.

85. Rubin, *The Fragmentation of Afghanistan*, xiii. On Taliban structures, see Anthony Davis, "How the Taliban Became a Military Force," in *Fundamentalism Reborn: Afghanistan and the Taliban*, ed. William Maley (New York: New York University Press, 1998), 55. For a study of the role of local business elites in building up the Taliban, see Ahmad, *Jihad & Co.*, chap. 4.

86. Some claim that the name Northern Alliance was given by Pakistani generals to depict the United Front as a regional alliance rather than a national one and therefore discredit it. See, for example, Barry, *Massoud*, 39.

87. On the limits of the Taliban state-building enterprise, see S. Yaqub Ibrahimi, "The Taliban's Islamic Emirate of Afghanistan (1996–2001): 'War-Making and State-Making' as an Insurgency Strategy," *Small Wars & Insurgencies* 28, no. 6 (2017): 947–72.

88. Stephen D. Biddle, "Allies, Airpower, and Modern Warfare: The Afghan Model in Afghanistan and Iraq," *International Security* 30, no. 3 (Winter 2005/06): 161.

89. Gary Berntsen and Ralph Pezzullo, *Jawbreaker: The Attack on Bin Laden and Al-Qaeda, a Personal Account by the CIA's Key Field Commander* (New York: Three Rivers, 2005); Gary C. Schroen, *First In: An Insider's Account of How the CIA Spearheaded the War on Terror in Afghanistan* (New York: Presidio, 2005); Doug Stanton, *Horse Soldiers: The Extraordinary Story of a Band of U.S. Soldiers Who Rode to Victory in Afghanistan* (New York: Scribner, 2009).

90. Giustozzi, *Empires of Mud*, 90.

91. Barfield, *Afghanistan*, 283, 294–97.

92. Eckart Schiewek, "Keeping the Peace without Peacekeepers," in *Building State and Security in Afghanistan*, ed. Wolfgang Danspeckgruber with Robert P. Finn (Princeton, NJ: Woodrow Wilson School of Public and International Affairs, 2007), 169, 188.

93. Ahmed Rashid, *Descent into Chaos: How the War against Islamic Extremism Is Being Lost in Pakistan, Afghanistan and Central Asia* (London: Allen Lane, 2008), 132.

94. Zalmay Khalilzad, "How to Nation-Build: Ten Lessons from Afghanistan," *National Interest*, July 18, 2005, 22. According to Rashid, the phrase *warlord strategy* was popularized by a 2002 Human Rights Watch report entitled *Afghanistan's Bonn Agreement, One Year Later, a Catalog of Missed Opportunities* (New York: Human Rights Watch, 2002). See Rashid, *Descent into Chaos*, 424.

95. William Taylor, quoted on "Rebuilding Afghanistan?," *CBS*'s *60 Minutes*, May 2, 2003.

96. Quoted on "Rebuilding Afghanistan?."

97. Michael Bhatia, "The Future of the Mujahideen: Legitimacy, Legacy and Demobilization in Post-Bonn Afghanistan," *International Peacekeeping* 14, no. 1 (2007): 94 (first quote); Khalilzad, "How to Nation-Build," 22–23 (second quote). See also Keith Stanski, "'So These Folks Are Aggressive': An Orientalist Reading of 'Afghan Warlords,'" *Security Dialogue* 40, no. 1 (2009): 73–94.

98. Quoted in "All Afghans, Even Taleban, Should Return—Afghan President to Hungarian Daily," *Népszabadság*, October 4, 2002.

99. Roy, "La difficile reconstruction," 37.

100. Interview with Afghan scholar 2, 2011.

101. Interview with former aide to Ahmad Shah Massoud 1, 2011. Weingrod defines political brokers as "specialists in bringing the more and the less powerful into contact."

Alex Weingrod, "Patronage and Power," in *Patrons and Clients in Mediterranean Societies*, ed. Ernest Gellner and John Waterbury (London: Duckworth, 1977), 47.

102. Jan Koehler, "Social Order within and beyond the Shadow of Hierarchy Governance: Patterns in Afghanistan" (SFB-Governance Working Paper 33, Berlin, 2012), 14.

103. Interview with Ismail Khan, March 19, 2011.

104. Interview with former Shura-i Nazar commander 1, 2011 (first quote); interview with former Shura-i Nazar commander 2, 2013 (second quote). As Driscoll notes in the context of post-Soviet Georgia and Tajikistan, "One might observe certain kinds of cosmetic disarmament—warlords may don suits, affix a party label pin, and reinvent themselves as party officials or vote brokers—but they maintain control of men and weapons" (*Warlords and Coalition Politics*, 31).

105. Koehler, "Social Order," 15.

106. Martin, *An Intimate War*, 222.

107. Abdulkader H. Sinno, *Organizations at War: In Afghanistan and Beyond* (Ithaca, NY: Cornell University Press, 2008), 273.

108. I first developed the concept of shape-shifting to describe warlord behavior in Romain Malejacq, "Warlords, Intervention, and State Consolidation: A Typology of Political Orders in Weak and Failed States," *Security Studies* 25, no. 1 (2016): 85–110. It has since been used in Mimmi Söderberg Kovacs and Ibrahim Bangura, "Shape-Shifters in the Struggle for Survival: Post-War Politics in Sierra Leone," in *Warlord Democrats in Africa: Ex-Military Leaders and Electoral Politics*, ed. Anders Themnér (London: Zed Books, 2017), 177–98.

2. The Game of Survival

1. Ismail Khan, speech given in Badagh, Injil District, Herat Province, March 20, 2011.

2. For Lezhnev, for example, warlords are "driven overwhelmingly by personal power, glory and monetary gain." Sasha Lezhnev, *Crafting Peace: Strategies to Deal with Warlords in Collapsing States* (Lanham, MD: Lexington Books, 2005), 2–3. And, for Robinson, "the pursuit of a narrow, commercial self-interest" is the raison d'être of warlordism. T. P. Robinson, "Twenty-First Century Warlords: Diagnosis and Treatment?," *Defence Studies* 1, no. 1 (Spring 2001): 123.

3. Jean-François Médard, "Charles Njonjo: Portrait d'un 'big man,' au Kenya," in *L'Etat contemporain en Afrique*, ed. Emmanuel Terray (Paris: L'Harmattan, 1987), 49–87; Jean-Patrice Lacam, "Le politicien investisseur: Un modèle d'interprétation de la gestion des ressources politiques," *Revue française de science politique* 38, no. 1 (1988); Jean-François Médard, "Le 'big man' en Afrique: Esquisse d'analyse du politicien entrepreneur," *Année sociologique* 42, no. 3 (1992); Jean-François Médard, "Le système politique bordelais (le 'système Chaban')," *Revue internationale de politique comparée* 13, no. 4 (2006): 657–79.

4. See, for example, Patrick Chabal and Jean-Pascal Daloz, *Africa Works: Disorder as Political Instrument* (Bloomington: Indiana University Press, 1999), 85; Mats Berdal,

"How 'New' Are 'New Wars'? Global Economic Change and the Study of Civil War," *Global Governance* 9, no. 4 (2003): 477–502; William Reno, *Warfare in Independent Africa* (New York: Cambridge University Press, 2011), 12. On warlords's political economies, see, for example, Mark Duffield, "Post-Modern Conflict: Warlords, Post-Adjustment States and Private Protection," *Civil Wars* 1, no. 1 (Spring 1998): 65–102; William Reno, *Warlord Politics and African States* (Boulder, CO: Lynne Rienner, 1998). Here I consider that warlords do not necessarily pursue short-term economic interests but remain driven by political goals (even though the warlords's communities can at times be of their own making). This challenges common assumptions about political choice in the context of weak state authority such as Fearon and Laitin's idea that weak institutions unleash self-interested actors, as well as Collier and Hoeffler's argument that resources are incitements to rent-seeking behavior—greed. See James D. Fearon and David D. Laitin, "Ethnicity, Insurgency, and Civil War," *American Political Science Review* 97, no. 1 (2003): 75–90; Paul Collier and Anke Hoeffler, "Greed and Grievance in Civil War," *Oxford Economic Paper* 56, no. 4 (2004): 563–95. I also differ from Driscoll, whose consolidation lottery model is based on "war economy" payoff. Jesse Driscoll, *Warlords and Coalition Politics in Post-Soviet States* (New York: Cambridge University Press, 2015), 41. Instead, I argue that these environments create opportunities in which actors do not necessarily see self-enrichment, but power, as their primary goal.

5. Bob Woodward, *Bush at War* (New York: Simon & Schuster, 2002), 35.

6. Lucian Pye, *Warlord Politics: Conflict and Coalition in the Modernization of Republican China* (New York: Praeger, 1971), 40–41.

7. Interview with Herat resident 1, 2011.

8. Pierre Bourdieu, "The Forms of Capital," in *Handbook of Theory and Research for the Sociology of Education*, ed. John G. Richardson (New York: Greenwood, 1986), 241.

9. F. G. Bailey, *Stratagems and Spoils: A Social Anthropology of Politics* (Oxford: Basil Blackwell, 1969), 1. Quoted in G. Whitney Azoy, *Buzkashi: Game and Power in Afghanistan* (Philadelphia: University of Pennsylvania Press, 1982), 17.

10. Bourdieu, "The Forms of Capital," 252. Calhoun further notes that "the rules of each game are both constraints on the players and the ways in which players get things done. Players usually have to treat them as fixed and unchanging, but in fact they are historically produced." Craig Calhoun, "Pierre Bourdieu," in *Blackwell Companion to Major Social Theorists* (Malden, MA: Blackwell, 2000), 699.

11. Michael Mann, *The Sources of Social Power: Volume 1, A History of Power from the Beginning to A.D. 1760* (Cambridge, UK: Cambridge University Press, 1986); Timothy Earle, *How Chiefs Come to Power: The Political Economy in Prehistory* (Stanford, CA: Stanford University Press, 1997). Here I differ from Mccormick and Fritz, who consider only the "reciprocal and self-reinforcing military and economic foundations of warlord regimes." Gordon H. Mccormick and Lindsay Fritz, "The Logic of Warlord Politics," *Third World Quarterly* 30, no. 1 (2009): 83.

12. Michael Mann, *The Sources of Social Power, Volume 2. The Rise of Classes and Nation-States 1760–1914* (Cambridge, UK: Cambridge University Press, 1993), 7.

13. Niels Terpstra and Georg Frerks, "Governance Practices and Symbolism: De Facto Sovereignty and Public Authority in 'Tigerland,'" *Modern Asian Studies* 52, no. 3 (2018): 1001–42.

14. Bourdieu, "The Forms of Capital," 243, 252.

15. Pierre Bourdieu, "What Makes a Social Class? On the Theoretical and Practical Existence of Groups," *Berkeley Journal of Sociology* 32 (1987): 4. Social capital (or social power) is "the aggregate of the actual or potential resources which are linked to possession of a durable network of more or less institutionalized relationships of mutual acquaintance and recognition" (Bourdieu, "The Forms of Capital," 248). In sum, "the volume of the social capital possessed by a given agent . . . depends on the size of the network of connections he can effectively mobilize and on the volume of capital (economic, cultural or symbolic) possessed in his own right by each of those to whom he is connected" (Bourdieu, 249).

16. On patronage and social capital, see also Jeremy Boissevain, *Friends of Friends: Networks, Manipulators and Coalitions* (Oxford: Basil Blackwell, 1974); Alex Weingrod, "Patronage and Power," in *Patrons and Clients in Mediterranean Societies*, ed. Ernest Gellner and John Waterbury (London: Duckworth, 1977), 41–51; Robert Putnam, *Making Democracy Work: Civic Traditions in Modern Italy* (Princeton, NJ: Princeton University Press, 1993).

17. Mann, *Sources of Social Power: Volume 1*, 11.

18. Robert A. Dahl, *Modern Political Analysis* (Englewood Cliffs, NJ: Prentice-Hall, 1963), 35.

19. Lacam, "Le politicien investisseur," 27.

20. Weingrod, "Patronage and Power," 42.

21. On the use of religious capital (or power) in the Afghan context, see Noah Coburn, *Bazaar Politics: Power and Pottery in an Afghan Market Town* (Stanford, CA: Stanford University Press, 2011), 116–23. On extraversion, see Jean-François Bayart, *The State in Africa: The Politics of the Belly* (London: Longman, 1993), 20–32.

22. Interview with Robert Finn, former US ambassador to Afghanistan, October 5, 2011.

23. Reno, *Warfare in Independent Africa*, 11.

24. Walter Korpi, "Power Resources Approach vs. Action and Conflict: On Causal and Intentional Explanations in the Study of Power," *Sociological Theory* 3, no. 2 (Autumn 1985): 38.

25. Driscoll, *Warlords and Coalition Politics*, 52.

26. Coburn, for example, notes that violence did not have popular support in the village of Istalif after the fall of the Taliban: "During the jihad, Istalifis thought of relying on violence as Islamic, but to continue to use unnecessary violence later was seen as an individual's acknowledgement that he could not mobilize other forms of political capital. In this sense, commanders were shackled by the very thing that had brought them to power" (*Bazaar Politics*, 132).

27. Giustozzi, *Empires of Mud*, 227. On the role of violence in Afghan elections, see Noah Coburn and Anna Larson, *Derailing Democracy in Afghanistan: Elections in an Unstable Political Landscape* (New York: Columbia University Press, 2014), chap. 7.

28. Abdulkader H. Sinno, *Organizations at War: In Afghanistan and Beyond* (Ithaca, NY: Cornell University Press, 2008), 275.

29. Philip Münch, "Local Afghan Power Structures and the International Military Intervention: A Review of Developments in Badakhshan and Kunduz Provinces"

(Afghanistan Analysts Network Thematic Report 3, Kabul, 2013), 12. For more examples of warlord reconversion in the political arena, see Anders Themnér, ed., *Warlord Democrats in Africa: Ex-Military Leaders and Electoral Politics* (London: Zed Books, 2017).

30. Vadim Volkov, *Violent Entrepreneurs: The Use of Force in the Making of Russian Capitalism* (Ithaca, NY: Cornell University Press, 2002), 27.

31. Volkov, 3. Volkov argues that, in the Russian context, "the emergence of the private economy made a huge difference, providing the resource base and structuring the management of force to enable regular extraction" (15).

32. Giustozzi notes that land grabs were already widespread in northern Afghanistan in the 1990s (*Empires of Mud*, 138).

33. Diego Gambetta, *The Sicilian Mafia: The Business of Private Protection* (Cambridge: Harvard University Press, 1993), 79.

34. Gambetta, *The Sicilian Mafia*. Racketeering must be distinguished from extortion: extortion is "a particular act, a criminal offense, whereas a protection racket is an institutionalized relationship." Volkov, *Violent Entrepreneurs*, 29.

35. Duffield, "Post-Modern Conflict," 92. See also Federico Varese, "Is Sicily the Future of Russia? Private Protection and the Rise of the Russian Maffia," *Archives européennes de sociologie* 35, no. 2 (1994): 224–58. On private military and security companies in Afghanistan, see Christian Olsson, "Coercion and Capital in Afghanistan: The Rise, Transformation and Fall of the Afghan Commercial Security Sector," in *The Routledge Research Companion to Security Outsourcing*, ed. Joakim Berndtsson and Christopher Kinsey (Abingdon, UK: Routledge, 2016), 41–51.

36. Sarah Chayes, *The Punishment of Virtue: Inside Afghanistan after the Taliban* (New York: Penguin, 2006), 169.

37. Sinno, *Organizations at War*, 261.

38. Noah Coburn, *Losing Afghanistan: An Obituary for the Intervention* (Stanford, CA: Stanford University Press, 2016), 150.

39. Jennifer Brick Murtazashvili, *Informal Order and the State in Afghanistan* (New York: Cambridge University Press, 2016), 167.

40. Antonio Giustozzi, "Warlords into Businessmen: The Afghan Transition 2002–2005. Preliminary Findings from a Research Trip, May 2005" (paper presented at the Transforming War Economies Seminar, University of Plymouth, June 16–18, 2005), 4.

41. Korpi, "Power Resources Approach vs. Action and Conflict," 39, 37.

42. Interview with former Herat resident, 2009.

43. "Mohaqiq's Exclusive Interview with Hazaristan Times," *Hazaristan Times*, July 20, 2008; Thibauld Malterre, "Thousands March over Afghan Land Dispute," *Macau Daily Times*, July 23, 2008.

44. Olivier Roy, "Afghanistan: La difficile reconstruction d'un Etat," *Cahier de Chaillot* 73, no. 1 (2004): 42. This phenomenon can be traced back to the Soviet-Afghan war. As Brick Murtazashvili writes: "Various warlords and political parties fighting the Soviet-backed government in Kabul in the 1980s and 1990s viewed the widespread legitimacy of [customary] organizations as a threat to their power and sought to dominate them by populating them with their own agents" (*Informal Order*, 37). She further notes that, after

2008, growing insecurity has "forced customary authority to dissimulate during periods of conflicts (as it had in the past) or be co-opted by these commanders" (126).

45. Münch, "Local Afghan Power Structures."

46. Coburn, *Bazaar Politics*, 113. Here I differ from de Waal's political marketplace model, which puts a strong emphasis on violence and the accumulation of economic resources. Alex de Waal, *The Real Politics of the Horn of Africa: Money, War and the Business of Power* (Cambridge, UK: Polity, 2015). Coburn also explains why what he calls religious capital (which implies a certain degree of piety) is particularly difficult to combine with other forms of capital (in particular, economic capital): "Religious figures were required to shun wealth or they would be perceived as 'less Muslim.' For the same reason, mullahs were rarely seen as threatening violence and usually did not associate themselves with commanders or the police" (*Bazaar Politics*, 117).

47. On straddling practices, see Médard, "Le 'big man' en Afrique"; Jean-François Bayart, "L'historicité de l'État importé," in *La greffe de l'État: Les trajectoires du politique, 2*, ed. Jean-François Bayart (Paris: Karthala, 1996), 11–39; Jean-François Bayart, Stephen Ellis, and Béatrice Hibou, "From Kleptocracy to the Felonious State?," in *The Criminalization of the State in Africa*, ed. Jean-François Bayart, Stephen Ellis, and Béatrice Hibou (Oxford: James Currey, 1999), 1–31.

48. Pye, *Warlord Politics*, 62.

49. Georgi M. Derluguian, *Bourdieu's Secret Admirer in the Caucasus: A World-System Biography* (Chicago: University of Chicago Press, 2005), 4.

50. Here I follow Yama Torabi's usage of Erving Goffman's concept of face—"an image of self delineated in terms of approved social attributes" (Erving Goffman, *Interaction Ritual: Essays in Face-to-Face Behavior* [Garden City, NY: Doubleday Anchor Books, 1967], 5) in the context of post-2001 Afghanistan. Yama Torabi, "State-, Nation- et Peace-Building comme processus de transactions: L'interaction des intervenants et des acteurs locaux sur le théâtre de l'intervention en Afghanistan, 2001–08" (PhD diss., Institut d'Études Politiques de Paris, 2009), 214–65. Barry uses the same image for Burhanuddin Rabbani (Michael Barry, *Massoud: De l'islamisme à la liberté* [Paris: Audibert, 2002], 121) and Notin a similar idea for Massoud (Jean-Christophe Notin, *La guerre de l'ombre des Français en Afghanistan 1979–2011* [Paris: Fayard, 2011], 328, 490). For examples of similar practices in different contexts, see also Médard, "Le 'big man' en Afrique"; Volkov, *Violent Entrepreneurs*; Denis M. Tull, "A Reconfiguration of Political Order? The State of the State in North Kivu (DR Congo)," *African Affairs* 102, no. 408 (2003): 429–46; Tanja R. Müller, "From Rebel Governance to State Consolidation: Dynamics of Loyalty and the Securitisation of the State in Eritrea," *Geoforum* 43, no. 4 (2012): 793–803.

51. Pierre Bourdieu, *Language and Symbolic Power* (Cambridge, UK: Polity, 1991), 192.

52. Max Weber, "Politics as a Vocation," in *From Max Weber: Essays in Sociology*, ed. H. H. Gerth and C. Wright Mills (New York: Oxford University Press, 1946), 79.

53. Weber, 79.

54. James C. Scott, "Prestige as the Public Discourse of Domination," *Cultural Critique* 12 (Spring 1989): 146.

55. Romain Malejacq, "Meeting with a Warlord," *Afghanopoly* (blog), entry July 20, 2011. See also Romain Malejacq and Dipali Mukhopadhyay, "The 'Tribal Politics' of

Field Research: A Reflection on Power and Partiality in 21st-Century Warzones," *Perspectives on Politics* 14, no. 4 (2016): 1011–28.

56. Loïc Wacquant, "Symbolic Power in the Rule of the 'State Nobility,'" in *Pierre Bourdieu and Democratic Politics: The Mystery of Ministry*, ed. Loïc Wacquant (Cambridge, UK: Polity, 2005), 134.

57. Scott, "Prestige as the Public Discourse of Domination," 146.

58. Interview with Thomas Barfield, Afghanistan scholar, October 27, 2011.

59. Coburn, *Losing Afghanistan*, 68.

60. Mccormick and Fritz similarly note the importance, for warlords, of keeping popular perceptions of weakness low ("The Logic of Warlord Politics," 102).

61. Thomas Hobbes, *Leviathan or the Matter, Forme and Power of a Commonwealth Ecclesiasticall and Civil* (Oxford: Clarendon, 1909), 66.

62. Chayes, *Punishment of Virtue*, 188.

63. Olivier Roy, "Afghanistan: Internal Politics and Socio-economic Dynamics and Groupings" (UNHCR Writenet Paper 14, Paris, 2003), 7.

64. Carter Malkasian, *War Comes to Garmser: Thirty Years of Conflict on the Afghan Frontier* (New York: Oxford University Press, 2016), 91.

65. Rajiv Chandrasekaran, *Little America: The War within the War for Afghanistan* (New York: Vintage Books, 2012), 91. A similar tactic was used against Dostum, who was reported to feel deeply threatened by US bombers flying over his compound. See Zalmay Khalilzad, *The Envoy: From Kabul to the White House, My Journey through a Turbulent World* (New York: St Martin's, 2016), 202–3.

66. Scott, "Prestige as the Public Discourse of Domination," 163.

67. Scott, 163.

68. Borhan Osman, "The Fall of Kunduz: What Does It Tell Us about the Strength of the Post-Omar Taleban?," Afghanistan Analysts Network, September 30, 2015.

69. Karl W. Deutsch, *The Nerves of Government: Models of Political Communication and Control* (New York: Free Press, 1966), 121. See also Médard, "Charles Njonjo," 57–58.

70. Abner Cohen, *Two-Dimensional Man* (London: Routledge and Kegan Paul, 1974), 31. Quoted in Azoy, *Buzkashi*, 1982, 84. As Mccormick and Fritz point out, warlords have an "incumbent's advantage" ("The Logic of Warlord Politics," 99). Because information is incomplete, a warlord's authority can be assessed only "after a challenge has been made" (Mccormick and Fritz, 100). See also Coburn, *Bazaar Politics*, 203.

71. Coburn, 221.

72. Interview with former Shura-i Nazar commander 1, 2011.

73. Martine van Bijlert, "Imaginary Institutions: State-Building in Afghanistan," in *Doing Good or Doing Better: Development Policies in a Globalizing World*, ed. Monique Kremer, Peter van Lieshout, and Robert Went (The Hague: Amsterdam University Press, 2009), 158.

74. Driscoll, *Warlords and Coalition Politics*, 52.

75. Van Bijlert, "Imaginary Institutions," 158, 161.

76. Mujib Mashal and Jawad Sukhanyar, "Face-Off between Strongmen Exposes Afghanistan's Political Rifts," *New York Times*, March 23, 2016.

77. G. Whitney Azoy, quoted in Stephen Thorne, "'Ritual' of Buzkashi a Metaphor for Afghan Culture and Politics: Anthropologist," Canadian Press Newswire, August 30, 2004.

78. Earle, *How Chiefs Come to Power*, 3.

79. Scott, "Prestige as the Public Discourse of Domination," 152.

80. Kimberly Marten, *Warlords: Strong-Arm Brokers in Weak States* (Ithaca, NY: Cornell University Press, 2012), 99.

81. Olivier Roy, "Afghanistan—War as a Factor of Entry into Politics," *Central Asian Survey* 8, no. 4 (1989): 52. Giustozzi mentions "transformations caused by several years of war, in which the traditional notables had been supplanted by military leaders (the 'new Khans')" (*Empires of Mud*, 54). See also Olivier Roy, "The New Political Elite in Afghanistan," in *The Politics of Social Transformation in Afghanistan, Iran, and Pakistan*, ed. Myron Weiner and Ali Banuazizi (Syracuse, NY: Syracuse University Press, 1994), 72–100. Yet, preexisting forms of customary governance have not completely withered away in rural Afghanistan. See Brick Murtazashvili, *Informal Order*, 26–30.

82. Frederick Barth, *Political Leadership among Swat Pathans* (London: Athlone, 1996), 215.

83. Gilles Dorronsoro, *Revolution Unending: Afghanistan, 1979 to the Present* (New York: Columbia University Press, 2005), 119. As the Pashto saying indicates: "There is no Khan without *Dostarkhwan* [tablecloth]." Quoted in Peter Tomsen, *The Wars of Afghanistan: Messianic Terrorism, Tribal Conflicts, and the Failures of Great Powers* (New York: Public Affairs, 2011), 35. See also Joshua Partlow, *A Kingdom of Their Own: The Family Karzai and the Afghan Disaster* (New York: Alfred A. Knopf, 2016), 127. In this sense, Bayart's metaphor of the "politics of the belly" quite literally applies to khans (and warlords). See Bayart, *The State in Africa*.

84. Mukhopadhyay uses the term *neo-khan* to describe how warlord turned governor Gul Agha Sherzai developed his own brand of provincial governance: "the product of utilizing weak formal institutions in combination with robust forms of informal power." Dipali Mukhopadhyay, *Warlords, Strongman Governors, and the State in Afghanistan* (New York: Cambridge University Press, 2014), 167.

85. For a concrete example, see Brick Murtazashvili, *Informal Order*, 168.

86. Azoy, *Buzkashi*, 1982, 24. For a more comprehensive discussion of the concept, see Azoy, 30–38.

87. Brick Murtazashvili, *Informal Order*, xxxi.

88. Brick Murtazashvili, 79. "Broadly speaking," the Afghan historian Hasan Kakar explained, "the term *arbab* was used in western Afghanistan and the term malik in eastern Afghanistan." M. Hasan Kakar, *Government and Society in Afghanistan: The Reign of Amir Abd Al-Rahman Khan* (Austin: University of Texas Press, 1979), 58. Quoted in Brick Murtazashvili, 79. On the *malik* as bridge (*pul*) between people and government, see also Coburn, *Bazaar Politics*, 77.

89. Mukhopadhyay, *Warlords, Strongman Governors*, 196.

90. On the "reinforcing feedback effects between domestic and international support," see Reyko Huang, "Rebel Diplomacy in Civil War," *International Security* 40, no. 4 (Spring 2016): 120. See also Romain Malejacq, "From Rebel to Quasi-state: Governance, Diplomacy and Legitimacy in the Midst of Afghanistan's Wars (1979–2001)," *Small Wars &*

Insurgencies 28, no. 4–5 (2017): 867–86; Sukanya Podder, "Understanding the Legitimacy of Armed Groups: A Relational Perspective," *Small Wars & Insurgencies* 28, no. 4–5 (2017): 686–708. Coburn points out that, at the local level, too much stress on acquiring external connections can undermine the authority of the *malik*: "A malik gained social capital through connections with the government and international groups. . . . Yet, a malik who was too close to the government was viewed with suspicion about his potential to betray his people" (*Bazaar Politics*, 113–14).

91. Dipali Mukhopadhyay, "Warlords as Bureaucrats: The Afghan Experience" (Carnegie Paper 101, Washington, DC, 2009).

92. On neopatrimonialism and warlords in Afghanistan, see Weeda Mehran, "Neopatrimonialism in Afghanistan: Former Warlords, New Democratic Bureaucrats?," *Journal of Peacebuilding & Development* 13, no. 2 (2018): 91–105.

93. Jean-François Médard, "Political Clientelism in France: The Center-Periphery Nexus Examined," in *Political Clientelism, Patronage and Development*, ed. Shmuel N. Eisenstadt and René Lemarchand (London: Sage, 1981), 136. Here Médard cites Luigi Graziano, "A Conceptual Framework for the Study of Clientelistic Behavior," *European Journal of Political Research* 4, no. 2 (1976): 164. Médard also draws on Henri Mendras, "Un schéma d'analyse de la paysannerie occidentale," *Peasant Studies Newsletter* 1, no. 3 (1972): 79–93. See also Pierre Grémion, *Le pouvoir périphérique: Bureaucrates et notables dans le système politique français* (Paris: Seuil, 1976).

94. Michael Bhatia, "Armed Groups in Afghanistan," in *Afghanistan, Arms and Conflict: Armed Groups, Disarmament and Security in a Post-War Society*, ed. Michael Bhatia and Mark Sedra (New York: Routledge, 2008), 86.

95. Quoted in Dorronsoro, *Revolution Unending*, 123.

96. Roy, "La difficile reconstruction," 39.

97. Pye, *Warlord Politics*, 41.

98. Ariel I. Ahram and Charles King, "The Warlord as Arbitrageur," *Theory and Society* 41, no. 2 (2012): 170.

99. Conrad Schetter, Rainer Glassner, and Masood Karokhail, "Beyond Warlordism: The Local Security Architecture in Afghanistan," *Internationale Politik Und Gesellschaft* 2 (2007): 139. According to Antonio Giustozzi and Noor Ullah, "What characterises warlords is that their leadership is exercised over the military class. In other words, their strength is their military legitimacy. This, together with their control over a territory, gives them in turn a political role, but without the benefits of political legitimacy." Antonio Giustozzi and Noor Ullah, "'Tribes' and Warlords in Southern Afghanistan, 1980–2005" (Crisis States Working Paper 7 [Series 2], London, 2006), 2.

100. Van Bijlert, "Imaginary Institutions," 158–59.

3. Ismail Khan, the Armed Notable of Western Afghanistan

1. Interview with Herat resident 2, 2011.

2. *Tajik*, in the context of Afghanistan and as used in this book, does not refer to a separate ethnolinguistic group, but rather to the non-Hazara Persian-speaking populations of Afghanistan.

3. The role of the different actors in staging and coordinating the Herat uprising remains unclear. Ismail Khan, for example, has claimed that the mutineers had been in contact with the city's religious leaders—who were to give them the green light—before the rebellion. See Radek Sikorski, *Dust of the Saints: A Journey to Herat in Time of War* (New York: Paragon House, 1990), 230. Roy and Dorronsoro maintain that contacts had also been previously established between Jamiat militants and officers of the Seventeenth Division; Roy even claims that Ismail Khan (among others) was a secret member of Jamiat, which Ismail Khan has always denied, including during our interview of June 24, 2018. See Olivier Roy, *Islam and Resistance in Afghanistan* (Cambridge, UK: Cambridge University Press, 1986), 108; Gilles Dorronsoro, *Revolution Unending: Afghanistan, 1979 to the Present* (New York: Columbia University Press, 2005), 102.

4. Giustozzi notes that "the Iranians allowed Ismail Khan and his men to move relatively freely across its territory, but never agreed to supply significant quantities of military hardware." Antonio Giustozzi, *Empires of Mud: Wars and Warlords in Afghanistan* (New York: Columbia University Press, 2009), 233.

5. According to Giustozzi's estimates, a quarter of Ismail Khan's funds during the jihad came from the Jamiat headquarters in Peshawar, "another quarter from taxes and the rest from international support organisations, presumably Islamic charities and private donors" (233).

6. For background information conveyed in this section, I used anonymous interviews as well as the following sources: Roy, *Islam and Resistance*, 107–9; Chantal Lobato, "Civils et résistants dans la province d'Hérat à l'automne 1989," *Afghanistan Info* 26 (1989): 7; Sikorski, *Dust of the Saints*, 225–33; Ahmed Rashid, *Taliban: Militant Islam, Oil and Fundamentalism in Central Asia*, 2nd ed. (New Haven, CT: Yale University Press, 2001), 37–38; Dorronsoro, *Revolution Unending*, 98–102; Peter B. DeNeufville, "Ahmad Shah Massoud and the Genesis of the Nationalist Anti-Communist Movement in Northeastern Afghanistan, 1969–1979" (PhD diss., University of London, 2006), 145–56; Giustozzi, *Empires of Mud*, 207–10, 213, 221, 242. I also consulted "Ismail Khan, Anti-Taliban Key to Western Afghanistan," AFP, October 3, 2001.

7. Interview with Herat resident 3, 2011.

8. Interview with religious leader, 2018.

9. Interview with Herat resident 4, 2011.

10. Giustozzi, *Empires of Mud*, 214.

11. Interview with Ismail Khan, June 24, 2018.

12. Rashid, *Taliban*, 38.

13. Giustozzi, *Empires of Mud*, 272.

14. Interview with former Herat resident, 2011.

15. Interview with Ismail Khan, June 24, 2018. Dorronsoro even claims that Ismail Khan turned down President Rabbani's offer to appoint him minister of defense in lieu of Ahmad Shah Massoud in 1992 (*Revolution Unending*, 253).

16. Interview with Herat resident 1, 2011. For information conveyed in this section, in addition to anonymous interviews and the sources cited above, I relied on the following: Gilles Dorronsoro, "La politique de pacification en Afghanistan," in *Stratégies de la guérilla*, ed. Gérard Chaliand (Paris: Payot & Rivages, 1994), 468; Veronica Doubleday, "Printemps 1994 à Hérat," *Afghanistan Info* 35 (1994): 13–14; Bernard Dupaigne, "Hérat,

un modèle et une chance pour l'Afghanistan," *Afghanistan Info* 34 (1994): 7–10; Dorronsoro, *Revolution Unending*, 126; Ahmed Rashid, *Descent into Chaos: How the War against Islamic Extremism Is Being Lost in Pakistan, Afghanistan and Central Asia* (London: Allen Lane, 2008), 126; Giustozzi, *Empires of Mud*, 87–100, 226, 239, 242–43, 250, 274.

17. Dupaigne, "Hérat, un modèle et une chance," 7–10. For information conveyed in this section, in addition to anonymous interviews and the sources cited above, I relied on the following: Olivier Roy, "Iran: Vers une évolution de la politique afghane," *Afghanistan Info* 18 (1987): 15; Bernard Dupaigne, "Hérat: Les O.I. et les ONG," *Afghanistan Info* 34 (1994): 10; Bernard Dupaigne, "Etat des lieux en décembre 93," *Afghanistan Info* 34 (1994), 11; Rashid, *Taliban*, 27; Dorronsoro, *Revolution Unending*, 133, 245, 252; Rashid, *Descent into Chaos*, 127; Giustozzi, *Empires of Mud*, 226, 261.

18. For information conveyed in this section, in addition to anonymous interviews, I relied on the following sources: Etienne Dubuis, "Extraordinaire retournement de situation: La prise de Hérat par les Talibans," *Afghanistan Info* 37 (1995): 7; Rashid, *Taliban*, 39; Dorronsoro, *Revolution Unending*, 251–52; Giustozzi, *Empires of Mud*, 215–17, 257–58.

19. Michael Griffin, quoted in Gary Thomas, "Afghan Warlord Brings Stability to Region, but at a Price," VOA News, November 22, 2002.

20. Quoted in Barry Bearak, "Taliban Opposition Confirms Death of Its Battle Commander," *New York Times*, September 16, 2001.

21. On "Interview with Sotiris Mousouris," CNN's *Live Today*, November 15, 2001.

22. Quoted in "Afghan Northern Alliance Commander Says Foreign Troop Support Unnecessary," *Al-Sharq Al-Awsat*, October 11, 2001.

23. Quoted in "US Should Provide Afghan Opposition Military Aid, Not Troops: Khan," AFP, October 11, 2001.

24. Quoted in "'Foreign Troops Should Go Home,'" *Times*, November 17, 2001.

25. Quoted in Behrouz Mehri, "Hatred Drove Afghan People to Rise Up against Taliban: 'Lion of Herat,'" AFP, November 16, 2001.

26. Ivan Watson on "Iran and US Seem to Be Competing for Favor of Afghanistan's Warlords and Ruling Government," NPR's *Morning Edition*, July 19, 2002.

27. Quoted in Margaret Coker, "Iranian Influence, and Guns, Felt in Western Afghanistan," Cox News Service, February 1, 2002.

28. According to Giustozzi, "Iranian trucks were reported unloading weapons in Ismail Khan's armories" as late as 2004 (*Empires of Mud*, 236).

29. Quoted in Coker, "Iranian Influence."

30. Rashid, *Descent into Chaos*, 126.

31. Interview with Robert Finn, former US ambassador to Afghanistan, October 5, 2011. Finn mentioned that, under Ismail Khan's governorship, Herat had an honor guard for ceremonial duties, such as welcoming ministers and foreign delegations on official visits. This clear marker of sovereignty was disbanded in 2004 when Ismail Khan lost his governorship.

32. On "Iran and US Seem to Be Competing for Favor."

33. Rashid, *Descent into Chaos*, 125.

34. Quoted in Kim Sengupta, "Last-Minute Hitch Could Stall Peace-Keeping Deal; Warlord Insists Western Soldiers Are Not Wanted," *Independent*, December 31, 2001.

35. Quoted in Susan B. Glasser, "Karzai Team Sent to Calm Unruly Area; Afghan Militia Leader Evasive about Truce," *Washington Post*, July 25, 2002.

36. For information conveyed in this section, in addition to anonymous interviews and the sources cited above, I relied on Rashid, *Descent into Chaos*, 143; Jean-Christophe Notin, *La guerre de l'ombre des Français en Afghanistan 1979–2011* (Paris: Fayard, 2011), 737–38. I also consulted the following news sources: Suzanne Goldenberg, "Global Aid for Kabul, Iranian Arms for Herat," *Guardian*, January 24, 2002; "No Evidence of Iranian Interference in Afghanistan: UN Official," AFP, January 24, 2002; "Governor of Herat, Afghanistan, Ismail Khan," NPR's *Weekend Edition Sunday*, February 3, 2002; "Afghan Leader to Visit Iran," IPR Strategic Business Information Database, February 5, 2002; "Afghan Warlord Denies Receiving Arms and Cash from Iran," AFP, February 10, 2002; Amy Waldman, "Courted by U.S. and Iran, an Afghan Governor Plays One Side off the Other," *New York Times*, April 3, 2002; Borzou Daragahi, "Afghan Governor Spurs Instability Fears," *Washington Times*, April 13, 2002; "Donald H. Rumsfeld Holds News Conference," FDCH Political Transcripts, April 28, 2002; Chris Otton, "Rumsfeld Seeks to Counter Tehran Influence in Western Afghanistan," AFP, April 28, 2002; "Ex-Mujaheddin Commander Opts for War," *Moscow News*, May 15, 2002; "Herat Province . . . ," IPR Strategic Business Information Database, May 19, 2002; "Warlords in Afghanistan, like Ismail Khan, Reluctant to Give Up Power after Election for New Government," ABC News's *World News Tonight*, June 11, 2002; Regan Morris, "U.S. Commander Seeks to Shore Up Ties to the Men Who Wield Real Power in Afghanistan," AP, July 24, 2002; Bay Fang, "The Great Game 2002," *U.S. News & World Report*, August 12, 2002; "Afghan Herat Governor Says Kabul Visit 'Effective and Useful,'" Herat TV, August 18, 2002; Chris Otton, "Afghan President Gets Full Support from Herat Boss Ismail Khan," AFP, August 28, 2002; Glenn Kessler, "Study Cites Repression by Afghan Governor," *Washington Post*, November 5, 2002.

37. Rashid, *Descent into Chaos*, 125.

38. Quoted in Alfons Luna, "Ismail Khan, Lord of the Infinite Distance between Kabul and Herat," AFP, February 12, 2002.

39. Although numbers differ widely, it is usually agreed that Ismail Khan amassed a vast fortune while he was in control of the custom revenues. Sinno, for example, gauges Ismail Khan's income from trade with Iran at up to $300 million per year. Abdulkader H. Sinno, *Organizations at War: In Afghanistan and Beyond* (Ithaca, NY: Cornell University Press, 2008), 264. Rashid estimates that Ismail Khan earned "between three and five million dollars every month in customs revenue from the crossing point at Islam Qila on the Iran-Afghanistan border" (*Descent into Chaos*, 127).

40. Interview with governor of Herat Province, 2011.

41. Interview with Herat resident 1, 2011.

42. Interview with Afghan NGO worker, 2011.

43. Quoted in Fang, "The Great Game 2002."

44. Giustozzi, *Empires of Mud*, 236.

45. Rashid, *Descent into Chaos*, 126 (first quote); Giustozzi, *Empires of Mud*, 242 (second quote). Both Rashid and Giustozzi believe that Ismail Khan's prison experience in the 1990s changed him for the worse (Rashid, *Descent into Chaos*, 126; Giustozzi, *Empires of Mud*, 273). Others argue that prison had the opposite effect on him. In a response to a

blog post recounting my meeting with Ismail Khan, someone wrote: "You should have met Ismail Khan between 1992–1995 in Herat when he took power after the communists. . . . Back then he was a blood-sucking vampire, the prison 'reformed' him." The Lost Flaneur, September 13, 2011, comment on "Meeting with a Warlord," *Afghanopoly* (blog), entry July 20, 2011. Some interpret this change of attitude as a sign of Iran's ideological influence. See, for example, "Women Remove Their Burkas," *Bristol Evening Post*, November 21, 2001; Waldman, "Afghan Governor Plays One Side Off the Other."

46. Richard Newell, *The Politics of Afghanistan* (Ithaca, NY: Cornell University Press, 1972), 26. An alternative explanation is that Ismail Khan became more conservative over time, but most importantly that the international and domestic settings changed, the pressure for liberalization being much more important in the post-2001 period than during the warlord era. It should also be noted that Veronica Doubleday, who visited Herat in 1994, was already describing a process of harsh Islamization ("Printemps 1994 à Hérat"). Giustozzi writes that, during Ismail Khan's first emirate, "one would certainly hesitate to describe the environment of Herat as liberal" (*Empires of Mud*, 226).

47. Interview with Herat resident 1, 2011.

48. For information conveyed in this section, in addition to anonymous interviews and the sources cited above, I consulted the following news sources: Amy Waldman, "The Warlord, in Charge Again, Thanks the West but Wants It Gone," *New York Times*, November 17, 2001; David Rohde, "Afghan Women Push for Their Rights," *Deseret News*, November 21, 2001; "Afghan Strongman Ismail Khan Keeps Order," Cox News Service, February 8, 2002; "Warlords in Afghanistan"; "Herat Province . . ."; Daragahi, "Afghan Governor Spurs Instability Fears"; "Afghan Government Moves to Disarm Private Armies," AFP, July 15, 2002.

49. Quoted in Kathy Gannon, "Afghan Chiefs Gripe over U.N. Deal," AP, December 10, 2001. On the mujahideen's claim to rule post-2001 Afghanistan, see Michael Bhatia, "The Future of the Mujahideen: Legitimacy, Legacy and Demobilization in Post-Bonn Afghanistan," *International Peacekeeping* 14, no. 1 (2007), 90–107.

50. Interview with Ismail Khan, June 24, 2018.

51. Quoted in "Ismail Khan Keeps Order." During the interviews I held separately with both Karzai and Ismail Khan in 2018, they spoke very positively of each other. Karzai called Ismail Khan "a patriot," "a very good governor and a good minister," to whom he would have offered "any position." Ismail Khan told me that "the relationship with Karzai was always really good," while blaming Zalmay Khalilzad for any tension with Kabul in the early 2000s.

52. Quoted in Daragahi, "Afghan Governor Spurs Instability Fears."

53. Eric Westerwelt on, "New Report Showing the United States Supporting Governor in Western Afghanistan Who Is Charged with Human Rights Abuses," NPR's *Morning Edition*, November 6, 2002.

54. Quoted in Luna, "Lord of the Infinite Distance."

55. Interview with former president Hamid Karzai, June 30, 2018.

56. Quoted in Otton, "Afghan president Gets Full Support."

57. Quoted in Fang, "The Great Game 2002."

58. Interview with former Western diplomat, 2011.

59. Quoted in Alexandre Peyrille, "Warlords Pocket Afghan Customs Dues," AFP, May 12, 2002.

60. Quoted in Morris, "U.S. Commander Seeks to Shore Up Ties." Giustozzi affirms that, by the summer of 2004, "Herat was sending cash to Kabul to the tune of $8 million a month" (*Empires of Mud*, 235).

61. For information conveyed in this section, in addition to anonymous interviews and the sources cited above, I consulted the following news sources: "Herat Governor Argues Bonn Conference Decisions," *Ria Novosti*, December 7, 2001; Arkady Dubnov and Aleksei Slobodin, "The Jihad," *Vremya Novostei*, December 7, 2001; Carlotta Gall, "Iranian Influence Felt in Afghanistan's West," *New York Times*, January 22, 2002; "Afghan Leader to Visit Iran"; "Afghan Leader Visits Herat for Talks with Regional Chief," AFP, February 6, 2002; Guy Dinmore and Roula Khalaf, "America's New Enemy," *Financial Times*, February 1, 2002; "Karzai Flies to Herat to Meet Warlord Ismail Khan," AP, February 6, 2002; "Karzai Vows to Bring Afghan Warlords to Heel through Peaceful Means," AFP, July 26, 2002.

62. Human Rights Watch, *All Our Hopes Are Crushed: Violence and Repression in Western Afghanistan* (New York: Human Rights Watch, 2002).

63. Human Rights Watch, *Afghanistan's Bonn Agreement One Year Later: A Catalog of Missed Opportunities* (New York: Human Rights Watch, 2002).

64. Interview with UN official, 2011.

65. Giustozzi claims that "[the] Iranians, who had been consulted beforehand by the UN, thought it better to accept the change in the hope of establishing good relations with his successor and were 'rewarded' with the appointment of the former ambassador of Ismail Khan in Teheran [*sic*], Khairkhwa" (*Empires of Mud*, 262).

66. Phone interview with Ahmed Rashid, journalist, May 10, 2012.

67. Phone interview with Ahmed Rashid, journalist, May 10, 2012.

68. Giustozzi, *Empires of Mud*, 261. It has been alleged (most notably by Ismail Khan himself) that members of Karzai's cabinet had encouraged Amanullah Khan to wage a war against Ismail Khan: "They used Amanullah to depose me," he stated emphatically. Quoted in Ann Rachel Marlowe, "Interview with a Warlord," *LA Weekly*, October 15, 2004.

69. Amy Waldman, "Political Bid to Quell Unrest in Afghanistan," *New York Times*, August 29, 2004.

70. Sinno, *Organizations at War*, 274.

71. Interview with former president Hamid Karzai, June 30, 2018.

72. Dipali Mukhopadhyay, *Warlords, Strongman Governors, and the State in Afghanistan* (New York: Cambridge University Press, 2014), 245.

73. For information conveyed in this section, in addition to anonymous interviews and the sources cited above, I relied on Giustozzi, *Empires of Mud*, 259. I also consulted the following news sources: Fang, "The Great Game 2002"; Carlotta Gall, "Afghans Ask U.S. to Help Cool Conflict," *International Herald Tribune*, August 18, 2004; Anthony Loyd, "Afghan Warlord Closes In on Prize City," *Times*, August 25, 2004; Pamela Constable, "Afghans Riot over Dismissal of Governor in Herat," *Washington Post*, September 13, 2004; Carlotta Gall, "Region's New Governor Says Violence in Herat Is Ended;

Denounces Warlord," *New York Times*, September 14, 2004; Griff Witte, "Former Afghan Governor May Be behind Muslim Riot," *Houston Chronicle*, February 26, 2006.

74. Frederick Barth, *Political Leadership among Swat Pathans* (London: Athlone, 1996), 214.

75. Interview with human rights activist, 2011.

76. Ismail Khan, speech given in Badagh, Injil District, Herat Province, March 20, 2011.

77. Bhatia, "Future of the Mujahideen," 90.

78. The "power to make war successfully" can in fact be conceived as a source of legitimacy. Ariel I. Ahram and Charles King, "The Warlord as Arbitrageur," *Theory and Society* 41, no. 2 (2012): 171.

79. Ismail Khan, speech given in Badagh, Injil District, Herat Province, March 20, 2011. Ismail Khan has made similar statements multiple times since. See, for example, Fabrizio Foschini, "Guns, Girls and Grizzled Warriors: Ismail Khan's Mujahedin Council Project in the West," Afghanistan Analysts Network, November 17, 2012.

80. Bhatia, "Future of the Mujahideen," 90.

81. Interview with Ismail Khan, June 24, 2018.

82. Interview with former military officer, 2011.

83. Interview with human rights activist, 2018.

84. Ismail Khan, speech given in Badagh, Injil District, Herat Province, March 20, 2011.

85. Mirwais Sadeq was the former minister of labor and social affairs in the Afghan Interim Authority (2001–2) and, at the time of his death, minister of civil aviation in the transitional government (2002–4). He was not killed during the jihad but rather during skirmishes with forces loyal to one of Ismail Khan's rivals.

86. Interview with Herat resident 1, 2011.

87. Rashid, *Descent into Chaos*, 126.

88. G. Whitney Azoy, *Buzkashi: Game and Power in Afghanistan* (Philadelphia: University of Pennsylvania Press, 1982), 14 (first quote); Renee Montagne on "Democracy in Afghanistan: The Warlord of Herat," NPR's *Morning Edition*, May 18, 2004 (second quote). Ismail Khan is even reported to have invited journalists to admire him riding his white horse in the sunset. See "Return to Power of Ismail Khan in Herat, Afghanistan," NPR's *All Things Considered*, July 17, 2002.

89. Azoy, *Buzkashi*, 1982, 38. Partlow, for example, reports that President Karzai's cousin, Hashmat Karzai, also had his own private zoo, in which "he kept peacocks and pit bulls, a pelican, a hyena, and three ostriches from Pakistan." Joshua Partlow, *A Kingdom of Their Own: The Family Karzai and the Afghan Disaster* (New York: Alfred A. Knopf, 2016), 280. This is not unique to Afghanistan. Marten reports that, in Chechnya, Ramzan Kadyrov "regularly showed off his mansion and personal zoo, his constantly renewed fleet of imported luxury cars, and his stable of thoroughbred racing horses to visitors." Kimberly Marten, *Warlords: Strong-Arm Brokers in Weak States* (Ithaca, NY: Cornell University Press, 2012), 123.

90. Azoy, *Buzkashi*, 1982, 23. According to Azoy, "Such an emphasis on exploits helps explain why this society has never gotten a good press for political organization" (23).

91. Quoted in "Ismail Khan Keeps Order." His escape was mentioned in the introductory speech given at the gathering of former mujahideen I attended in 2011. Ismail Khan also gave me a detailed account of it during our interview of June 24, 2018. See also Giustozzi, *Empires of Mud*, 217.

92. Interview with Ismail Khan, June 24, 2018.

93. Conversation with aide to Ismail Khan, 2011.

94. Interview with UN official, 2011.

95. Giustozzi, *Empires of Mud*, 272.

96. Ahram and King, "The Warlord as Arbitrageur," 170.

97. Interview with human rights activist, 2018.

98. Dorronsoro, *Revolution Unending*, 119.

99. See Giustozzi, *Empires of Mud*, 230.

100. See "Afghanistan's Parliament Rejects over Half the Cabinet for Second Time," *Telegraph*, January 16, 2010. In a December 2009 memorandum, US ambassador to Afghanistan Karl Eikenberry described Ismail Khan as "the worst of Karzai's choices . . . known for his corruption and ineffectiveness at the energy ministry." Quoted in Brett Blackledge, "Karzai Ignored U.S. Bid to Oust Former Warlord," *Virginian-Pilot*, January 1, 2011.

101. Interview with former aide to Ahmad Shah Massoud 1, 2018.

102. Ismail Khan, speech given in Badagh, Injil District, Herat Province, March 20, 2011.

103. Quoted in Morris, "U.S. Commander Seeks to Shore Up Ties." At the gathering of commanders I attended at Ismail Khan's palace in 2018, a banner hung above the speakers read (in both Arabic and Dari): "And hold fast to the rope of God, altogether, and do not become divided" (sura 3:103), in *The Quran*, trans. Talal Itani (Dallas: ClearQuran, 2012). Accessed online.

104. Conversation with Gilles Dorronsoro, Afghanistan scholar, 2011. The doubt still persists. In 2002, William Maley wrote that Ismail Khan was of "mixed [Pashtun] and Tajik ancestry" [William Maley, *The Afghanistan Wars* (Basingstoke, UK: Palgrave Macmillan, 2002), 65] while, according to Jean-Pierre Guinhut, former French ambassador in Afghanistan (2002–2005), Ismail Khan "is more Persian than Tajik" (translated by the author). Quoted in Notin, *La guerre de l'ombre*, 738.

105. Ismail Khan, speech given in Badagh, Injil District, Herat Province, March 20, 2011.

106. Barth, *Political Leadership*, 214.

107. Interview with Ismail Khan, June 24, 2018. Ismail Khan initially called on the insurgents to negotiate with him and other former mujahideen leaders during a speech he gave for the anniversary of the Herat rebellion in March 2018. See "Ismail Khan Invites Insurgent Groups to Talk with Mujahideen," Tolo News, March 16, 2018; "Taliban Welcomes Former Herat Governor's Call for Peace Talks," Tolo News, March 20, 2018. On the talks between the Taliban and representatives of the Afghan opposition, see Abdul Qadir Sediqi and Rupam Jain, "Russia Plays Power Broker as U.S.-Taliban Talks Gather Steam," Reuters, January 31, 2019; Sayed Salahuddin, "Afghan Government Frozen out of Moscow Peace Talks with the Taliban," *Washington Post*, February 4, 2019.

108. Interview with human rights activist, 2011.

109. Interview with Herat bureaucrat, 2011. Some, for instance, argue that Ismail Khan would not be a minister without Iranian support; others claim that his government position is key to his power. A US report indicates that "our repeated interventions directly with Karzai . . . did not overcome Karzai's deeply personal bonds with Khan." Quoted in Blackledge, "Karzai Ignored U.S. Bid."

110. Interview with Ismail Khan, March 19, 2011.

111. See, for example, "Ismail Khan Blasts Government for Lack of Mujahidin in Cabinet," Tolo News, January 17, 2015; "Security Sector Given to Leftists Supported by Soviets: Ismail Khan," Khaama Press, January 17, 2015; "Ismail Khan Labels New Cabinet 'Communists' and 'Dual Citizens', Calls for Mujahideen Leadership," Tolo News, February 8, 2015; "No Stability If Jihadi Leaders Remain Sidelined, Ismail Khan Warns," Khaama Press, February 9, 2015; Margherita Stancati, "Afghan City Rises as Opposition Hub," *Wall Street Journal*, March 15, 2015; Lynne O'Donnell, "Afghan Warlord Warns of ISIS Rise," AP, April 2015; "Herat Will Become Insecure within Weeks If Govt Keep Looking the Other Way: Ismail Khan," *Afghanistan Times*, April 28, 2015; "Afghan Warlord's Anger at Being 'Sidelined' by Ghani," *Express Tribune*, June 19, 2015; "Afghanistan: Ismaïl Khan ou la 'génération moudjahidine' mise sur la touche," AFP, June 19, 2015; "Ismail Khan Warns Afghan Government for Sidelining Mujahideen Leaders," Khaama Press, June 19, 2015; Fahim Masoud, "Ismail Khan, Former Warlord, on ISIS, Afghan Governance, and His Country's Future," International Policy Digest, October 21, 2015; "Ismail Khan Urges Government to Implement Mujahideen's Suggestions for Security," Khaama Press, February 16, 2016; Jawed Ziaratjayee, "Jamiat Official Calls for Early Elections to Fix Current Crisis," Tolo News, June 7, 2017.

4. Dostum, the Ethnic Entrepreneur

1. On Dostum being denied a visa to the United States, see Matthew Rosenberg, "Afghanistan's Vice President Is Barred from Entering U.S.," *New York Times*, April 25, 2016. On government control of militia behavior, see Jessica A. Stanton, "Regulating Militias: Governments, Militias, and Civilian Targeting in Civil War," *Journal of Conflict Resolution* 59, no. 5 (2015): 899–923. On the Afghan model of warfare, see Stephen D. Biddle, "Allies, Airpower, and Modern Warfare: The Afghan Model in Afghanistan and Iraq," *International Security* 30, no. 3 (Winter 2005/06): 161–76.

2. Interview with European diplomat, 2008.

3. G. Whitney Azoy, *Buzkashi: Game & Power in Afghanistan*, 3rd ed. (Long Grove, IL: Waveland, 2012), 24, 167.

4. James D. Fearon and David D. Laitin, "Explaining Interethnic Cooperation," *American Political Science Review* 90, no. 4 (1996): 716.

5. According to Azoy, there are two versions of the story of how Dostum earned his nickname: the first one is that Dostum, as a boy, called everyone "my friend" affectionately; the second is that he started calling everyone "my friend" when he was a teenager, to mock the people he bullied (*Buzkashi*, 2012, 40). Williams claims that Dostum gained his nickname while in the army, because he addressed men in his unit as "my friend." See Brian Glyn Williams, *The Last Warlord: The Life and Legend of Dostum, the Afghan*

Warrior Who Led US Special Forces to Topple the Taliban Regime (Chicago: Chicago Review, 2013), 103.

6. "The Five-Star General of the North and Afghan Events," *Cheragh*, March 29, 2005.

7. Antonio Giustozzi, "The Ethnicisation of an Afghan Faction: Junbesh-I-Milli from Its Origins to the Presidential Elections" (Crisis States Working Paper 67 [Series 1], London, 2005), 5. See also "The Five-Star General."

8. One of these new allies, General Abdul Mumin, had previously been in charge of protecting the Hairatan border post with Uzbekistan on behalf of the regime and was now in control of it, therefore playing a major role in generating additional revenues. Giustozzi estimates that the custom revenues associated with the Hairatan border post amounted to tens of millions of dollars annually in the 1990s. Antonio Giustozzi, *Empires of Mud: Wars and Warlords in Afghanistan* (New York: Columbia University Press, 2009), 134.

9. For information conveyed in this section, in addition to anonymous interviews and the sources cited above, I relied on the following sources: Anthony Davis, "The Battleground of Northern Afghanistan," *Jane's Intelligence Review* 6, no. 7 (1994): 323–27; Kamal Matinuddin, *The Taliban Phenomenon: Afghanistan 1994–1997* (Oxford: Oxford University Press, 1999), 48–49; Antonio Giustozzi, *War, Politics and Society in Afghanistan, 1978–1992* (Washington, DC: Georgetown University Press, 2000), 222–23; Willem Vogelsang, *The Afghans* (Malden, MA: Wiley-Blackwell, 2002), 322–24; Jean-José Puig, *La pêche à la truite en Afghanistan* (Paris: Éditions de La Martinière, 2005), 329–30; Giustozzi, *Empires of Mud*, 56–57; Peter Tomsen, *The Wars of Afghanistan: Messianic Terrorism, Tribal Conflicts, and the Failures of Great Powers* (New York: Public Affairs, 2011), 477–82; Williams, *The Last Warlord*, 93, 95, 102, 120. See also Patrick Cockburn, "Rashid Dostum: The Treacherous General," *Independent*, December 1, 2001.

10. For more on Junbesh, see Giustozzi, "Ethnicisation of an Afghan Faction"; Giustozzi, *Empires of Mud*, chaps. 6–13.

11. Interview with Afghan scholar 3, 2008.

12. On the idea of storing power, see Walter Korpi, "Power Resources Approach vs. Action and Conflict: On Causal and Intentional Explanations in the Study of Power," *Sociological Theory* 3, no. 2 (1985). Stanton claims that Dostum controlled a 20,000-man militia in 1997. Doug Stanton, *Horse Soldiers: The Extraordinary Story of a Band of U.S. Soldiers Who Rode to Victory in Afghanistan* (New York: Scribner, 2009), 54. Garanich reports that "at one time, Dostum claimed to have upwards of 100,000 troops in his command." Gleb Garanich, "Rebels Use U.S. Strikes to Gain Ground," *Toronto Star*, October 16, 2001. According to Cockburn, estimates range from 25,000 to 40,000 soldiers ("The Treacherous General"). Finally, Giustozzi mentions 110,000 men "on paper" but claims that "Dostum never fielded more than 20,000 men at the same time" (*Empires of Mud*, 106, 166).

13. Gilles Dorronsoro, "Kabul at War (1992–1996): State, Ethnicity and Social Classes," *South Asia Multidisciplinary Academic Journal*, 2007, para. 14 (accessed online); Giustozzi, *Empires of Mud*, 135.

14. Quoted in "Afghanistan's Dostum Advocates Integration of Militias into Independent Army," *Der Spiegel*, February 25, 2002. Junbesh's former foreign affairs

representative, General Abdul Malik Pahlawan, told me the same thing in an interview conducted on November 9, 2008.

15. Giustozzi, *Empires of Mud*, 171. See also Puig, *La pêche à la truite*, 331.

16. Chris Stephen, "Prized City Awaits a Feared Warlord's Revenge," *Guardian*, October 25, 2001.

17. Ahmed Rashid, *Taliban: Militant Islam, Oil and Fundamentalism in Central Asia*, 2nd ed. (New Haven, CT: Yale University Press, 2001), 56–57.

18. Abdulkader H. Sinno, *Organizations at War: In Afghanistan and Beyond* (Ithaca, NY: Cornell University Press, 2008), 192. Giustozzi notes that "Dostum's diplomatic efforts in 1992–1998 turned out to be insufficient to save Junbesh, mainly because of the relatively low caliber of his interlocutors" (*Empires of Mud*, 172).

19. Interview with Antonio Giustozzi, Afghanistan scholar, October 11, 2008. On Dostum's relations with Uzbekistan, see also Gilles Dorronsoro, *Revolution Unending: Afghanistan, 1979 to the Present* (New York: Columbia University Press, 2005), 262; Giustozzi, *Empires of Mud*, 136–37. On Dostum's involvement in drug trafficking, Deepali Gaur Singh writes: "It was also commonly believed that General Rashid Dostum, the leader of the ethnic Uzbek militia, was also involved in earning huge profits by exporting drugs via Uzbekistan. In May 1996, a Russian daily newspaper, *Komsomolskaya Pravda*, published exposes about an elaborate drug trafficking network between Afghanistan, Uzbekistan and Chechnya involving 'senior officials' of the states. The story, which was never refuted by anyone in authority, named Russians and Chechens linked to the KGB and General Rashid Dostum. . . . According to these reports, opium was collected in the southern Afghan province of Helmand, which was one of the largest producers of opium, and then sent to Termez in Uzbekistan, from where it was airlifted to Samarkand by General Dostum's own helicopter force, each carrying two-thirds of one metric ton at a time." Deepali Gaur Singh, *Drugs Production and Trafficking in Afghanistan* (Kabul: Shah M. Book, 2007), 80.

20. For information on Turkey's relations with Dostum in the 1990s, see also Giustozzi, "Ethnicisation of an Afghan Faction"; Giustozzi, *Empires of Mud*, 113, 137. Another well-informed source claims that Turkey was giving Dostum $1 million a month during that period (interview with Afghan scholar 4, 2011). Interviewed on October 11, 2008, Antonio Giustozzi believed that Turkey's financial support to Junbesh remained minimal at the time.

21. Giustozzi, *Empires of Mud*, 113.

22. I have heard different stories regarding Beg's airplane crash: some point toward Dostum as being responsible; others toward Iran. Giustozzi argues that it was the Taliban's doing ("Ethnicisation of an Afghan Faction," 4).

23. Although there is no clear evidence, many believe that Rasul Pahlawan (Malik's brother), one of Junbesh's strongest commanders, was assassinated by Dostum in 1996 because he opposed the reconciliation effort between Junbesh and Jamiat, a move that Dostum considered crucial to the long-term future of Junbesh, after the Taliban had become a threat. See Giustozzi, *Empires of Mud*, 163.

24. Interview with former governor of Faryab Province, 2011.

25. Interview with former European diplomat, 2011. See also "Bin Laden Cave Complexes to Be Searched; General Dostum Wields Power in NW Afghanistan," CNN's

Live Event/Special, December 24, 2001; Eckart Schiewek, "Keeping the Peace without Peacekeepers," in *Building State and Security in Afghanistan,* ed. Wolfgang Danspeckgruber with Robert P. Finn (Princeton, NJ: Woodrow Wilson School of Public and International Affairs, 2007), 167–211.

26. Quoted in Sudarsan Raghavan, "Charismatic Uzbek Chieftain Important to Afghan Future," Knight Ridder, October 14, 2001.

27. Giustozzi, *Empires of Mud,* 88. Giustozzi also claims that the role later given to Dostum by the CIA "was the result of contacts between Dostum's representatives in Tashkent and the Agency, which had been going on already some months prior to the 9/11 attacks" (136).

28. For information conveyed in this section, in addition to anonymous interviews and the sources cited above, I relied on the following: Rashid, *Taliban,* 27, 52; Vogelsang, *The Afghans,* 326, 331–33; Puig, *La pêche à la truite,* 331; Giustozzi, *Empires of Mud,* 115–16, 137, 154–55; Jean-Christophe Notin, *La guerre de l'ombre des Français en Afghanistan 1979–2011* (Paris: Fayard, 2011), 510; Fotini Christia, *Alliance Formation in Civil Wars* (New York: Cambridge University Press, 2012), 70; Williams, *The Last Warlord,* 188–93. I also consulted the following news sources: Peter Baker and Susan B. Glasser, "Rebels Capture Northern Areas, Cut Off Taliban Supply Route," *Washington Post,* October 10, 2001; Julius Strauss and Ahmed Rashid, "West's Ally General Is Known for Brutality," *Gazette,* October 24, 2001.

29. Quoted in Giustozzi, *Empires of Mud,* 155.

30. Stanton, *Horse Soldiers,* 197.

31. Quoted in Justin Huggler, "American Aircraft Carry Out First Carpet Bombing Raids on Front Line," *Independent,* November 1, 2001.

32. Stanton, *Horse Soldiers,* 253.

33. A journalist reported that US Special Forces had become so intimate with Dostum and his men that they swam in his new indoor pool almost a year after the beginning of the US-led intervention (Christopher Torchia, "Afghan Commander Gets Indoor Pool," AP, September 7, 2002), while Khalilzad recalls meeting with US Special Forces who considered that the United States should have made Dostum president of the country for his role in fighting the Taliban. Zalmay Khalilzad, *The Envoy: From Kabul to the White House, My Journey through a Turbulent World* (New York: St Martin's, 2016), 134. See also Notin, *La guerre de l'ombre,* 669, 779.

34. Online communication with former European diplomat, 2012.

35. Stanton also reports that Dostum was in contact with US congressmen as well as political actors in Pakistan and Russia (*Horse Soldiers,* 148–49). Giustozzi notes the importance for Dostum of "claiming a monopoly over foreign relations" in the 1990s but does not account for the importance of these personal networks in the post-2001 international environment (*Empires of Mud,* 113).

36. Quoted in Raghavan, "Charismatic Uzbek Chieftain."

37. Ravi Nessman, "Once Feared Warlord Says He Is Ready for Political Life in the New Afghanistan," AP, January 15, 2002. Notin reports that Dostum also prepared a greeting card for Jacques Chirac in which he wished the French president a happy new year and falsely presented himself as Afghanistan's minister of defense (*La guerre de l'ombre,* 716).

38. Quoted in "Turkey Can Help Train Afghan Army, Says Afghan Warlord Dostum," AP, January 23, 2002.

39. A Western diplomat mentioned payments of $300,000 a month made to Dostum by the Turkish government (interview with Western diplomat 2, 2012).

40. For information conveyed in this section, in addition to anonymous interviews and the sources cited above, I also consulted the following news sources: Frederic Frommer, "Lobbyist Adds Afghan Warlord to List of Unusual Clients," AP, December 16, 2001; "Japanese Lawmaker Says Afghan Warlord Willing to Disarm," Pakistan Newswire, December 21, 2001; "Afghan Gen Dostum Back in Mazar-e Sharif after High-Level Meetings in Kabul," Balkh Radio, December 25, 2001; "Northern Afghan Warlord to Visit Family in Turkey," AP, January 15, 2002; "Afghan Deputy Defence Minister Meets Turkish Prime Minister," TRT2, January 22, 2002; "Turkish PM Discusses Afghan Issue with Afghan Deputy PM," Xinhua General News Service, January 23, 2002; Jeffrey Schaeffer, "Afghan Soldiers Bid Farewell to U.S. Special Forces," AP, December 19, 2001; Anna Badkhen, "Reports of Rape, Looting by Afghan Militiamen," *San Francisco Chronicle*, February 15, 2002; Ann Rachel Marlowe, "'Warlords' and 'Leaders,'" *National Review*, February 18, 2002; Robert Young Pelton, "The Legend of Heavy D & the Boys: In the Field with an Afghan Warlord," *National Geographic Adventure*, March 2002; Tod Robberson, "Warlord Dostum de-Facto Leader in Northern Afghanistan," *Dallas Morning News*, April 19, 2002; Burt Herman, "In New Afghanistan, Dostum Trades Battle Garb for Business Suit and Turns to Politics," AP, April 28, 2002; "US Official Observes Narcotics Destruction in Afghan North," Jowzjan TV, May 14, 2003; "Afghan Northern Leader Meets Officials in Kabul," Jowzjan TV, May 24, 2003; "Programme of Afghan Jowzjan TV News in Dari 1640 Gmt 3 Jun 03," Jowzjan TV, June 4, 2003; "Afghan Provincial Governor Upbeat on Government's Achievements," Jowzjan TV, November 13, 2003; Sara Carter, "The Art of Warlord," *Washington Times*, October 12, 2008.

41. Khalilzad, *The Envoy*, 134.

42. Even though Juma Khan Hamdard was not officially a member of Junbesh, he was in fact closely affiliated with it. Two of the four divisions of the Eighth Army Corps actually paid direct allegiance to General Dostum. Junbesh also engaged in reaching out to the division commanders of the other Army Corps based in northern Afghanistan (Sixth and Seventh) and eventually managed to turn two of the divisions that made up the Seventh Army Corps (under Ata's command) in favor of General Dostum. See Schiewek, "Keeping the Peace," 169.

43. Schiewek, 192.

44. Interview with Robert Finn, former US ambassador to Afghanistan, October 5, 2011. In more general terms: "The specialists do not disarm, but if their land, labor, and resources are more productive in the absence of violence then this arrangement creates an additional cost to fighting; herein lies the solution to the credible commitment to nonviolence. If each violence specialist captures a larger economic return (a rent) from the land, labor, and resources he or she controls when there is peace and if those rents are large enough, then it is possible for both specialists to credibly believe that the other specialist is better off by refraining from fighting." Douglas C. North, John Joseph Wallis, and Barry R. Weingast, *Violence and Social Orders: A Conceptual*

Framework for Interpreting Recorded Human History (New York: Cambridge University Press, 2009), 19.

45. Quoted in Carlotta Gall, "Two Afghan Warlords Coexist, Warily," *New York Times*, April 28, 2002.

46. Peter B. Golden, *Central Asia in World History* (New York: Oxford University Press, 2011), 137. See, for example, Cockburn, "The Treacherous General."

47. Torchia, "Afghan Commander Gets Indoor Pool"; Ilene Prusher, "Afghan President Renews Bid to Rein in Northern Warlords," *Christian Science Monitor*, November 12, 2003; Catherine Philip, "From a Brutal Warlord to 'Our Hero of Peace' Now He Wants to Be Afghanistan's President," *Times*, September 29, 2004. While I personally came to doubt the existence of these things, it is possible that these reports referred to Dostum's private house, as opposed to the guest house, which is where I stayed. See also Brian Murphy, "Warlord Backs Plans to Leave Cities, Balks at Disarming Militia," AP, February 7, 2002.

48. Robberson, "Dostum de-Facto Leader." NPR reports that Afghan rugs bearing Dostum's face could even be purchased in Mazar-i Sharif. "General Abdurrashid Dostum Committed to a Unified Afghanistan," NPR's *All Things Considered*, January 15, 2002. I purchased one in Kabul as late as 2013, as well as Dostum calendars in Sheberghan in 2014 and pictures of various Afghan leaders (including one of Dostum riding a horse) on the streets of Mazar-i Sharif in 2008.

49. For information conveyed in this section, in addition to anonymous interviews and the sources cited above, I relied on the following: Ali A. Jalali, "Rebuilding Afghanistan's National Army," *Parameters* 32, no. 3 (2002): 72–86; Antonio Giustozzi, "Military Reform in Afghanistan," in *Confronting Afghanistan's Security Dilemma: Reforming the Security Sector*, ed. Mark Sedra (Bonn: Bonn International Center for Conversion, 2003), 23–31; Schiewek, "Keeping the Peace," 174; Giustozzi, *Empires of Mud*, 134, 168, 187–88; Stanton, *Horse Soldiers*, 276; Dipali Mukhopadhyay, *Warlords, Strongman Governors, and the State in Afghanistan* (New York: Cambridge University Press, 2014), 290–96. I also consulted the following news sources: "Afghan Alliance Commander Tells Iranian Radio of Gains in North," Voice of the Islamic Republic of Iran, October 11, 2001; Judy Woodruff and Harris Whitbeck, "Dostum Appointed Deputy Defense Minister," CNN's *Live Today*, December 24, 2001; Edward Cody, "In Afghanistan, Most Politics Is Still Local," *Washington Post*, January 16, 2002; Pamela Constable, "Operation Transformation for Afghan with a Dark Past," *Washington Post*, May 29, 2002; "Coalition to Stay in Afghanistan until Peace Restored, Says Envoy in Kyrgyzstan," Kyrgyz Radio, October 8, 2002; "Afghanistan to Remain United, Envoy to Kyrgyzstan Says," *Vecherniy Bishkek*, December 3, 2002; April Witt, "An Afghan Boss Loses His Bite," *Washington Post*, May 23, 2003.

50. Khalilzad, *The Envoy*, 137, 201.

51. Quoted on "Abdurrashid Dostum," NPR's *Weekend All Things Considered*, December 2, 2001.

52. Quoted in David Rohde, "Boycott Threat Is Early Test for Afghan Leadership Pact," *New York Times*, December 7, 2001.

53. Quoted in "Afghan Warlord Dostum Promises No Return to Fighting," AFP, December 9, 2001.

54. Quoted in "Ethnic Uzbek Warlord Dostum Reconciled to Afghan Interim Government," Voice of the Islamic Republic of Iran, December 9, 2001.

55. Quoted in Carlotta Gall, "Afghan Has No Doubt Country Needs Him," *New York Times*, December 27, 2001.

56. Quoted in Murphy, "Warlord Backs Plans to Leave Cities."

57. Online communication with former UK official, 2012.

58. Interview with former president Hamid Karzai, June 30, 2018.

59. Quoted on CNN International's *Q&A with Zain Verjee*, March 20, 2002.

60. On "Deputy Defence Chief Says Terrorism Still a Threat to Afghanistan," Balkh Radio, March 22, 2002.

61. Interview with former European diplomat, 2011.

62. Giustozzi mentions a few examples, such as eradicating poppy, handing over custom posts, backing off from threatening to boycott the presidential election, and demobilizing his troops. See Giustozzi, *Empires of Mud*, 172.

63. Human Rights Watch, *Paying for the Taliban's Crimes: Abuses against Ethnic Pashtuns in Northern Afghanistan* (New York: Human Rights Watch, 2002).

64. Chief of staff of President Hamid Karzai, quoted in Witt, "An Afghan Boss Loses His Bite." Giustozzi argues that being appointed as special adviser was actually Dostum's "greatest achievement" as he had been authorized to dismantle the Seventh Army Corps, commanded by Ata, but that the latter's refusal to do so rendered the position merely ceremonial (*Empires of Mud*, 156, 175).

65. On "Afghan Commander Mounts Robust Defense Position, Pledges Security for North," Balkh TV, May 26, 2003.

66. Mukhopadhyay, *Warlords, Strongman Governors*, 82.

67. Quoted in Bradley Graham, "Rumsfeld Meets Afghan Militia Chiefs," *Saint Paul Pioneer Press*, December 5, 2003.

68. On October 10, 2003, Pamela Constable mentioned in the *Washington Post* that Dostum had even been offered the vice presidency but had turned it down, hoping to be appointed first deputy minister of defense instead. Former president Hamid Karzai denied this when we met on June 30, 2018.

69. Quoted in Mukhopadhyay, *Warlords, Strongman Governors*, 97. Giustozzi notes that the demobilization campaign was relaunched after Dostum decided to run in the presidential elections (*Empires of Mud*, 191).

70. For information conveyed in this paragraph, in addition to anonymous interviews and the sources cited above, I relied on the following sources: Yaqub Ibrahimi, "Army Develops despite Militia Disarmament Issues" Institute for War and Peace Reporting, September 29, 2004; Schiewek, "Keeping the Peace," 180–81, 192, 200; Giustozzi, *Empires of Mud*, 192. I also consulted the following news sources: "Afghan Northern Alliance Commander Outlines Plans for Offensive," *Der Spiegel*, October 13, 2001; Raghavan, "Charismatic Uzbek Chieftain"; "The Peace-Seeking Missile Profile General Abdul Rashid Dostum," *Herald*, December 1, 2001; "Northern Alliance Commander Puts Boycott on New Afghan Government," Ria Novosti, December 6, 2001; "Uzbek Warlord to Boycott Afghan Accord," *Globe and Mail*, December 6, 2001; Mike Blanchfield, "Uzbek Warlord Threatens to Boycott Bonn Regime over Lack of Representation," *Vancouver Sun*, December 7, 2001; "General Dostum Disagrees with Distribution of Ministerial

Posts in Afghanistan's Interim Government," Ria Novosti, December 15, 2001; Peter Beaumont, "Warlords Hear Karzai Vow to Build an Era of Peace," *Guardian*, December 23, 2001; Woodruff and Whitbeck, "Dostum Appointed"; "Live from Afghanistan: Tracing al Qaeda Footsteps; Former Warlord Becomes Part of Government; What Is the Next Target in War on Terror?," CNN's *Live Event/Special*, December 24, 2001; "New Afghan Deputy Minister Dostum Says Differences Resolved," Voice of the Islamic Republic of Iran, December 25, 2001; Jeffrey Schaeffer, "Afghanistan's New Deputy Defense Minister Says Remnant of Taliban," AP, December 27, 2001; Martin Arostegui, "New Afghan Deal Calms North," United Press International, December 28, 2001; "Is Pakistan Too Dangerous for Americans?; Why Would Afghan Warlord Free Taliban Prisoners," CNN's *Wolf Blitzer Reports*, March 22, 2002; Susan B. Glasser, "Afghans Take a First Step toward Democracy," *Washington Post*, April 16, 2002; Gall, "Two Afghan Warlords"; Niko Price, "Afghan Warlord Fighting Kills Six," AP, May 1, 2002; Constable, "Operation Transformation"; David Blair, "SAS Peace Deal Helps Tame the Warlords," *Telegraph*, July 9, 2002; Todd Pitman, "U.N. to Visit Afghan Warlord after Offer to Cooperate with Mass Killing Investigation," AP, September 1, 2002; "President Karzai Orders Dostum Back to Kabul," *Morning Star*, May 23, 2003; Pamela Constable, "Afghan Militia Leaders Sign Truce," *Washington Post*, October 10, 2003; Pamela Constable, "Afghan Militias Cling to Power in North," *Washington Post*, October 28, 2003; "Afghan Interior Minister Says Heavy Weapons' Collection in North 'Going Ahead,'" Balkh TV, November 22, 2003; Michael Evans, "Warlord's Arms Deal Bolsters Peace Push," *Times*, December 4, 2003; Kim Sengupta, "Afghan Warlord Agrees to Hand Over His Weapons to British Team," *Independent*, December 4, 2003; "Warlord Summitry," *Washington Post*, December 11, 2003; "Afghan General Dostum Says Can Crush Al-Qa'idah If Given Official Post," Al Jazeera, December 26, 2003; "Afghan Northern Commander, Dostum, Says Capable of Crushing Al-Qa'idah," Al Jazeera, December 26, 2003; "Afghan Paper Warns against Perks for Senior Officials," *Erada*, January 24, 2004; "Afghan Paper Responds to Criticism against Gen Dostum,'" *Parcham-i Azadi*, March 14, 2004; "Afghan Warlord Challenges Karzai in Presidential Election," Xinhua General News Service, July 23, 2004.

71. Quoted in Burt Herman, "Afghan Strongman Turned Presidential Candidate, Dostum in Fight for Political Life," AP, October 25, 2004.

72. Giustozzi, "Ethnicisation of an Afghan Faction," 16.

73. Quoted in Carol Harrington, "Ruthless Dostum a Rival for Karzai," *Toronto Star*, September 20, 2004.

74. Quoted in Hamida Ghafour, "Warlord with Shifting Loyalties 'Hero of Peace' in Afghan Vote," *Globe and Mail*, October 7, 2004.

75. Interview with former mujahideen government official, 2008.

76. The same had occurred before. For example, on April 16, 2002, Susan B. Glasser, covering the election of the *loya jirga* representatives, reported in the *Washington Post* that, in a Jowzjan village, "soldiers stood in the green fields with Kalashnikovs and grenade launchers."

77. Herman, "Afghan Strongman Turned Presidential Candidate."

78. The horse is not only a status marker all over Central Asia (and hence northern Afghanistan). It is also of symbolic importance in Islamic culture. Various Quranic suras

and verses refer to the importance of the horse and the horse rider (e.g., 3:14, 16:8, and 100:1–11). Some suras and verses directly link the horse to warfare and success in battle (e.g., 8:6; 100:2). And a classical Arabic poem equates the horse to "el-Khayr," the supreme blessing. Akiko Motoyoshi Sumi, *Description in Classical Arabic Poetry* (Leiden: Brill, 2003), 47.

79. *Buzkashi* literally means "goat grabbing" or "goat dragging," but, as Azoy points out, "no special importance attaches itself to the change in carcass species—from goat to calf—which seems to have occurred in the last three of four generations" (*Buzkashi*, 2012, 4). See also Michael Barry, *Massoud: De l'islamisme à la liberté* (Paris: Audibert, 2002), 147.

80. G. Whitney Azoy, *Buzkashi: Game and Power in Afghanistan* (Philadelphia: University of Pennsylvania Press, 1982), 11 (first quote); Azoy, *Buzkashi*, 2012, 146 (second quote).

81. Quoted in Ghafour, "Warlord with Shifting Loyalties." While the article mentions eighteen horses in Dostum's stables in 2004, I counted about forty a decade later, potentially an indication that he has increased his role as a sponsor of *buzkashi*.

82. Giustozzi, "Ethnicisation of an Afghan Faction," 17.

83. The appointments of the Turkmens Roz Mohammad Noor, as governor of Jowzjan, and Noor Mohammad Qarqin, as minister of education, as well as of other Turkmens from the North to government posts tend to support the theory that Karzai was trying to bypass Dostum.

84. Quoted in Robberson, "Dostum de-Facto Leader."

85. Niels Terpstra and Georg Frerks, "Governance Practices and Symbolism: De Facto Sovereignty and Public Authority in 'Tigerland,'" *Journal of Modern Asian Studies* 52, no. 3 (2018): 1036. See also Zachariah Mampilly, "Performing the Nation-State: Rebel Governance and Symbolic Processes," in *Rebel Governance in Civil War*, ed. Ana Arjona, Nelson Kasfir, and Zachariah Mampilly (New York: Cambridge University Press, 2015), 74–97.

86. "Afghan Paper Says Government 'Caves In' to Compromise with Dostum," *Eqtedar-i Melli*, March 9, 2005 (first quote); "Afghan Paper Evaluates Northern General's Government Appointment," *Mojahed*, March 12, 2005 (second quote); online communication with former European diplomat, 2012 (third quote).

87. Under Article 153 of the 2004 Afghan constitution: "Judges, Attorneys, Officers of the Armed Forces, Police and officials of the National Security shall not become members of political parties during their term of office."

88. Interview with former aide to Ahmad Shah Massoud 1, 2011.

89. Interview with former European diplomat, 2011.

90. For information conveyed in this section, in addition to anonymous interviews and the sources cited above, I relied on the following: Giustozzi, *Empires of Mud*, 173; Haseeb Humayoon, *The Re-election of Hamid Karzai* (Washington, DC: Institute for the Study of War, 2010), 14–15. I also consulted the following news sources: Arostegui, "New Afghan Deal Calms North"; Philip, "'Our Hero of Peace'"; Hamida Ghafour, "Warlord on the Election Trail with Horsepower," *Telegraph*, October 8, 2004; "Afghan Commentary Evaluates Benefits of Gen Dostum's New Military Post," Afghan Islamic Press News Agency, March 2, 2005; "Afghan Paper Weighs Up Impact of Dostum's New 'Sym-

bolic' Appointment," *Kabul Weekly*, March 4, 2005; "Afghan Paper Says Government 'Caves In'"; "Afghan Paper Says People Disappointed at Dostum Getting Government Post," *Farda*, March 9, 2005; "Afghan Daily Warns Government against Attempts to Marginalize Dostum," *Cheragh*, March 29, 2005; "Afghan Paper Analyses Politics behind Dostum's Removal, Elevation," *Rozgaran*, May 2, 2005.

91. Mukhopadhyay, *Warlords, Strongman Governors*, 294.

92. Mukhopadhyay, 289.

93. Mukhopadhyay, 300 (first quote); M. K. Bhadrakumar, "Bad Blood Spreads to Afghanistan's North," Asia Times Online, May 30, 2007 (second quote). Quoted in Mukhopadhyay, 306–7.

94. Quoted in Arash Dabestani, "North Afghan Factions Clash," *International Herald Tribune*, May 31, 2007.

95. Phone conversation with former European diplomat, 2017. For Juma Khan Hamdard's declarations, see "Afghan Governor Says Iran, Russia Support Northern Gen Dostum," Afghan Islamic Press News Agency, May 28, 2007.

96. Quoted in "Afghan Warlord Dostum Is 'Everyone's Friend,'" Knight Ridder, December 11, 2008.

97. "President Karzai Appoints New Governors," *Wikileaks Cable 2007KABUL2505_a*, August 3, 2007.

98. Quoted in Mukhopadhyay, *Warlords, Strongman Governors*, 305.

99. For background information on the Juma Khan Hamdard incident, in addition to anonymous interviews and the sources cited above, I relied on Yaqub Ibrahimi, "Commanders Line Up behind Karzai," Institute for War and Peace Reporting, September 15, 2004; Brian Glyn Williams, "Dostum: Afghanistan's Embattled Warlord," *Terrorism Monitor* 6, no. 8 (2008), accessed online; Giustozzi, *Empires of Mud*, 155–56; Mukhopadhyay, *Warlords, Strongman Governors*, 299–304. I also consulted the following news sources: "2nd Ld Police Kill 3 Protestors in N. Afghanistan: Official," Xinhua General News Service, May 28, 2007; Abdul Waheed Wafa and Carlotta Gall, "Rise in Violence in North Shows Afghanistan's Fragility," *New York Times*, May 29, 2007; "Afghan MP Sees 'Clues' to Dostum's Involvement in Jowzjan Violence," *Pajhwok Afghan News*, June 2, 2007; Tahir Qadiry, "Afghanistan: Officials Blame Uzbek Warlord for 'Rebellion,'" Inter Press Service, June 5, 2007; "Afghan Weekly Calls for Sensible Solution to Dostum's Case," *Kabul Weekly*, February 23, 2008.

100. Interview with former European diplomat, 2011.

101. Quoted in Rosie DiManno, "Kabul's Big, Bad Warlord," *Toronto Star*, May 13, 2008.

102. Mohammad Aleem Sayee, quoted on "Kabul Siege Underscores Warlord Threat to Rule of Law," Radio Free Europe, February 3, 2008.

103. Abdul Jabar Sabit, quoted on "Afghanistan: Prosecutor Suggests 'Some People' Cannot Be Tried," Radio Free Europe, February 6, 2008.

104. Quoted in Carter, "The Art of Warlord."

105. Interview with former NDS director Amrullah Saleh, June 19, 2018.

106. Interview with Western diplomat 3, 2012.

107. Quoted in "Foreign Ministry Confirms Afghan Warlord Dostum Is in Turkey," Anatolia News Agency, December 4, 2008.

108. Quoted in "Afghan Warlord Dostum in Turkey Comments on Exile, Alleged House Arrest," *Milliyet*, December 5, 2008.

109. For information conveyed in this section, in addition to anonymous interviews and the sources cited above, I relied on Giustozzi, *Empires of Mud*, 183. I also consulted the following news sources: "Head of Afghan Islamic Turks Body Accuses Ex-Jonbesh Leader Dostum," ATN, January 5, 2007; "Afghan Politicians Accuse Gen Dostum of Establishing Links with Taleban," ATN, January 14, 2007; "Afghan Paper Urges Government to Rein In Tensions in North," *Rah-i Nejat*, June 1, 2007; "Afghan Turk Council Head Arrested on Terror Charges," Ayna TV, November 7, 2007; "Afghan Ministry Says 'Drunk' Northern Leader Attacked Rival's House," Afghan Islamic Press News Agency, February 3, 2008; "Famous Afghan Warlord in Standoff with Police," AFP, February 3, 2008; "Afghan Ex-Defence Minister Condemns 'Intolerable' Dostum House Siege," Ayna TV, February 4, 2008; "Pro-Dostum Demo in Afghan North Calls for Interior Minister's Dismissal," Ayna TV, February 4, 2008; "We Should Prevent Tensions," *Daily Afghanistan*, February 4, 2008; "Afghan Opposition Front Describes Siege of Northern General's House Conspiracy," Tolo TV, February 5, 2008; "Afghan Police Arrest Three Men after 'Warlord Attack,'" AFP, February 5, 2008; "Battered Afghan Turk Leader Urges Official Prosecution of Dostum," ATN, February 5, 2008; "Afghan Paper Warns against Hasty Action in Dealing with Dostum's Incident," *Hasht-i Sobh*, February 6, 2008; "Afghan Chief of Staff Suspended as Part of Investigations into Alleged Assault," Tolo TV, February 18, 2008; "Afghan Daily Says Police Plan to Arrest Northern General Dostum," *Arman-i Melli*, May 18, 2008; "Afghan Party Leader Leaves for Turkey after End of House Arrest," *Arman-i Melli*, December 3, 2008; "Afghan Warlord Dostum Departs for Turkish Exile," *Vatan*, December 4, 2008.

110. Interview with former NDS director Amrullah Saleh, June 19, 2018.

111. Interview with Afghan scholar 5, 2015. According to a former European diplomat interviewed in 2011, the deal entailed other elements, such as the replacement of Mohammad Hashim Zare, a fairly independent individual known as not being aligned with Dostum, with Mohammad Aleem Sayee, a Dostum ally, as governor of Jowzjan Province. There were also rumors that Karzai had offered Dostum a ministry in the new government.

112. Quoted in Jeremy Page, "Brutal Ally Back to Boost Karzai's Flagging Campaign," *Times*, August 18, 2009. On Ata and his competition with Dostum, see Mukhopadhyay, *Warlords, Strongman Governors*, chap. 2.

113. Quoted in Joshua Partlow, "Militia Commander Dostum Campaigns for Karzai," *Washington Post*, August 18, 2009.

114. Quoted in Fisnik Abrashi, "Karzai Pressured to Rein In Warlords," AP, July 20, 2009.

115. Esadullah Oguz, "Will Elections Bring Peace to Afghanistan?," Right Vision News, July 22, 2009.

116. Quoted in "Gen Dostum Tells Supporters to Back Karzai in Afghan Presidential Poll," Ayna TV, August 2, 2009. On the internal politics of and tension within Junbesh, see Robert Peszkowski, "Reforming Jombesh: An Afghan Party on Its Winding Road to Internal Democracy" (Afghanistan Analysts Network Briefing Paper 3, Kabul, 2012).

117. Quoted on "Afghan Gen Dostum Addresses His Followers, Urges Party Unity," Ayna TV, August 19, 2009.

118. Interview with former president Hamid Karzai, June 30, 2018.

119. Quoted in Hal Bernton and Jonathan Landay, "U.S. Fears Reform beyond Karzai's Reach," *Saint Paul Pioneer Press*, November 3, 2009.

120. Quoted in Golnar Motevalli, "Afghanistan's Dostum Denies Karzai Vote Deal," Reuters, August 19, 2009. For information conveyed in this section, in addition to anonymous interviews and the sources cited above, I relied on the following sources: Obaid Ali and Thomas Ruttig, "How Disenchantment with General Dostum Split the Uzbek Vote Bank," Afghanistan Analysts Network, May 22, 2014; Khalilzad, *The Envoy*, 223–24. I also consulted the following news sources: "Afghan Paper Says Karzai 'Trying to Use' Gen Dostum to Win Upcoming Polls," *Arman-i Melli*, June 3, 2009; "Afghan General Reinstated in Post," Tolo TV, June 11, 2009; "Afghan Paper Analyzes Gen Dostum's Reinstatement," *Hasht-i Sobh*, June 15, 2009; James Risen, "U.S. Inaction Seen after Taliban P.O.W.'s Died," *New York Times*, July 10, 2009; "Paper Sceptical about Karzai Coalition with Gen Dostum's Party," *Hasht-i Sobh*, July 15, 2009; Jean MacKenzie, "Hero on Horseback, or Mass Murderer?," *Global Post*, July 17, 2009; Golnar Motevalli, "Former Militia Leader Backs Karzai," *Vancouver Sun*, August 18, 2009; "Afghan General Assures Support to US, NATO, in Fighting Taleban," ATN, August 20, 2009; "Effects of Gen. Dostum's Return on Presidential Election Result," *Daily Outlook Afghanistan*, August 27, 2009; "US Embassy Says No Meeting Held with Afghan Gen Dostum," Tolo TV, August 31, 2009; "Afghan Northern General Is Obstacle to US Plan to Put Pressure on Russia," *Arman-i Melli*, September 21, 2009; Pamela Constable and Joshua Partlow, "In Kabul, a Collective Sigh of Relief," *Washington Post*, November 3, 2009; "Britain to Raise Dostum Appointment with Afghan Leader," AFP, January 25, 2010; "US Envoy Voices Concern about Reinstatement of Gen Dostum," Tolo TV, February 2, 2010.

121. Interview with former president Hamid Karzai, June 30, 2018.

122. Interview with former NDS director Amrullah Saleh, June 19, 2018.

123. Interview with Abdul Qader Dostum, February 12, 2014. See also Humayoon, *The Re-election*, 14–15.

124. In June 2013, portrayals of Tamerlane and Babur, the Timurid leader who founded the Mughal empire in the sixteenth century, still decorated the outside walls of the Dostum Foundation. Dostum even named one of his sons Babur. The creation of the Dostum Foundation can also be seen as an attempt to promote the Dostum name and redeem the general's image with foreigners, as evidenced by Batur Dostum asking me directly for contacts among the international community and by the fact that the foundation's website is available not only in Dari and Uzbeki but also in Turkish, English, and Arabic.

125. Dostum had taken an earlier trip to Mecca, in 1992, to try to break the image of a godless communist he had acquired during the Soviet-Afghan war. He even declared himself a mujahideen. Antoine Sfeir, ed., "Afghanistan," in *The Columbia World Dictionary of Islamism* (New York: Columbia University Press, 2007), 14; Brian Glyn Williams, *Afghanistan Declassified: A Guide to America's Longest War* (Philadelphia: University of Pennsylvania Press, 2011), 164.

126. Quoted in Spencer Ackerman, "Nothing Could Go Wrong with Turning Over the War to a War Criminal," Washington Independent, September 22, 2009.

127. Interview with Western diplomat 1, 2014.

128. Interview with former president Hamid Karzai, June 30, 2018.

129. For information conveyed in this section, in addition to anonymous interviews and the sources cited above, I relied on Thomas Ruttig, "New Trouble in the Jombesh: Dostum reasserts leadership," Afghanistan Analysts Network, February 17, 2013; Ali and Ruttig, "Disenchantment with General Dostum." I also consulted the following news sources: "Programme Summary of Afghan Aina TV News 1430 Gmt 7 Sept 11," Ayna TV, September 7, 2011; "Programme Summary of Afghan Aina TV News in Dari 1430 Gmt 12 Nov 11," Ayna TV, November 13, 2011; "Afghan Gen Dostum Opposes Hasty US Military Pull-Out, Warns of Taleban Comeback," Ayna TV, May 16, 2012.

130. Interview with General Dostum's media adviser, 2015. See also Sultan Faizy, "Working with General Abdul Rashid Dostum," *Diplomat*, April 24, 2015. Dostum and his team seemed to have embraced the label since (or at least do not seem bothered by it as long as it has no pejorative connotation). In the beginning of 2018, Batur Dostum traveled to the United States to attend the New York premiere of the movie *12 Strong*, a movie that depicts Dostum's collaboration with US forces in 2001, and to participate in a promotional event of *The Last Warlord*, a very flattering biography of General Dostum by Brian Williams (who worked as an adviser on the set of *12 Strong*), held at the University of Massachusetts Dartmouth.

131. Azam Ahmed, "Afghan First Vice President, an Ex-Warlord, Fumes on the Sidelines," *New York Times*, March 18, 2015. The hotline has since been discontinued.

132. See, for example, Mujib Mashal, "Afghan Vice President Raises Concerns by Turning to Militias in Taliban Fight," *New York Times*, August 18, 2015; Human Rights Watch, *Afghanistan: Forces Linked to Vice President Terrorize Villagers* (New York: Human Rights Watch, 2016); Shawn Snow, "Afghanistan: General Dostum Micromanages Kunduz War," *Diplomat*, October 11, 2016; Shawn Snow, "Dostum Seeks to Cement His Position in Northern Afghanistan," *Diplomat*, October 26, 2016.

133. In one such example he met and even posed with Kremlin-backed Chechen leader Ramzan Kadyrov. See Frud Bezhan, "Afghanistan's Dostum Turns to Old Ally Russia for Help," Radio Free Europe, 2015.

134. Interview with Afghan scholar 6, 2015.

135. On the Ishchi case and Dostum's return, see Mujib Mashal and Fahim Abed, "Afghan Vice President Seen Abducting Rival," *New York Times*, November 27, 2016; Catherine Putz, "Did Afghanistan's Vice President Abduct a Rival?," *Diplomat*, December 2, 2016; Mujib Mashal and Fahim Abed, "Afghanistan Vice President Accused of Torturing Political Rival," *New York Times*, December 13, 2016; "Afghan Vice-President Dostum Accused of Sex Assault," BBC News, December 14, 2016; Anisa Shaheed, "Watchdog Calls for Independent Probe into Eshchi Incident," Tolo News, December 15, 2016; "Ischi Calls for Job Suspension, Travel Ban on Dostum," *Heart of Asia*, January 23, 2017; Mujib Mashal, "Afghanistan Orders Arrest of Vice President's Guards in Rape and Torture," *New York Times*, January 24, 2017; James MacKenzie, "Security

Forces Surround Afghan VP's House over Abuse Case," Reuters, February 21, 2017; Ayaz Gul, "Afghan Officials Send High-Profile Sexual Assault Case to Court," VOA News, July 12, 2017; Catherine Putz, "Kabul's Dostum Problem," *Diplomat*, July 13, 2017; Catherine Putz, "Where in the World Is Abdul Rashid Dostum?," *Diplomat*, July 18, 2017; Massoud Ansar, "ARG Urged to Pave the Way for Dostum's Return," Tolo News, September 10, 2017; Massoud Ansar, "Dostum Could Return Soon after Almost a Year in Turkey," Tolo News, April 2, 2018; Arif Musavi, "Protesters Burn Tires, Close Kabul-Balkh Highway," Tolo News, July 7, 2018; Massoud Ansar, "MPs Accuse Ghani of Fueling Faryab Crisis," Tolo News, July 9, 2018; Rod Nordland, "Accused of Rape and Torture, Exiled Afghan Vice President Returns," *New York Times*, July 22, 2018; Mujib Mashal, "'No Shame': Afghan General's Victory Lap Stuns a Victim of Rape," *New York Times*, August 7, 2018.

136. Giustozzi argues that Junbesh's secularism participated in isolating the party and might have contributed to precipitating the conflict with the center (*Empires of Mud*, 199). He also argues that Junbesh's regionalist platform, combined with the refusal to take a separatist stand, structurally put Junbesh "in a position to have to bargain with Kabul, whoever might have been in control of it." Giustozzi therefore concludes that Junbesh's "only real option was to ally with the weaker factions hoping to force the centre to a compromise that was never likely to be implemented" (154).

137. On Junbesh ethnic politics, see Giustozzi, "Ethnicisation of an Afghan Faction."

138. Ahram and King, "The Warlord as Arbitrageur," 176.

139. Interview with member of Afghan parliament, 2008.

140. Interview with Robert Finn, former US ambassador to Afghanistan, October 5, 2011.

141. Fahim Abed and Mujib Mashal, "Gun Battle between Ethnic Factions Roils Afghanistan's Capital," *New York Times*, September 1, 2016.

142. Quoted in Mujib Mashal, "Afghan Vice President Hints That Turmoil Awaits If He Is Not Respected," *New York Times*, October 25, 2016. See also Azam Ahmed, "Afghan First Vice-President.

143. Interview with Afghan scholar 2, 2011. This tends to confirm Marten's hypothesis that "warlords may become irreplaceable in minority population areas when ethnic or sectarian tension is high." Kimberly Marten, *Warlords: Strong-Arm Brokers in Weak States* (Ithaca, NY: Cornell University Press, 2012), 197.

144. In addition to Ayna TV, launched in 2004, Dostum launched a second television channel, Batur TV (or B-TV), in 2013. Named after and presided over by his eldest son, the channel broadcasts only in Uzbeki and Turkmen. On the concept of brand, see Jean-François Médard, "Le système politique bordelais (le 'système Chaban')," *Revue internationale de politique comparée* 13, no. 4 (2006): 657–79; Clifford Bob, *The Marketing of Rebellion: Insurgents, Media, and International Activism* (New York: Cambridge University Press, 2005), 47.

145. Interview with former European diplomat, 2011.

146. Ben Arnoldy, "Dostum's Return to Afghanistan: A Nod to 'Warlord Politics,'" *Christian Science Monitor*, August 17, 2009.

5. Massoud and Fahim

1. Massoud was declared a "national hero" by then chairman of the Afghan Interim Authority Hamid Karzai on April 28, 2002, during a parade celebrating the tenth anniversary of the mujahideen's victory over communism. Azoy describes: "Most of all, it commemorated a dead man, the iconic martyr Ahmad Shah [Massoud]. His portrait, ubiquitous that day in a dozen variations, both bolstered and challenged national identity." Whitney Azoy, "Masood's Parade: Iconography, Revitalization, and Ethnicity in Afghanistan," *Expedition* 45, no. 1 (2003): 39–40. The American anthropologist continues: "The language of words . . . was no match for stagecraft and the sheer power of iconographic image. And just as they had taken Kabul, the Tajiks took hold of this parade" (Azoy, 44). See also Jon Lee Anderson, *The Lion's Grave: Dispatches from Afghanistan* (New York: Grove, 2002), 195–98.

2. Azoy, "Masood's Parade," 45.

3. Interview with Antonio Giustozzi, Afghanistan scholar, October 11, 2008.

4. Quoted in Jon Boone, "Afghan President Hamid Karzai Picks Ex-Warlord as Election Running Mate," *Guardian*, May 4, 2009.

5. The exact number differs in various accounts. In previous literature and in what I gathered from interviews, estimates range from twenty-five to forty-five men, some of them having joined along the way. See Michael Barry, *Massoud: De l'islamisme à la liberté* (Paris: Audibert, 2002), 144; Peter B. DeNeufville, "Ahmad Shah Massoud and the Genesis of the Nationalist Anti-Communist Movement in Northeastern Afghanistan, 1969–1979" (PhD diss., University of London, 2006), 5, 12.

6. Online communication with former Shura-i Nazar commander 1, 2018. On the rivalry between Massoud and Pahlawan Ahmad Jan, see Barry, *Massoud*, 146–50, 155–60.

7. Klaus Schlichte and Ulrich Schneckener, "Armed Groups and the Politics of Legitimacy," *Civil Wars* 17, no. 4 (2015): 418. The quotation applies to Massoud but was written as a general observation. These efforts were not unique to Massoud and his mujahideen. Slogans painted on rocks, for example, were also reported in the area under Ismail Khan's control. Radek Sikorski, *Dust of the Saints: A Journey to Herat in Time of War* (New York: Paragon House, 1990), 103.

8. Online communication with former Shura-i Nazar commander 1, 2012.

9. Zachariah Mampilly, "Performing the Nation-State: Rebel Governance and Symbolic Processes," in *Rebel Governance in Civil War*, ed. Ana Arjona, Nelson Kasfir, and Zachariah Mampilly (New York: Cambridge University Press, 2015), 85. The quotation applies to Massoud but was written as a general observation. On performances and symbolism, see also Niels Terpstra and Georg Frerks, "Governance Practices and Symbolism: De Facto Sovereignty and Public Authority in 'Tigerland,'" *Modern Asian Studies* 52, no. 3 (2018): 1001–42.

10. Steve Coll, *Ghost Wars: The Secret History of the CIA, Afghanistan and Bin Laden, from the Soviet Invasion to September 10, 2001* (London: Penguin Books, 2004), 121.

11. Arjona, Kasfir, and Mampilly, "Introduction" in *Rebel Governance in Civil War*, 5.

12. For information conveyed in this section, in addition to anonymous interviews and the sources cited above, I relied on the following: Olivier Roy, *Islam and Resistance in Afghanistan* (Cambridge, UK: Cambridge University Press, 1986), 69–79; Jean-José Puig, "Le commandant Massoud," in *Stratégies de la guérilla*, ed. Gérard Chaliand (Paris: Payot & Rivages, 1994), 411–52; Barry, *Massoud*, 49, 55–57, 73–75, 77–78, 107–8, 126–27, 129–34, 143–47, 185, 189, 192–94, 213–16, 218–19, 254; William Maley, *The Afghanistan Wars* (Basingstoke, UK: Palgrave Macmillan, 2002), 65; Barnett R. Rubin, *The Fragmentation of Afghanistan: State Formation and Collapse in the International System*, 2nd ed. (New Haven, CT: Yale University Press, 2002), 103–4, 233, 237; Willem Vogelsang, *The Afghans* (Oxford: Blackwell, 2002), 315; Coll, *Ghost Wars*, 109–19, 290; Philippe Morillon, *Le testament de Massoud* (Paris: Presses de la Renaissance, 2004), 13–14, 64; Sediqa Massoud, with Chékéba Hachemi and Marie-Françoise Colombani, *Pour l'amour de Massoud* (XO Éditions, 2005), 29–30, 32, 38–41, 53, 63, 131, 144, 212; De-Neufville, "Ahmad Shah Massoud," 7, 11, 74–75, 85–91, 96–98, 100, 102–4, 145, 159–60, 162, 169–71, 173–77, 179, 188–89, 196–98, 229–36, 257, 260–61, 266–68, 270–71, 277–78, 280, 282; Abdulkader H. Sinno, *Organizations at War: In Afghanistan and Beyond* (Ithaca, NY: Cornell University Press, 2008), 132; Antonio Giustozzi, *Empires of Mud: Wars and Warlords in Afghanistan* (New York: Columbia University Press, 2009), 282; Marcela Grad, *Massoud: An Intimate Portrait of the Legendary Afghan Leader* (St. Louis, MO: Webster University Press, 2009), 67–77; Jean-Christophe Notin, *La guerre de l'ombre des Français en Afghanistan 1979–2011* (Paris: Fayard, 2011), 20–21, 122–24, 153, 219–22, 240–41, 279; Jennifer Brick Murtazashvili, *Informal Order and the State in Afghanistan* (New York: Cambridge University Press, 2016), 58. I also consulted Peter Baker and William Branigin, "Even after Death, 'Lion' Remains King of the Rebels," *Washington Post*, October 11, 2001.

13. Bridget Coggins, "Rebel Diplomacy: Theorizing Violent Non-state Actors' Strategic Use of Talk," in *Rebel Governance in Civil War*, ed. Ana M. Arjona, Nelson Kasfir, and Zachariah Mampilly (New York: Cambridge University Press, 2015), 110. See also Schlichte and Schneckener, "Armed Groups and the Politics of Legitimacy," 419.

14. Interview with former Shura-i Nazar representative in Washington, 2011.

15. Interview with former Shura-i Nazar head of intelligence, 2011.

16. Edward Girardet was allegedly "the first Western journalist to provide a detailed account of Massoud's war in the Panjshir" (Coll, *Ghost Wars*, 602). He relates his 1981 trip to Panjshir as follows: "Together with two French doctors and a nurse of the Paris-based Aide Médicale Internationale (AMI), one of three French humanitarian organizations operating clandestine hospitals inside Afghanistan, I had arranged to accompany a 50-horse guerrilla caravan to the strategic Panjshir Valley, 40 miles north of Kabul. Also on the trip were two French filmmakers, Jérôme Bony and Christophe de Ponfilly, who, like myself, hoped to report on the struggle of a besieged resistance-held region in Soviet-occupied Afghanistan." Edward Girardet, "Journey to the Panjshir," *Christian Science Monitor*, December 31, 1981. See also Barry, *Massoud*, 161; Notin, *La guerre de l'ombre*, 154–65.

17. Gilles Dorronsoro, *Revolution Unending: Afghanistan, 1979 to the Present* (New York: Columbia University Press, 2005), 131.

18. On the trade of gems from the Panjshir Valley, see Barry, *Massoud*, 196; Coll, *Ghost Wars*, 345; Massoud, with Hachemi and Colombani, *Pour l'amour de Massoud*, 192; Grad, *Massoud*, 69; Notin, *La guerre de l'ombre*, 455, 482, 502.

19. On the relationship between France and Massoud, see Notin, *La guerre de l'ombre*.

20. Coll relates that Massoud's ISI stipend increased from $50,000 to $100,000 a month and that he soon thereafter received his "first, albeit small" batch of Stinger missiles (*Ghost Wars*, 219–20). For information conveyed in this section, in addition to anonymous interviews and the sources cited above, I relied on Puig, "Le commandant Massoud," 425; Barry, *Massoud*, 193, 284–85; Rubin, *The Fragmentation of Afghanistan*, 254; Vogelsang, *The Afghans*, 315; Coll, *Ghost Wars*, 8–10, 123–24, 151, 181, 198, 211, 218, 225, 233; Morillon, *Le testament de Massoud*, 14, 47; Massoud, with Hachemi and Colombani, *Pour l'amour de Massoud*, 80–84, 127–28; Giustozzi, *Empires of Mud*, 286; Notin, *La guerre de l'ombre*, 183, 201–2, 207–8, 213, 222–23, 227, 240, 242–44, 249–50, 324–29, 334, 354, 381–86, 390–91, 400, 412, 416, 426–27, 444, 452, 490–91, 553.

21. Rubin, *The Fragmentation of Afghanistan*, 247; Coll, *Ghost Wars*, 262–63; Thomas Barfield, *Afghanistan: A Cultural and Political History* (Princeton, NJ: Princeton University Press, 2010), 248–53.

22. Robert H. Jackson, *Quasi-states: Sovereignty, International Relations and the Third World* (Cambridge, UK: Cambridge University Press, 1990). Clapham calls this "letter-box sovereignty" in the sense that they controlled the most important buildings in the national capital, and thus symbolically "received the invitation to represent the state . . . in the United Nations and other international bodies." Christopher Clapham, *Africa and the International System: The Politics of State Survival* (Cambridge, UK: Cambridge University Press, 1996), 20.

23. Interview with Afghan scholar 2, 2011. On the relationship between Massoud and Rabbani and the role of the latter, see also Giustozzi, *Empires of Mud*, 285. To improve their relations, a marriage was organized between Ahmad Shah Massoud's brother Ahmad Zia and Burhanuddin Rabbani's daughter in the mid-1980s. See Barry, *Massoud*, 203; Massoud, with Hachemi and Colombani, *Pour l'amour de Massoud*, 129; Notin, *La guerre de l'ombre*, 278.

24. Coll, *Ghost Wars*, 286.

25. At the time, Panjshir was part of Parwan Province. The Panjshir Province was created in 2004.

26. On politics of international recognition, see Bridget Coggins, "Friends in High Places: International Politics and the Emergence of States from Secessionism," *International Organization* 65, no. 3 (Summer 2011): 433–67.

27. Most NGOs remained based in Peshawar. Those based in Dushanbe, however, played a very important role in the Afghan resistance. The Aga Khan Foundation did a lot in terms of reconstruction; ACTED served as an intermediary between Massoud and France and traded currencies with Massoud, who needed US dollars.

28. Interview with former military attaché, 2008.

29. For information conveyed in this section, in addition to anonymous interviews and the sources cited above, I relied on Coll, *Ghost Wars*, 47, 186, 345, 464; Sinno, *Organizations at War*, chaps. 7–8; Giustozzi, *Empires of Mud*, 202, 286.

30. Giustozzi, *Empires of Mud*, 285.

31. Reyko Huang, "Rebel Diplomacy in Civil War," *International Security* 40, no. 4 (Spring 2016): 91. Huang does not use the expression *wartime diplomat* in reference to Massoud but in the context of civil war more broadly.

32. Interview with Abdullah Abdullah, former minister of foreign affairs of Afghanistan, February 7, 2011. It is worth noting that most of these Afghan Tajiks in exile did not work full time at these embassies. Morillon gives the example of an Afghan architect in Rennes, France, who also presided over an association named Bretagne-Afghanistan and kept close contacts with Panjshir, even traveling there on a regular basis (*Le testament de Massoud*, 39).

33. Interview with Ahmad Wali Massoud, February 13, 2011.

34. Coll, *Ghost Wars*, 507. See also Notin, *La guerre de l'ombre*, 456, 559–60, 593.

35. Interview with Ahmad Wali Massoud, February 13, 2011.

36. Massoud was in contact with the Uzbek authorities as well and traveled a couple of times to Tashkent, where he met with President Karimov and the head of Uzbekistan's national intelligence agency. Massoud also took a diplomatic trip to New Delhi in 2000. India offered only limited political support but built a military hospital in the northeastern city of Farkhar, in the zone under his control. Philippe Morillon seems to believe that India was also providing weapons (*Le testament de Massoud*, 44). Coll mentions cash payments (*Ghost Wars*, 519).

37. The fact that, toward the end of the resistance, Massoud decided to send Engineer Esaq, one of his most trusted aides, to represent him in the United States is particularly telling of the importance he gave to US support.

38. Quoted in Coll, *Ghost Wars*, 346.

39. "A/S Raphel Discusses Afghanistan," declassified cable, April 22, 1996, released by the National Security Archive. Quoted in Coll, 329.

40. Asked about Massoud's involvement in drug trafficking, one of his former aides explains: "Massoud didn't always control the commanders, and especially not the pilots. They couldn't control what was being flown in the helicopters to Dushanbe." Interview with former aide to Ahmad Shah Massoud 1, 2018. See also Notin, *La guerre de l'ombre*, 454.

41. Coll, *Ghost Wars*, 562.

42. Coll, 575.

43. For information conveyed in this section, in addition to anonymous interviews and the sources cited above, I relied on the following: Morillon, *Le testament de Massoud*, 23, 30, 98, 114, 118–19; Coll, *Ghost Wars*, 9–10, 14, 151, 218, 233, 336, 345–47, 460–72, 660; Massoud, with Hachemi and Colombani, *Pour l'amour de Massoud*, 225. I also consulted Peter Bergen, "Iranian Troops on Alert against Afghanistan," CNN, September 15, 1998; "Iran Army Forces Parade Near Afghan Border," CNN, November 1, 1998.

44. Interview with former Shura-i Nazar commander 1, 2011.

45. Interview with former military attaché, 2009 (first quote); Baker and Branigin, "Even after Death" (second quote).

46. Interview with former NDS director Amrullah Saleh, June 19, 2018.

47. Interview with former aide to Ahmad Shah Massoud 2, 2018.

48. Interview with former NDS director Amrullah Saleh, June 19, 2018.

49. Interview with former Shura-i Nazar representative in Washington, 2011.

50. Interview with former Shura-i Nazar commander 1, 2011.

51. Some argue that the Shura-i Nazar collapsed when a number of Jamiatis decided to collaborate with Karzai and others refused to do so. According to Olivier Roy, as long as the inhabitants of Afghanistan's northeast do not feel threatened, the Shura-i Nazar will not be reactivated. Olivier Roy, "Afghanistan: La difficile reconstruction d'un Etat," *Cahier de Chaillot* 73, no. 1 (2004): 40–42. The Afghanistan scholar David Isby makes a similar argument. See "Afghanistan's Gamble," *Washington Times*, July 29, 2004.

52. Giustozzi, *Empires of Mud*, 289.

53. Gary C. Schroen, *First In: An Insider's Account of How the CIA Spearheaded the War on Terror in Afghanistan* (New York: Presidio, 2005), 90.

54. Schiewek notes that "more than 1,200 positions were filled in the last week of November and the first week of December." Eckart Schiewek, "Keeping the Peace without Peacekeepers," in *Building State and Security in Afghanistan*, ed. Wolfgang Danspeckgruber with Robert P. Finn (Princeton, NJ: Woodrow Wilson School of Public and International Affairs, 2007), 186. The ministry of foreign affairs was used to appoint most of the diplomats in the years that followed, which only added to the fact that most in-position diplomats already belonged to the Shura-i Nazar.

55. Halima Kazem, "Brewing Power Struggle in Kabul," *Christian Science Monitor*, October 17, 2003.

56. Quoted in Kazem.

57. Partlow reports the following anecdote regarding Karzai's arrival in Kabul after the fall of the Taliban regime: "'Where are your men?' Fahim asked him on that airstrip, in an exchange that Karzai would recount for years to demonstrate the trust he laid at the feet of an ethnic rival. 'You are my men,' Karzai replied." Joshua Partlow, *A Kingdom of Their Own: The Family Karzai and the Afghan Disaster* (New York: Alfred A. Knopf, 2016), 55. The story is also reported in DeNeufville, "Ahmad Shah Massoud," 28. It is worth noting, when discussing the relationship between Fahim and Karzai, that during his time as head of intelligence, the former had the latter arrested: "Acting on a tip that he was plotting against the government, Fahim sent intelligence officers to Hamid Karzai's Kabul home. They arrested the deputy foreign minister and drove him to an interrogation center downtown, not far from the presidential palace. For several hours Fahim's operatives worked on Karzai, accusing him of collusion with Pakistan. . . . Several people [Karzai] talked to afterward said that he was beaten up and that his face was bloodied and bruised. Some accounts place Fahim himself in the cell during parts of the interrogation" (Coll, *Ghost Wars*, 286–87). See also Notin, *La guerre de l'ombre*, 478, 703.

58. Larry Goodson, "Afghanistan's Long Road to Reconstruction," *Journal of Democracy* 14, no. 1 (2003): 94.

59. Quoted in Anderson, *The Lion's Grave*, 196.

60. Partlow, *A Kingdom of Their Own*, 61.

61. Quoted in Frederick Starr, "Thievery, Treachery, Treason . . . : The Struggle Post-Taliban and What the U.S. Should Do," *National Review*, July 14, 2003. For information conveyed in this section, in addition to anonymous interviews and the sources cited above, I relied on the following: Barry, *Massoud*, 56, 165, 190–91; Schroen, *First In*, 16;

DeNeufville, "Ahmad Shah Massoud," 16, 240–41; Schiewek, "Keeping the Peace," 190; Notin, *La guerre de l'ombre*, 251, 669; Peter Tomsen, *The Wars of Afghanistan: Messianic Terrorism, Tribal Conflicts, and the Failures of Great Powers* (New York: Public Affairs, 2011), 597. I also consulted the following news sources: "Muhammad Fahim Appointed Interim Commander of Northern Alliance Troops," Ria Novosti, September 13, 2001; "New Northern Alliance Chief Likes Classics, Speaks English," Japan Economic Newswire, October 2, 2001; Susan B. Glasser and Pamela Constable, "Tension Rises between Two Key Afghans," *Washington Post*, August 5, 2002; Pamela Constable, "Afghan President, Rival Show Signs of Détente," *Washington Post*, August 16, 2002; "Rebuilding Afghanistan?," CBS's *60 Minutes*, May 2, 2003; Keith Richburg, "Key Afghan Minister to Back Karzai Rival," *Washington Post*, July 29, 2004.

62. Interview with Afghan scholar 2, 2011.

63. Quoted in Kathy Gannon, "Afghan Defense Ministry Sees U.N. Peacekeepers as Symbolic," *Southeast Missourian*, December 20, 2001.

64. Quoted in Gannon.

65. Kathleen Kenna, "Afghanistan Sees Limited Duties for Peacekeepers," *Toronto Star*, December 20, 2001.

66. Quoted in "Russia Prepared to Help Afghanistan Remove Mines, Generate Electricity," Interfax, February 11, 2002.

67. Quoted in Pamela Constable, "Operation Transformation for Afghan with a Dark Past," *Washington Post*, May 29, 2002.

68. Quoted in Glasser and Constable, "Tension Rises."

69. Zalmay Khalilzad, *The Envoy: From Kabul to the White House, My Journey through a Turbulent World* (New York: St Martin's, 2016), 136.

70. Quoted in "Afghanistan: Defense Minister Denies Rift with Karzai," Facts on File World News Digest, August 17, 2002.

71. Charles Hanley, "'We're a Team,' Says Afghan Chief Defense Chief, Rejecting Reports of Tension with President," AP, August 17, 2002.

72. Quoted in Glasser and Constable, "Tension Rises."

73. Rachel Morarjee, "Afghan Defence Minister Seen as Brake on Factions' Disarmament," AFP, July 27, 2004. Other news reports mention similar numbers. See also Barbara Stapleton, "Disarming the Militias—DDR and DIAG and the Implications for Peacebuilding," in *Peacebuilding in Afghanistan: Local, Regional and Global Perspectives*, ed. Maria Aschenbrenner and Hely Marouf (Stockholm: Swedish Committee for Afghanistan, 2008), 122–36. It is claimed that, by the end of its mandate in July 2005, 36,431 weapons (including 10,888 heavy weapons) had been collected through the Afghanistan New Beginnings Programme (Sinno, *Organizations at War*, 265).

74. For information conveyed in this section, in addition to anonymous interviews and the sources cited above, I relied on the following: Antonio Giustozzi, "Bureaucratic Façade and Political Realities of Disarmament and Demobilisation in Afghanistan," *Conflict, Security & Development* 8, no. 2 (2008): 183; Khalilzad, *The Envoy*, 181–83. I also consulted the following news sources: "Afghan Opposition Ready for Attack on Kabul," AFP, November 5, 2001; Michael R. Gordon, "U.N. Envoy Tries to Pave Holes in Road to Coalition," *New York Times*, December 12, 2001; John F. Burns, "Afghan Defense Chief Acts to Counter Talk of a Rift," *New York Times*, August 18, 2002; James Risen

and Mark Landler, "Accused of Drug Ties, Afghan Official Worries U.S.," *New York Times*, August 27, 2009.

75. Interview with former aide to Ahmad Shah Massoud 1, 2018.

76. Interview with Panjshiri politician, 2018.

77. Interview with Afghan scholar 2, 2011.

78. Interview with former aide to Ahmad Shah Massoud 1, 2018.

79. Stephen Graham, "Karzai Announces Candidacy for Re-election, Drops Key Warlord from His Election Ticket," AP, July 26, 2004.

80. According to *Payam-i Mujahed*, an Afghan newspaper closely linked to the Shura-i Nazar, "British Prime Minister Tony Blair was behind Karzai's decision to drop defence minister Marshal Fahim as his first running mate as Blair wanted to make Fahim a scapegoat for Britain's failure to curb Afghanistan's drugs cultivation and trafficking" ("Afghan Weekly Criticizes Foreign Interference in Elections," *Payam-i Mujahed*, August 24, 2004). Interviewed on June 19, 2018, former NDS director Amrullah Saleh confirmed this version. Torabi argues that the United States decided to favor the political process at the expense of military gains because of the approaching US presidential elections. Yama Torabi, "State-, Nation- et Peace-Building comme processus de transactions: L'interaction des intervenants et des acteurs locaux sur le théâtre de l'intervention en Afghanistan, 2001–08" (PhD diss., Institut d'Études Politiques de Paris, 2009), 244. Khalilzad claims that it was mostly Jean Arnault, the special representative of the UN secretary-general in Afghanistan (backed by the Japanese ambassador to Afghanistan Kinichi Komano), who pressured Karzai into dropping Fahim (*The Envoy*, 213).

81. Quoted in Richburg, "Key Afghan Minister to Back Karzai Rival."

82. Fahim actually kept a position as a special adviser to the president but called himself a "symbolic adviser" as Karzai never asked for his advice. See "Afghan Presidential Adviser Says President's Grip on Power Weak," *Payam-i Mujahed*, June 11, 2007.

83. Giustozzi, *Empires of Mud*, 293. See also Roy, "La difficile reconstruction," 41.

84. For information conveyed in this section, in addition to anonymous interviews and the sources cited above, I consulted the following news sources: Carlotta Gall, "Dispute Prompts Afghan Leader to Delay Trip," *New York Times*, July 26, 2004; Morarjee, "Afghan Defence Minister Seen as Brake"; "Samina Ahmed Discusses the Upcoming Elections in Afghanistan," NPR's *Morning Edition*, July 29, 2004; Carlotta Gall, "Afghans Ask U.S. to Help Cool Conflict," *International Herald Tribune*, August 18, 2004.

85. Quoted in Giustozzi, *Empires of Mud*, 138.

86. On Fahim's involvement in the Sherpur scandal, see Partlow, *A Kingdom of Their Own*, 207.

87. Quoted in Ron Synovitz, "Afghanistan Land Grab Scandal in Kabul Rocks the Government," Radio Free Europe, September 16, 2003.

88. Pratap Chatterjee, "Paying Off the Warlords," CBS News, November 18, 2009.

89. Chatterjee.

90. Chatterjee. For information on ZWG, I also consulted the company's official website, which has since been discontinued.

91. Carlos Ortiz, *Private Armed Forces and Global Security: A Guide to the Issues* (Santa Barbara, CA: Praeger, 2010), 50. I also consulted the snapshot description of the company provided on the Bloomberg website.

92. Interview with former member of the Shura-i Nazar, 2018.

93. Interview with former president Hamid Karzai, June 30, 2018.

94. Quoted in Dexter Filkins, "Afghan Leader Outmaneuvers Election Rivals," *New York Times*, June 24, 2009.

95. Mahmood Karzai and Hasin Fahim were later involved in the Kabul Bank scandal, like many other high-ranking officials. As shareholders, they had access to the US-funded salaries of Afghan civil servants, which gave them "an opportunity to earn millions of dollars in interest," as well as tremendous investment opportunities. Dexter Filkins, "Letter from Kabul: The Afghan Bank Heist," *New Yorker*, February 14, 2011. On the Kabul Bank scandal, see also Martine van Bijlert, "The Kabul Bank Investigations; Central Bank Gives Names and Figures," Afghanistan Analysts Network, May 2, 2011.

96. Interview with former aide to Ahmad Shah Massoud 1, 2018.

97. Interview with Afghan scholar 2, 2011.

98. Interview with Afghan scholar 2, 2011.

99. Quoted in G. Whitney Azoy, *Buzkashi: Game & Power in Afghanistan*, 3rd ed. (Long Grove, IL: Waveland, 2012), 160. While Dostum had already been fond of *buzkashi*, Fahim's interest for the game was brand new (and could be purely instrumental). Azoy writes: "As [military commanders] displaced the old khans in real world power, so they became the new powers behind buzkashi." Whitney Azoy, "The New Buzkashi Elite," *Afghanistan Info* 58 (2006): 18.

100. G. Whitney Azoy, *Buzkashi: Game and Power in Afghanistan* (Philadelphia: University of Pennsylvania Press, 1982), 15.

101. On Fahim and *buzkashi*, see Azoy, *Buzkashi*, 2012, 154–65.

102. Interview with Robert Finn, former US ambassador to Afghanistan, October 5, 2011.

103. Interview with Afghan scholar 2, 2011.

104. For information conveyed in this section, in addition to anonymous interviews, I relied on the following sources: Roy, "La difficile reconstruction," 41; Haseeb Humayoon, *The Re-election of Hamid Karzai* (Washington, DC: Institute for the Study of War, 2010), 17; Kai Eide, *Power Struggle over Afghanistan: An Inside Look at What Went Wrong and What We Can Do to Repair the Damage* (New York: Skyhorse, 2012), chap. 20. See also Boone, "Karzai Picks Ex-Warlord"; Chatterjee, "Paying Off the Warlords."

105. Giustozzi, *Empires of Mud*, 282.

106. Coburn also underlines how, in post-2001 Afghanistan, the *pakol* at times came to symbolize the threat of violence: "In Istalif, especially among young men, wearing the [pakol] had come to symbolize a willingness to resort to violence and a desire to ally oneself with, or show support for, former mujahideen" (*Bazaar Politics*, 109).

107. Clifford Bob, *The Marketing of Rebellion: Insurgents, Media, and International Activism* (New York: Cambridge University Press, 2005), 162. Here Clifford Bob does not refer to Ahmad Shah Massoud but to Commandant Marcos of Mexico.

108. For Massoud on women's rights, see, for example, Barry, *Massoud*, 33–34; Massoud, with Hachemi and Colombani, *Pour l'amour de Massoud*, 12, 220, 243; Torabi, "State-, Nation- et Peace-Building," 21.

109. Clifford Bob originally uses the idea of "inventing an icon" to describe the marketing strategy of Commandant Marcos and the Zapatistas in Mexico. See Bob, *The Marketing of Rebellion*, 161–64.

110. Interview with Ahmad Wali Massoud, February 13, 2011. According to Fahim Dashti, the *Kabul Weekly* director, interviewed on February 19, 2011, the main objective of *Kabul Weekly* is to "promote Massoud's vision." Wazmah Osman writes that "the television stations Noor and Badakhshan, which are financed by the Tajik political party Jamiat-e Islami, have been one of the most prolific producers of such docudramas in homage to their late leaders Burhanuddin Rabbani and Ahmad Shah [Massoud]." Wazmah Osman, "Brought to You by Foreigners, Warlords, and Local Activists: TV and the Afghan Culture Wars," in *Modern Afghanistan: The Impact of 40 Years of War*, ed. Nazif M. Shahrani (Bloomington: Indiana University Press, 2018), 157.

111. Azoy, "Masood's Parade," 41.

112. Giustozzi, *Empires of Mud*, 282.

113. Interview with Afghan scholar 2, 2011. Giustozzi notes that, during the jihad, already "the sense of superiority of Panjshiri fighters was often resented among combatants from other regions" and that, after Massoud's death, "the tension between [his] role as Islamist activist turned community leader and his role at the helm of a coalition of the northeastern military class . . . came into the open" (*Empires of Mud*, 283, 288).

114. Quoted in "Afghan Defence Chief to Support Karzai's Rival in Presidential Polls," Hindokosh News Agency, August 4, 2004.

115. Interview with former president Hamid Karzai, June 30, 2018.

116. Interview with former Shura-i Nazar commander 1, 2011.

Conclusion

1. Lucian Pye, *Warlord Politics: Conflict and Coalition in the Modernization of Republican China* (New York: Praeger, 1971), 10.

2. Thomas Barfield, *Afghanistan: A Cultural and Political History* (Princeton, NJ: Princeton University Press, 2010), 247.

3. On the ethnicization of Junbesh, see Antonio Giustozzi, "Ethnicisation of an Afghan Faction: Junbesh-I-Milli from Its Origins to the Presidential Elections" (Crisis States Working Paper 67 [Series 1], London, 2005).

4. The *chapan*, regularly worn by Dostum, was popularized outside Afghanistan by former president Karzai (hence showing that he was the president not only of the Pashtuns but of all Afghans).

5. Peter B. Golden, *Central Asia in World History* (New York: Oxford University Press, 2011), 137.

6. Merriam Webster, s.v. "resilience."

7. A full video recording of President Obama's West Point speech is available on the official website of the White House. The 2014 deadline was announced later, during the Afghanistan-Pakistan Annual Review of December 16, 2010. The full video recording of that speech is also available on the official website of the White House.

8. Ismail Khan, speech given in Badagh, Injil District, Herat Province, March 20, 2011; Ismail Khan made similar declarations at similar gatherings. See, for example, Graham Bowley, "Afghan Warlord's Call to Arms Rattles Officials" *New York Times*, November 12, 2012; Graham Bowley, "Freewheeling Afghan City Fearful of U.S. Pullout," *New York Times*, November 18, 2012.

9. Interview with Martine van Bijlert, co-director and co-founder of the Afghanistan Analysts Network, November 8, 2015.

10. Interview with Ismail Khan, June 24, 2018.

11. Mike Martin, *An Intimate War: An Oral History of the Helmand Conflict* (New York: Oxford University Press, 2014), 250.

12. Ismail Khan, speech given in Badagh, Injil District, Herat Province, March 20, 2011.

13. Pye, *Warlord Politics*, 15.

14. Interview with Afghan scholar 2, 2011.

15. Interview with former Shura-i Nazar commander 1, 2011.

16. Antonio Giustozzi, *Empires of Mud: Wars and Warlords in Afghanistan* (New York: Columbia University Press, 2009), 298.

17. Douglas C. North, John Joseph Wallis, and Barry R. Weingast, *Violence and Social Orders: A Conceptual Framework for Interpreting Recorded Human History* (New York: Cambridge University Press, 2009), 23.

18. For a similar discussion, see Timothy Earle and Georgi Derluguian, "Strong Chieftaincies out of Weak States, or Elemental Power Unbound," in *Troubled Regions and Failing States: The Clustering and Contagion of Armed Conflicts*, ed. Kristian B. Harpviken (Bingley, UK: Emerald, Cop, 2010), 57. For an analysis of a succession crisis, see Médard on René Cassagne. Jean-François Médard, "Le système politique bordelais (le 'système Chaban')," *Revue internationale de politique comparée* 13, no. 4 (2006): 677.

19. Giustozzi, *Empires of Mud*, 214.

20. See, for example, "Old Political Rivals Eye Political Cooperation after Recent Upheavals in Kabul," Khaama Press, June 12, 2017; "Ata Mohammad Noor, Mohaqiq, and Gen. Dostum Meet in Turkey," Khaama Press, June 28, 2017.

21. Quoted in Claire Billet, "Ahmad Massoud: Au nom du père," *Le Figaro*, September 9, 2016 (translated by the author). Already in 2001, then aged twelve, he had declared: "I want to follow in my father's footsteps. I want to secure our country's independence. I want to be my father's successor." Quoted in Ron Synovitz and Hamid Mohmand, "Son Recalls Dream of Afghanistan's 'Lion of Panjshir,'" Gandhara, September 10, 2016. See also AFP, "Lion of Panjshir: Ahmad Shah Masood's Son Ready to Take Up His Afghan Destiny," *Express Tribune*, September 1, 2016; Christina Lamb, "Son of Afghans' Greatest 'Lion' Rises to Be Peacemaker," *Sunday Times*, September 4, 2016.

22. Interview with Adib Fahim, July 1, 2018.

23. Quoted in "The introduction of Adib Fahim as the first deputy of the Afghan National Directorate of Security," June 1, 2015, available on the official website of the Office of the Chief Executive of the Islamic Republic of Afghanistan. The chief executive officer position, akin to prime minister, was created as part of a power-sharing agreement following the 2014 election.

24. Interviewed on July 1, 2018, Adib Fahim explained: "We have a foundation, like the Massoud Foundation, the Marshal Fahim Foundation. . . . In the past four years, we've celebrated my father's death with a different theme every year, with statements and examples from his life, clips on TV, billboards, etc." And indeed, as of July 2018, posters and billboards of both Marshal Fahim and Ahmad Shah Massoud were still to be seen all over the capital city. On Adib Fahim, see also Mujib Mashal, "Afghan Princelings: Are the Children of the *Mujahedin* Ready to Rule?," *Time*, August 13, 2012. I also consulted Adib Fahim's official website.

25. Babur Dostum and Mustafa Kamal Dostum, both of whom were involved in the military operations launched by their father in the North, received medals from President Ghani, "in recognition of courage demonstrated against enemies," in October 2015. "President Ghani Confers Medal to Gen. Dostum's Sons," Bakhtar News, October 20, 2015. Their brother, Yar Mohammad, was appointed as commander of the Sheberghan garrison in 2017. Tamim Hamid, "MoD Was Not Aware of Appointment of Dostum's Son," Tolo News, August 16, 2017.

26. Interview with former aide to Ahmad Shah Massoud 2, 2018. Another aide to Massoud used a surprisingly similar metaphor when asked the same question (interview with former aide to Ahmad Shah Massoud 1, 2018).

27. Joel S. Migdal and Klaus Schlichte, "Rethinking the State," in *The Dynamics of States: The Formation and Crises of State Domination*, ed. Klaus Schlichte (Aldershot, UK: Ashgate, 2005), 4.

28. Noah Coburn, *Bazaar Politics: Power and Pottery in an Afghan Market Town* (Stanford, CA: Stanford University Press, 2011), 203.

29. Thomas Blom Hansen and Finn Stepputat, "Introduction" in *Sovereign Bodies: Citizens, Migrants and States in the Postcolonial World*, ed. Thomas Blom Hansen and Finn Stepputat (Princeton, NJ: Princeton University Press, 2005), 3–4. Quoted in Coburn, *Bazaar Politics*, 183.

30. For a similar argument, see Stephen D. Krasner and Thomas Risse, "External Actors, State-Building, and Service Provision in Areas of Limited Statehood: Introduction," *Governance* 27, no. 4 (2014): 545–67. Driscoll likewise argues that "state-building is a constantly renewing process of contracting and bargaining between violence entrepreneurs." Jesse Driscoll, *Warlords and Coalition Politics in Post-Soviet States* (New York: Cambridge University Press, 2015), 30.

31. Arnold Wolfers, *Discord and Collaboration: Essays on International Politics* (Baltimore: Johns Hopkins University Press, 1962), chap. 1.

32. Hendrik Spruyt, *The Sovereign State and Its Competitors: An Analysis of System Change* (Princeton, NJ: Princeton University Press, 1996), 5. Robert Gilpin defines system change as "a transformation in the nature of the constitutive units" (the decline of empires in favor of feudal organization, for example). See Robert Gilpin, *War and Change in World Politics* (Cambridge, UK: Cambridge University Press, 1981), 39–40.

33. James N. Rosenau, *The Adaptation of National Societies: A Theory of Political System Behavior and Transformation* (Cambridge: Harvard University Press, 1970), 4.

34. Conversation with William Reno, 2012.

35. Aryn Baker, lecture given at the American Institute for Afghanistan Studies, Kabul, November 12, 2009.

36. Perry Anderson, *Lineages of the Absolutist State* (London: NLB, 1974), 18.

37. Christopher Hill, 'Comment' (on the Transition from Feudalism to Capitalism), *Science and Society*, 17, no. 4 (Fall 1953), 351. Quoted in Anderson, 18.

38. Médard, "Le système politique bordelais," 657.

39. Quoted in Brian Glyn Williams, "Afghanistan's Warlord Alliance," *Jane's Intelligence Digest*, November 2, 2007, 4.

40. Quoted in "Afghan Ex-Defence Minister Condemns 'Intolerable' Dostum House Siege," Ayna TV, February 4, 2008. See also "Afghan Opposition Front Describes Siege of Northern General's House Conspiracy," Tolo TV, February 5, 2008.

41. Interview with Adib Fahim, July 1, 2018.

42. Karim Amini, "New Political Front 'Emerging' amid Ongoing Tension within Govt," Tolo News, June 28, 2017; Khwaja Basir Fitri, "Three-Party Alliance in Turkey Draws Scorn at Home," Pajhwok Afghan News, July 1, 2017.

43. On the reconstruction of Afghanistan as a "highly intrusive attempt at social engineering," see Christoph Zuercher, "Is More Better? Evaluating External-Led State Building after 1989" (CDDRL Working Paper 54, Stanford, 2006), 8.

44. Dipali Mukhopadhyay, *Warlords, Strongman Governors, and the State in Afghanistan* (New York: Cambridge University Press, 2014), 322.

45. As Tilly pointed out, rulers stand to benefit when these networks are integrated into public politics. Tilly's understanding of trust networks can be extended to warlords: "Rulers have usually coveted the resources embedded in such networks, have often treated them as obstacles to effective rule, yet have never succeeded in annihilating them and have usually worked out accommodations producing enough resources and compliance to sustain their regimes." Tilly, *Trust and Rule*, (New York: Cambridge University Press, 2005), 6.

46. Peter B. Evans, *Embedded Autonomy: States and Industrial Transformation* (Princeton, NJ: Princeton University Press, 1995), 248. See also Mukhopadhyay, *Warlords, Strongman Governors*.

47. Haruhiro Fukui, "Introduction: On the Significance of Informal Politics," in *Informal Politics in East Asia*, ed. Lowell Dittmer, Haruhiro Fukui, and Peter N. S. Lee (New York: Cambridge University Press, 2000), 12. Waterbury raises the question of whether patronage is a "good" and "functional" thing. John Waterbury, "An Attempt to Put Patrons and Clients in Their Place," in *Patrons and Clients in Mediterranean Societies*, ed. Ernest Gellner and John Waterbury (London: Duckworth, 1977), 333. "Answers to these questions can only come in light of one's ideological preferences. If one believes that classless societies in which power and wealth are evenly distributed are utopian nonsense, then a good case can be made for the positive, 'integrative' functions of patronage which mitigate class cleavages and social conflict and link the powerless to the larger system. An unheeding aristocracy and an unapproachable bureaucracy could deny any real access to the powerless, while patronage evokes the *obligé* of the powerful and the need to perform on the part of the bureaucrats" (Waterbury, 333). On political clientelism and corruption, see Jean-François Médard, "Clientèlisme politique et corruption," *Revue tiers monde* 41, no. 161 (2000): 75–87.

48. Paul Staniland, "States, Insurgents, and Wartime Political Orders," *Perspectives on Politics* 10, no. 2 (2012): 257. For a similar argument, see Christoph Zürcher, Carrie

Manning, Kristie D. Evenson, Rachel Hayman, Sarah Riese, and Nora Roehner, *Costly Democracy: Peacebuilding and Democratization after War* (Stanford, CA: Stanford University Press, 2013).

49. Jeremy M. Weinstein, "Autonomous Recovery and International Intervention in Comparative Perspective" (Center for Global Development Working Paper 57, Washington, DC, 2005), 5.

Index

Italicized page numbers indicate photographs. Page numbers followed by n or nn indicate notes and page numbers followed by t indicate tables.